ROUTLEDGE LIBRARY EDITIONS:
URBAN EDUCATION

Volume 1

TEACHERS AND CRISIS

TEACHERS AND CRISIS
Urban School Reform and Teachers' Work Culture

DENNIS CARLSON

LONDON AND NEW YORK

First published in 1992 by Routledge, Chapman and Hall, Inc.

This edition first published in 2018
by Routledge
2 Park Square, Milton Park, Abingdon, Oxon OX14 4RN

and by Routledge
711 Third Avenue, New York, NY 10017

Routledge is an imprint of the Taylor & Francis Group, an informa business

© 1992 by Routledge, Chapman and Hall, Inc.

All rights reserved. No part of this book may be reprinted or reproduced or utilised in any form or by any electronic, mechanical, or other means, now known or hereafter invented, including photocopying and recording, or in any information storage or retrieval system, without permission in writing from the publishers.

Trademark notice: Product or corporate names may be trademarks or registered trademarks, and are used only for identification and explanation without intent to infringe.

British Library Cataloguing in Publication Data
A catalogue record for this book is available from the British Library

ISBN: 978-1-138-57853-1 (Set)
ISBN: 978-1-351-23745-1 (Set) (ebk)
ISBN: 978-1-138-08918-1 (Volume 1) (hbk)
ISBN: 978-1-138-57850-0 (Volume 1) (pbk)
ISBN: 978-1-315-10930-5 (Volume 1) (ebk)

Publisher's Note
The publisher has gone to great lengths to ensure the quality of this reprint but points out that some imperfections in the original copies may be apparent.

Disclaimer
The publisher has made every effort to trace copyright holders and would welcome correspondence from those they have been unable to trace.

Teachers and Crisis

Urban School Reform and Teachers' Work Culture

DENNIS CARLSON

NEW YORK · LONDON

Published in 1992 by
Routledge
An imprint of Routledge, Chapman and Hall, Inc.
29 West 35 Street
New York, NY 10001

Published in Great Britain by
Routledge
11 New Fetter Lane
London EC4P 4EE

Copyright © 1992 by Routledge, Chapman and Hall, Inc.

Printed in the United States of America on acid free paper.

All rights reserved. No part of this book may be reprinted or reproduced or utilized in any form or by any electronic, mechanical or other means, now known or hereafter invented, including photocopying and recording, or in any information storage or retrieval system, without permission in writing from the publishers.

Library of Congress Cataloging in Publication Data
Carlson, Dennis.
 Teachers and crisis : urban school reform and teachers' work culture / Dennis Carlson.
  p. cm.—(Critical social thought)
 Includes bibliographical references (p.).
 ISBN 0-415-90269-X : —ISBN 0-415-90270-3 (pbk.)
  1. Education, Urban—United States—Case studies. 2. Teachers—United States—Political activity—Case studies. 3. Teachers—United States—Social conditions—Case studies. 4. Teachers' unions—United States—Case studies. 5. Educational change—United States—Case studies. I. Title. II. Series.
LC5131.C37 1992
370.19'348'0973—dc20   91-27912
                                                    CIP

British Library Cataloguing-in-Publication Data also available.

This book is dedicated to Carl and Peggy Carlson

Contents

Acknowledgments		ix
Series Editor's Introduction		xi
Introduction		1
1	Crisis Tendencies in Urban Education	25
2	Teachers and Crisis: Teachers' Work Culture in Sociohistorical Perspective	65
3	Teachers and Basic Skills Restructuring in Midstate	105
4	Teachers and Basic Skills Restructuring in Urbanville	127
5	Role Formalization and "Playing the Game" in Urbanville Schools	155
6	"Classroom Management" in the Basic Skills Era	185
7	Beyond the Crisis in Urban Schooling	217
Notes		255
Index		277

Acknowledgments

No list of acknowledgments is ever complete, since a book's ideas and meanings are sedimented in the author's life across many years. Nevertheless, let me indicate some of the major influences on my scholarly thinking that led to this book. As a graduate student at the University of Wisconsin-Madison in the Department of Educational Policy Studies in the mid to late 1970s, I was fortunate enough to work with individuals like Philip Altbach, who encouraged me to write and publish; Carl Kaestle and Herbert Kliebard, who taught me the importance of historicizing my research; Philip Wexler, who introduced me to critical theory; and Michael Apple, who served as a constant source of inspiration and new ideas for many of us. The theoretical and conceptual foundation and the progressive political commitments I established at Wisconsin have continued to guide my research. In the 1980s, my work was also influenced by several colleagues and friends: Jean Anyon, at Rutgers University; Madeleine Grumet, then at Hobart and William Smith Colleges; and William Pinar, then at the University of Rochester. I completed writing this book at Miami University, as a member of the Center for Education and Cultural Studies. Here, I have been influenced by three colleagues and friends who have contributed immeasurably to my understanding of culture as discourse and practice: Henry Giroux, Peter McLaren, and Richard Quantz. I had the opportunity to finalize many of my ideas for this book while conducting a doctoral seminar on the urban

Acknowledgments

school crisis at Miami University during the summer of 1990, and I want to thank all those who participated. Kent Peterson, a friend and companion, has provided support and encouragement throughout this and other writing projects. Finally, I would like to thank the teachers and the local teacher union, along with the participant observer at "McKinley Middle School," who agreed to participate in this study under the condition of anonymity for teachers and school sites. They are the real heroes of this story.

An earlier version of Chapter One appeared as "Managing the Urban School Crisis: Recent Trends in Curricular Reform," *Journal of Education*, 171 (no. 3, 1989), pp. 89–108.

An earlier version of Chapter Two appeared as "Teachers as Political Actors: From Reproductive Theory to the Crisis of Schooling," *Harvard Educational Review*, 57 (no. 3, 1987), pp. 283–307.

Some of the data in this book was originally presented and discussed in papers delivered at the American Educational Research Association annual meetings. These include:

Chapter Three: 1986 AERA paper entitled, "Semiotics and State Educational Policy: A Case Study of the 'Selling' of School Reform."

Chapter Four: 1990 AERA paper entitled, "Of Basic Skills, Curriculum Restructuring and Crisis Tendencies in American Education."

Chapter Five: 1988 AERA paper entitled, "An Urban Teachers Union and Curriculum Politics: A Case Study of Contestation in the Schools."

Series Editor's Introduction

A number of books in this series have examined the effects on schools of either the management-oriented strategies for "school improvement" or of the economic crisis. They have provided crucial grounding for our growing understanding of the complexities of education in an unequal society and they have helped us see what is possible and what is not in schools throughout the country. Some have looked at a wide range of reform proposals in action, challenging our accepted wisdom about "what works."[1] Others have zeroed in on how declining economies have a major impact on teaching and curriculum, on class, gender, and race relations within schools and local communities, and on the changing political and cultural identities of students.[2]

Teachers and Crisis follows and markedly expands on this tradition. Like its influential predecessors, it too examines "reform" in the midst of a very visible crisis in our economy. Like the others it gets inside schools to give a close up view of what actually goes on in the daily lives of teachers and students. Yet, Dennis Carlson takes us into the gritty realities of inner-city schools, schools where teachers must struggle daily to create an education worthy of its name in situations that seem almost to have been purposely set up to deny both these teachers and their students real chances to accomplish this.

We must always be wary of crisis talk. The ability to define something as a crisis is often related to a group's power in the larger social arena. Dominant sectors of society can declare crises over specific things,

Series Editor Introduction

while less powerful segments can hardly get their lives and needs on the national agenda for public discussion. Yet, by any stretch of the imagination our urban areas *are* in crisis. The realities of unemployment, housing, health care, legal services, homelessness, education, the destruction of communities, and more, all of this constitutes a tragedy of immense proportions.[3] In many ways, the anger, alienation and despair that are generated out of those conditions—conditions to which the powerful often give no more than lip service—can best be described as simply the pornography of poverty. Greed and profit have taken their toll and have made our sense of the common good wither markedly.[4]

Schools are situated within the midst of all this. They exist not cut off from decades of "benign neglect," decay, and faltering communities, but at the very middle of the maelstrom that is both cause and effect of this situation.

Faced with an economic crisis and a crisis in authority relations and culture, many urban school systems have moved in familiar directions—tightening control, bureaucratization, making the needs of business and industry the primary if not the only goal of education, and so on. For those of you with a sense of the history of urban education in the United States, all of this has a familiar ring to it.

As you know, administrative control over both teaching and curriculum is of course nothing new. Bureaucratization, what Arthur Wise so cleverly called "hyper-rationalization,"[5] has had a very long history in education. Consider the case of one young teacher in her first year of teaching in Boston at the turn of the century. She relates the story of what happened during an observation by the school principal. The teacher rather proudly watched one of the children in her class read aloud from the assigned textbook. Yet the principal was less than pleased with both the teacher's and the student's performances. Rules weren't followed. In the words of the teacher:

> The proper way to read in the public school in 1899 was to say, "page 35, chapter 4" and holding the book in the right hand, with the toes pointing at an angle of forty-five degrees, the head held straight and high, the eyes looking directly ahead, the pupil would lift up his voice and struggle in loud, unnatural tones. Now, I had attended to the position of the toes, the right arm, and the nose, but had failed to enforce the mentioning of page and chapter.[6]

The possibility of sanctions, given the teacher's failure to follow all of the procedures that the administration "knew" would guarantee

Series Editor Introduction

"appropriate learning," is made very real in the teacher's final words about the situation. "My heart sank."[7]

Yet, control was not always so personally visible as it was in the case of that young woman teacher from Boston. It was just as often vested in the mountains of regulations and the accompanying paperwork that were almost always ushered in during times of crisis. Schools and their teachers and students have always been blamed for economic crisis as dominant groups export the crisis onto other agencies.

The amount of paperwork, of administrative tasks, that urban teachers have been called upon to do because of this has always been exceptional. Again, the words of teachers from the past can help us understand this. Mary Abigail Dodge, a former elementary school teacher who devoted much of her later career to creating conditions in schools that would enable women teachers to exercise more control over their teaching and curricula, is at her ironic best in a brief poem she wrote about exactly this issue.

> Twas Saturday night, and a teacher sat
>   Alone, her task pursuing:
> She averaged this and she averaged that
>   Of all her class was doing.[8]

But for many teachers, the overadministered and over-regulated life they led, with its focus on input and output and its emphasis on "efficiency" and cheapness at all costs, signified something that went well beyond the classroom. It represented a picture of social life in general that was perilous not only for teachers but for students and communities as well. It substituted an ethic of the factory for that of the common good and the ideal of democracy. These teachers understand how past crises were being exported onto them.

We could well ponder Margaret Haley's comments at an annual meeting of the National Education Association at the beginning of this century. Haley, one of the founding members of the first teachers' union in the United States, argued that the time had come for teachers to fight for their rights. Not only were students' and teachers' experiences at stake, but the battle was about a dangerous vision of society as a whole. In her words:

> Two ideals are struggling for supremacy in American life today: one, the industrial ideal, dominating through the supremacy of commercialism, which subordinates the worker to the

Series Editor Introduction

product and the machine; the other, the ideal of democracy, the ideal of the educators, which places humanity above all machines, and demands that all activity shall be the expression of life.[9]

Now, not all educators are as committed as Haley. Nor should we assume that simply handing decisions over to teachers is sufficient to guarantee truly democratic educational policies and practices. However, my basic point is this. While the crisis in urban areas has often been defined in ways that support dominant groups' definitions of what needs to be done, there can be no doubt that such a crisis is real and extremely damaging. School systems have sought to cope with it in ways that often mirror past responses. More power to the top, more centralized determination of curricula and teaching, more testing. This is where Dennis Carlson enters.

Teachers and Crisis documents the latent effects of top-down "reform" strategies that seek to increase bureaucratic control of teaching and curricula. Its discussion of how teachers respond to the growing management offensives that abound in urban school districts is more than a little insightful. The whittling away of autonomy, the creation of a situation in which teachers slowly but surely "teach for the test," the immensely tense relations between teachers and the administration, all of this and more are the results of the "reforms" often put in place by urban school districts.

Carlson does not only talk abstractly about this. He engages in a detailed examination of a case study of a school in a city on the eastern seaboard of the United States, a city that has been the scene of serious unrest, a decaying economy and infrastructure, and a fiscal crisis that threatens its entire set of public services. Yet what Carlson has to say about all this is not limited to one case. Anyone who has any familiarity with the crisis in our cities will recognize not only the description of what is happening in many of our urban centers, but also what the conditions are in many of our schools.

Teachers and Crisis serves as a provocative statement about some of the more reductive approaches to school improvement that have fallen under the rubric of the "effective schools" literature. It also enables us to think more critically about the possible negative implications of national testing, a movement that is well on its way but which may have exactly the same deleterious consequences in urban schools as those documented here. Further, by placing these movements within the growing conservative reconstruction of what education is for, the

Series Editor Introduction

volume gives us a distressing picture of the dangers that may be awaiting us if conservative discourse and policies drown out alternatives.

Carlson is conceptually creative in his approach to making sense out of what is happening in inner-city schools. Unlike others who are critical, but see urban education through only one lens—say, a focus on class relations and social reproduction, or a Weberian approach that stresses bureaucratic rationalization[10]—he integrates elements of neo-marxist, Weberian, game theory and post-structural theories. Each of these is combined so that they provide both extensions and criticisms of the others. This critical integration is unique within the literature.

But the primary focus in this volume is on *teachers*. In all too many analyses of education, the daily lives of teachers are basically ignored. Yet, as I argue in *Education and Power* and *Teachers and Texts*,[11] schools are not only places where we attempt to answer "What knowledge is of most worth?" (or better still, "Whose knowledge is of most worth?"),[12] they are also—and profoundly—places where teachers *work*. We must always ask what the effects are of any attempts to rationalize and control the labor process of teachers. As Carlson so nicely recognizes, teachers are themselves raced and gendered and classed. And these dynamics, too, have effects on how they see their work and how they respond to changes in it.[13]

Of great importance to the story *Teachers and Crisis* wishes to tell is teachers as members of organized unions. I personally find this aspect of the story very significant. As president of a teachers' union in New Jersey in the 1960s, I have many memories of what it took collectively to make a difference and how important such organized action can be. I am not unaware of some of the contradictions within the teachers' union movement, however; nor is Carlson. His portrayal of how unions function in times of crisis and what they can and must do is quite perceptive.

Even with the power of his analysis of what is happening in many urban schools, Carlson does not stop there. He argues for a reconceptualization of curriculum and teaching and a reconstruction of schools based on workplace democratization. His proposals are articulate and could go a long way in altering the conditions that have deskilled and intensified the work of teachers.[14] In making this case, here too he recognizes the utter import of taking the gendered nature of teaching and the racial dynamics of the larger society into account in any attempt at altering what schools now do.

Series Editor Introduction

As both an analysis of the effects of the conservative reconstruction of education and a vision of the possibilities of a democratic agenda for change, *Teachers and Crisis* is a volume that deserves to be taken very seriously.

>Michael W. Apple
>The University of Wisconsin, Madison

Introduction

In this book I examine teachers' work culture in the basic skills era of urban school reform, an era which began in the mid to late1960s and continues into the 1990s. Much of what follows describes the results of a study I undertook of teachers' work culture and teacher unionism in one highly urban northeastern state which I call Midstate, one urban school district in that state which I call Urbanville, and one urban middle school I call McKinley School.[1] My intent is to locate teachers as institutional, social, and political actors within a drama of systemic educational crisis, and more particularly within the context of the conservative, bureaucratic state response to that multi-faceted crisis. The state's answer to this multifaceted crisis in urban education has been the institutionalization of a whole package of "basic skills" reforms over the 1970s and 1980s. By institutionalization I mean the production of a discourse and practice in urban school sites organized around: minimum competency testing to raise standards, a skill-based or performance-based curriculum designed to teach "functional literacy" skills, performance-based lesson and unit planning, time-on-task approaches to classroom management, teach-to-the-test approaches to instruction, and a bifurcation of management and labor roles in the school formalized in collective bargaining and the union contract. All of these elements of reform are dependent discursively upon the others and have participated in a common project in urban education. In interpreting teachers' responses to this package of reforms that has

Introduction

restructured urban schools, I focus on teacher unionism and collective bargaining and suggest how they have defined and shaped teachers' work culture in ways that have cultural and political consequences.

By way of examining teachers, the restructuring of their work, and the construction of teacher work culture during the basic skills era, I also mean to raise a number of much broader issues in education that are relevant to a discussion of the current crisis in urban schooling. The past few decades have been difficult one's for America's urban schools, which have been gripped by a number of interrelated crisis tendencies that threaten the survival of public education in its current form. The crisis in urban education has been an outgrowth of several developments. By the mid 1960s poor African-American and Hispanic students were becoming the majority in many urban schools across the nation and their cultures and languages clashed with that of the dominant white middle-class culture of the schools. Changes in the economy also had an impact on urban schools. In a rapidly deindustrializing economy, many of the well-paid, unionized industrial jobs were disappearing and being replaced by lower-paid, generally non-unionized jobs in the service industry, data processing, and paramedical and paralegal fields. Urban schools, according to the business community, were failing to graduate enough students with the generalizable "functional literacy" skills and "work attitudes" necessary for these new jobs, and necessary to improve American economic competitiveness and business profitability.

To meet these new expectations and challenges, urban schools also have had to make do with fewer fiscal resources. By the mid- to late 1960s, the declining urban tax base that resulted from "white flight" along with corporate flight to the suburbs had left urban schools in a state of fiscal insolvency. Urban schools faced an immediate and pressing crisis. Their plight was a visible symbol of inequities in school funding between the rich suburbs and the "starving" urban school districts, and it threatened to delegitimate the state's claim that public schools promoted equality of opportunity.

Finally, urban teachers were, by the late 1960s, beginning to assert their collective power in opposition to the administrative chain of command that kept them rigidly subordinated. Collective bargaining laws channeled much of this discontent into conflict over the hours and conditions of the wage-labor exchange, which legitimated some of teachers' grievances and concerns but did not directly threaten teachers' bureaucratic subordination and domination. In fact, collective bargaining and the dominant model of teacher unionism in urban America have developed coextensively with the basic skills model of school

Introduction

restructuring. Teacher unionism during the basic skills era has largely taken for granted the current hierarchical, bureaucratic structure and control of urban schools, it has narrowed teachers' interests to playing the "contract game," and in these ways it has depoliticized teachers' response to the urban school crisis and school restructuring. Nevertheless, the structured conflict between teachers and administrators that has resulted from collective bargaining undermines all efforts at reform by bureaucratic elites and generates conflicts and crisis tendencies that drive the system towards further change. Furthermore, I argue that teachers' work culture contains elements of a critique of the urban school crisis that potentially rearticulates teachers' interests consistent with democratic-progressive models of school reform and that challenges continued conservative, bureaucratic, state management of the urban school crisis and steerage of the system.

Beyond the issue of teacher trade unionism and the role it has played in shaping teachers' interests in response to the restructuring of their work during the basic skills era, I am interested in understanding teachers' work culture as the product of a complex interplay between the class, gender, and race power dynamics in which urban school teachers are involved. Of these three, class analysis is most developed in this book, at least partially because there is a rich theoretical tradition of Marxist and neo-Marxist work to draw upon which orients us to class issues; and I will have more to say about the contributions of class analysis to an understanding of teachers' work culture shortly. However, race also plays an inextricable role in defining power relations in urban schools. Most obviously, because urban schools participate in the construction of racial inequalities of achievement which help structure job market, income, and status inequalities, they are sites of much conflict along racial lines. Teachers' work, along with that of their students, is made more difficult and alienating under such conditions. Furthermore, the same model of bureaucratic top-down school reform that has de-skilled teachers and further subordinated them within the bureaucracy has had the effect of shifting more power over local educational decisions to the state, and this has served to maintain white control of schools in poor African-American and Hispanic communities. This suggests that to challenge their occupational disempowerment, teachers will need to help urban communities regain control of their schools and work to counter racial power relations and ideologies in the culture that contribute to the oppressive character of urban schooling.

Gender also plays a very important role in teachers' work culture and teachers will need to confront patriarchal ideologies in education

Introduction

in working for their occupational empowerment. The disempowerment of teachers during the basic skills era (and throughout the 20th century, for that matter) has been coextensive with the dominance of a bureaucratic-hierarchical discourse in education that reproduces a patriarchal as well as corporate model of institutional reform. Basic skills, performance-based, and cost-effective approaches to urban school reform have employed a highly masculinized language of technical rationality in holding a highly feminized teaching force accountable. Gender also proved to be a relevant factor in interpreting power relations within the local teacher union described in this study. Tendencies towards oligarchic leadership existed in the teacher union, with only a few leaders making all the important decisions and with widespread rank-and-file apathy and cynicism; and this oligarchic style of leadership was related to a patriarchal form of leadership by the union president. Finally, in Urbanville schools elementary school teachers, of whom approximately 90 percent were female, were much more subject to bureaucratic, top-down controls and supervision from administrators and had a more intensified working day than their secondary school cohorts, of whom 50 percent were male. For teachers, the fight for occupational empowerment clearly is inseparable from the struggle to challenge patriarchal ideology and practice in the schools and society.

Theoretical Groundings for a Study of Teachers' Work Culture and Urban School Crisis

In addressing these various issues having to do with teachers' work culture and urban school crisis, I draw upon concepts associated with a number of different discursive traditions of social theory and research, including neo-Marxism, Weberian interpretive sociology, neo-rationalism (with its concern with the situational construction of reality and the "rules of the game"), and poststructuralism. This is obviously a diverse and in some ways contradictory group of theoretic discourses. Yet it is also obvious that insights from each of these discursive traditions contributes in unique ways to a comprehensive critical analysis of teachers' work culture and teachers as actors in the schools. Each is limited, partial, and incomplete in its own way, and some combination of theories rather than a single meta-theory is needed in order to adequately account for the complexity of institutional phenomena. Consequently, I invoke concepts and themes from each of these traditions when appropriate throughout the book to frame issues, pose questions, and analyse empirical data.

Introduction

The Neo-Marxist Discourse

None of these discourses will be taken as a determinant or meta-discourse, although some play a much larger role than others in framing the overall set of issues raised in this book, and this has to do with their connections to democratic projects and movements in the culture. Marxist categories and themes (from classical Marxism, neo-Marxism, and the critical theory of the Frankfurt School) provide the most comprehensive framework for reading the case study text and addressing the various substantive issues having to do with urban school reform, teachers' work, and crisis tendencies in urban schooling. The importance of the Marxist tradition lies in its multifaceted critique of the social relations and worldviews of advanced capitalist societies, its interest in the dynamics that drive modern society (through contradictions and crisis tendencies), its commitment to the realization of democratic values in all spheres of social and economic life, and its emphasis on the importance of cultural struggle and movements.

But Marxist discourse faces its own crisis in the late 20th century. Aside from increasing political attacks from the Right, it has been limited by a structuralist model of the reproduction of power relations and the role of the state as an agent of capital. Marxism's conceptual limitations, related to its structural, functional, and deterministic tendencies, need to be taken seriously and addressed within educational theory. Over the past decade, women, racial minorities, and other oppressed groups have challenged Marxism's tendency to take class struggle as a privileged or superordinate category of struggle, and to treat other forms of struggle as explainable in terms of, and as subsumable under, an analysis of class-based beliefs, practices, and systemic dynamics. This is an important and, I think, accurate criticism of mainstream Marxism so long as it does not imply (as some do) that Marxist categories and themes have become irrelevant in critical discourse. We need, I believe, to draw extensively upon existing Marxist categories in guiding critical educational research and theory, although these categories need to be modified, and new categories from other theoretical discourses need to be drawn upon, in order to sufficiently account for the complexity of power relations and the various axes along which individuals constitute identities and organize collective movements. What is called for now is the development of more and better linkages between various critical discourses in education that are lateral rather than hierarchical—what Ernesto Laclau and Chantal Mouffe refer to as a democratic *articulation* of discourses.[2]

While Marxist discourse has been less influential in educational

Introduction

analysis in recent years, because of the political climate of the nation along with Marxism's conceptual limitations, it was the most influential critical discourse in education throughout much of the 1970s and 1980s. This is not to say that critical educational research always called itself Marxist, or drew explicitly upon Marxist or neo-Marxist categories and themes. But much critical research and discourse took for granted a number of important Marxist or neo-Marxist categories that significantly advanced our understanding of how schools operate, and in whose interests. Perhaps the most influential of these was the notion of *reproduction*. On the most functional and mechanistic level, this implied a structuralist analysis of how schools perform a role in socializing and skilling students for various positions in the production process and the corresponding labor hierarchy, and in legitimating inequalities constructed through the schooling process.[3] At the level of the situational construction of reality, reproductive theory implied an ethnographic, cultural account of how dominated groups, in an often ironic and paradoxical fashion, participate in "making" or producing a culture, constructing identities, and also resisting domination—all within the context of processes that basically serve to reproduce dominant power relations.[4] Related to both the structural and the cultural reproduction theory of schooling, and dependent conceptually upon it, was the presumption that a rough correspondence exists between the organization of school work and the organization of work in the economy, and that the organization of curriculum and instruction will therefore vary for students who are being prepared for different types of work.

This structural-functional reproductive theory of schooling, as formulated cogently in Samuel Bowles and Herbert Gintis' *Schooling in Capitalist America*, represented an important advancement over liberal-pluralist explanations of schooling.[5] It challenged the liberal belief that schools served to promote (1) egalitarianism or equality of opportunity, (2) the development of the full range of cognitive, critical, and aesthetic powers of individuals, and (3) the integration of individuals into society and community as fully participating members of a democracy.[6] In doing so it also implied that to achieve the liberal project, we would have to move beyond liberalism, to envision a new socioeconomic order in which formal democratic control was linked to workplace democratization, so that the organization of students' and teachers' work would correspond to the needs of citizens and workers in a democratic social and economic order. All of this is important in any critical assessment of education. What it lacks is an analysis of the active, dynamic, contested character of social life that places the rough

Introduction

correspondence between work in schools and work in the economy within the context of struggle, change, and possibility.

In fact, some existing Marxist and neo-Marxist categories may help counter the one-sided functionalism of reproductive theory and move us in the direction of "seeing" struggle and the constitution of identities around struggle along with the reproduction of dominant power relations. We may begin by including an analysis of interest construction, and whose interests are served within particular institutional discursive practices. Vulgar or deterministic Marxism is generally associated with the essentialist presumption that at some level individuals' and groups' interests are derivable from an "objective" assessment of their positions and roles within the forces that reproduce patterns of domination. We may say that urban school teachers' interests, for example, are derivable from an analysis of two basic "facts." First, teachers participate in the work of skilling, socializing, and disciplining disadvantaged students in ways that, whatever the intent, prepare most of these students for second-class citizenship and dead-end, low-skill jobs. Second, teachers are workers of a particular type, subject to disempowerment through the extention of bureaucratic and technical forms of control over their work.

These "facts" about urban school teaching do indeed play an important role in beginning any assessment of the construction of teachers' interests and identities in the schools. However, Marxism in this form provides too reductionistic and mechanistic a conception of interests to be of much value in examining and explaining the particular construction of interests by teachers. As Michael Apple observes, "[A] male worker who has lost his job can be antagonistic to the corporations who engaged in capital flight or can blame unions, people of color, or women 'who are taking men's jobs.' The response is *constructed*, not preordained. . . ."[7] Culture and hence history remains open rather than determined, and it may be constructed by individuals in very different ways. Now, having said this, let me suggest that such a bipolar opposition between an "open" and "closed" conception of interests needs to be questioned rather than taken for granted. Interests and meaning are always constructed within a material, objective infrastructure and they always refer back to that infrastructure, so that a sufficient or explanatory analysis of teachers' interests does not imply that we can ignore the material and technical conditions of teaching—over which teachers generally have little control.

Interests, as they are constituted within institutional sites by particular groups of actors, also need to be linked to movements and struggle. The neo-Marxist notion of *hegemony* suggests that the domination of

Introduction

one class or group within society and culture is achieved and maintained through the successful mobilization of a political movement that articulates general cultural themes consistent with the interests of the dominant group.[8] In America for example, the inordinate power of the business community and its freedom from public oversight is encouraged by a widespread (although perhaps less so now than in an earlier era) belief that "what is good for General Motors is good for the country." In public education, the hegemony of conservative, bureaucratic state reform initiatives has been associated with widespread belief that educational issues are about the effective management of the schools to raise student achievement levels rather than about the distribution of power in the culture (a political issue), and that the state is a neutral party in various struggles and conflicts in the culture. But hegemony is never complete or unchallenged. A *counter-hegemony*, by implication, involves the mobilization of a new political movement that rearticulates social values and themes consistent with the interests of a democratic coalition. In this regard, I am interested in teachers' work culture generally and teacher unionism more specifically in building a counter-hegemonic movement that addresses the urban school crisis in new ways.

Other concepts or categories that are useful in redirecting Marxist analysis in education to overcome deterministic tendencies are *contradiction* and *crisis*. These concepts have been developed in deterministic, mechanistic, and "scientific" ways (particularly in economic Marxism), but also in a less deterministic and active way in neo-Marxist cultural studies. In a general sense, *contradiction* implies incompatibility in the governing principles of a system of discursive practices that constitute power relations. These incompatibilities, Marx presumed, would eventually lead to the transformation of the existing system of power relations following a systemic crisis. Jürgen Habermas, who has done the most to develop the notion of crisis within an advanced capitalist context, challenges the notions that a decisive crisis will develop in advanced capitalist societies or that crisis will inevitably lead to system transformation.[9] While crisis tendencies of legitimation, rationality and motivation continue to push the current sociocultural, economic, and political systems to crisis, dominant groups may become ever more adept at managing crises, one at a time. Crisis and contradiction, from this less deterministic perspective, do not lead inevitably to transformation, although they provide the conditions that make transformative political action possible and perhaps even likely.

Many of the state-sponsored reform initiatives of the past several decades are understandable as forms of crisis management by hege-

Introduction

monic groups, although how successful they have been remains an open question. Arguably, crisis tendencies in the political, economic and sociocultural spheres have deepened during this period, although there were no signs that elite groups in education were losing their grip on steerage of the system. Each successive crisis was managed or muddled through in some fashion, and dominant groups continued to be fairly successful in articulating a public philosophy of education consistent with continued elite domination.[10] Nevertheless, superordinate groups in power relations always must be concerned with *crisis management*, that is, the shoring up of centralized steerage of a system in which deconstructive and oppositional forces—related to contradictions in both beliefs and practices—always threaten to overtake reproductive forces. Basic skills restructuring, consequently, must be understood as it arises out of various crisis tendencies in urban schooling, and as it responds and enters into these developing crisis tendencies and efforts at crisis management.

The Weberian Tradition

Aside from the Marxist tradition, the other major theory of capitalist, industrial, or modern society that emerged out the late 19th century is grounded in the work of Max Weber. Although the Weberian tradition of social theory has influenced mainstream conservative and liberal discourse on the schools more than critical discourse, it does encompass several notions and themes that need to be included in any critical assessment of bureaucratic state reform initiatives in education and their contradictions. Weber's analysis of modern industrial and bureaucratic society is in some ways compatible with Marx's analysis of capitalism. Both, for example, viewed the increasing rationalization of social and institutional authority as a basically progressive historical development in comparison to earlier despotic, charismatic, and feudal forms of social authority. Marx recognized that the rationalization of work processes and authority relations in capitalist society resulted in a vast increase in productivity and efficiency; but he also recognized that it resulted in the exploitation of workers, the degradation of labor, the progressive despoilment of the environment, and the fragmentation of community. For Marx, capitalist society would needed to be transformed if the promise of democratic values of equality and fraternity were to be realized.

Weber, however, generally took for granted the liberal belief that

Introduction

the rationalization of authority relations in bureaucratic organizations (in both industry and the state) resulted in a relatively benign and non-oppressive form of control, consistent with democratic steerage of society. Weber argued, very much like progressive reformers of the era, that *substantive* democracy, involving the direct democratic control of public institutions, was not feasible in a modern industrial society. The public could and should be involved in electing officials to represent their interests, but the rationalization of decision-making that was necessary to ensure that the state played a disinterested or neutral role in civil society also necessitated the delegation of authority to highly specialized, professional experts working within state agencies, who could apply standardized operating procedures and scientific-technical knowledge to resolve questions about how to achieve agreed-upon institutional goals. Weber was led to conclude that " 'democratization' ... does not necessarily mean an increasingly active share of the governed in the authority of the social structures." It could not imply "the minimization of the civil servants' ruling power in favor of the greatest possible 'direct' rule of the *demos*." Rather, democracy had to be reconstructed as a process whereby those governed select, and exert public opinion upon, those executive leaders who are chosen to govern.[11]

Both conservative and liberal discourses in education have taken for granted this Weberian construction of issues consistent with a managerial "end of ideology" thesis. According to this thesis, issues in advanced capitalism are no longer ideological, no longer involve conflicts over fundamentally different values and purposes. Rather, social problems and conflicts are said to require better management and administration consistent with supposedly consensual social goals. Questions of social policy are constructed around how institutions can be operated more "effectively." Within this general conceptual framework, conservatives generally support more top-down accountability by bureaucratic subordinates to central office and state officials, so that these officials can ensure that local schools organize instruction consistent with public mandates and economic needs. For example, over the past decade or so, effective schools research has been used by bureaucratic elites to support the claim that managerial principles derived from scientific research on effective urban schools (i.e., those with higher than expected test scores given the socioeconomic mix of the student population) can be used to make all urban schools effective. These principles include such things as a clear focus on teaching basic skills as the school mission, strong leadership by the principal, a high level of commitment among the staff to the importance of teaching for

Introduction

basic skills mastery, a commitment to increasing student "time on task," and so forth. The presumption, consistent with the end of ideology thesis, is that state support of the basis skills restructuring of urban schools along these lines has been a purely rational response to a self-evident problem in school effectiveness. In fact, it has been a response to deep-rooted conflicts, contradictions, and crisis tendencies in schools, urban communities, and the broader culture, all of which have political and social implications, since they organize and distribute power to serve some interests over others.

Liberal discourse in education has also generally endorsed this end of ideology thesis, although liberals have proposed a somewhat broader and more democratic conception of institutional effectiveness (including effectiveness in promoting equality of opportunity) and more decentralized approaches to promoting effectiveness. Bureaucratic decentralization of decision-making, according to the dominant liberal discourse, will free local administrators and teachers to be more adaptive and creative, and thus also more effective in the achievement of their assigned "missions." Teachers are to be treated more like professionals, which means allowing them much more individual autonomy in organizing curricular experiences for students. This too, however, presumes that our objective is to make the current system work more effectively in pursuit of taken for granted educational goals, under the steerage of state officials, in partnership with corporate leadership.

Aside from promoting and legitimating a view of the state as the disinterested or neutral guardian of the public interest in education, the end of ideology thesis also has been applied to the analysis of conflict management in the workplace. In the 1950s, a group of liberal-pluralist sociologists argued that the conflict between labor and capital that Marx saw as the driving force in capitalist society had been pretty much resolved and contained in advanced capitalist democracies such as America by the rationalization of conflict in the collective bargaining process, the formalization of worker rights and responsibilities in the contract, and the instrumentalization of worker interests around the wage package, and that we were, in the words of Daniel Bell, witnessing an "end of ideology."[12] For most of the post-World War II years, both conservatives and liberals have accepted this version of the end of ideology thesis and hailed it as the American solution to the labor "problem." It should hardly be surprising, consequently, that it has been so influential in constructing the roles of teachers and administrators, particularly in highly bureaucratized urban schools.

A critical response to this industrial relations end of ideology thesis

Introduction

consists of several elements. First, the notion that economic and workplace conflicts in advanced capitalist societies have been successfully managed to everyone's benefit provides state officials with a convenient legitimating rationale for imposing a rigid system of labor-management relations upon private and (more recently) public institutions, designed to ensure that conflict is properly channeled and regulated so that it will not become politicized or pose a significant threat to existing institutional power relations. In public schools, this implies that state-regulated and supervised collective bargaining has legitimated an organizational structure that keeps teachers rigidly subordinated and disempowered within a bureaucratic chain of command. Second, as a statement of existing conditions, the notion that workers (including teachers) have largely forsaken struggles over the realization of democratic ideals for struggles over higher salaries and better working conditions needs to be taken seriously. Critical theorists of the Frankfurt School advanced a very similar end of ideology argument in suggesting that modern society promoted a "one-dimensional" or instrumental reasoning among all classes that eliminated the possibility for a radical democratic rethinking of culture. From a less pessimistic critical perspective, we may say that the instrumentalization of motivation among workers in advanced capitalism may impede (but not prevent or prohibit) the development of the labor movement as a democratic-progressive force in society. Third, and in line with the last point, it is possible to suggest that conflicts and struggles organized around work have not been fully contained or instrumentalized in the era of collective bargaining. While Weberians have presumed that the current labor-management accord is a workable solution to problems of conflict in the workplace, it is better understood as one phase in an ongoing conflict that generates crisis tendencies that may not always be containable. Data presented in this study suggest that in urban schools, the current model of labor-management relations is not working very well for any of the involved parties, that teacher instrumentalism is more expedient than deeply internalized, and that the potential always exists for a politicization of issues around power and its distribution.

Aside from the end of ideology thesis, I make use of one other important Weberian concept in analyzing teachers and urban school reform, that of a *vicious cycle* of control. Weber recognized that bureaucratic controls were associated with a number of "irrationalities" having to do with an emphasis upon red tape and rule-following in serving individual and unique client needs. A number of American sociologists in the 1930s through 1950s focused their work upon an analysis of these and other bureaucratic "dysfunctions" and "unantici-

Introduction

pated consequences" as they were now called.[13] Out of this research emerged the notion that the "bureaucratic personality" is overly resistant to innovation and is not able to adapt effectively to changing work demands. Out of it also emerged the thesis that bureaucratic control is caught in an irresolvable dilemma—a vicious circle or cycle. On the one hand, bureaucratic managers are motivated to impose more and more impersonal rules and directives to more effectively hold bureaucratic subordinates accountable to central managerial steerage of the system; and on the other hand, the elaboration of rules and procedures and the rationalization of work processes lead to a decline in worker motivation and a decline in productivity that motivates management to decentralize authority and give subordinates more direct, discretionary control over their work. The decentralization of authority generates its own problems, since system managers can no longer guarantee that subordinates will organize their work in ways that are consistent with managerial goals and expectations, which motivates a return to more top-down, bureaucratic regulation and control, which sets up the next round of the vicious cycle.

Basic skills restructuring may be interpreted from this Weberian perspective as one phase in a vicious cycle of control in urban education associated with a reassertion of centralized control by managerial elites to overcome the problems associated with a preceding period of decentralization of authority. From the mid-1960s through the early 1970s and related to the counter-cultural movement, teachers and students pressured school systems to give them more autonomy to experiment with "open classrooms," "informal education," "alternative schools," and other approaches to providing instruction that radically decentralized educational decision-making to the classroom level. At the same time, system elites hoped that by decentralizing power within the bureaucratic chain of command to the actual "point of production" of educational outcomes—the classroom—that teacher and student discontent could be countered; and they were no doubt right in this assessment. Furthermore, alternative programs helped keep potential drop-outs motivated and in the system (so that school districts could continue to receive state aid to educate them) without a heavy investment in new technologies or curricular materials.

While this might seem a good, workable solution to the problems that confronted urban schools, the empowerment of teachers and students consistent with open classroom and alternative school programs also led to changes in what students were learning, how they learned it, and the dispositions and attitudes they were learning in the process, that were not consistent with bureaucratic state and corporate expecta-

Introduction

tions for schools, especially urban schools. Employers wanted disciplined, functionally literate workers to graduate from urban schools, and the alternative programs were producing critically-minded, autonomous, freethinkers who did not adapt well to the jobs and social roles that were available to them upon graduation. Basic skills restructuring thus represented, in effect, a reform movement designed to shift authority back to the top of the bureaucratic hierarchy to ensure that students were taught the literacy skills, self-discipline, and work dispositions they needed to find gainful employment in the new, semi-skilled work force. However, the centralization of authority in the hands of bureaucratic elites over the past several decades has generated its own problems of declining teacher and student morale and a tendency towards rule compliance rather than commitment. As Timar and Kirp remark in their neo-Weberian study of the basic skills reforms of the 1980s: "The critical question that state reform efforts raise is whether reform policies yield outcomes that are consistent with standards of excellence, or whether reforms lead only to more rules, formalistic compliance, evasion, paperwork, and legal proceedings. . . Do schools simply turn reforms into bureaucratized routines?"[14] The authors concluded that, for the most part, the schools have become bogged down in routine as a result of the past two decades of bureaucratic state reforms.

We may expect, consequently, that as these contradictions and dilemmas of reform through bureaucratic centralization (such as basic skills restructuring) become more apparent, reform efforts will shift once more in the direction of decentralization. We may already see signs of such a shift in the growing interest among state officials in the so-called "whole language" or "holistic" approaches to teaching literacy skills, which return control of the educative process to the child and the teacher, and personalize rather than standardize both curriculum and instruction. We must also bear in mind that from the perspective of educational elites the problem is that such informal educational approaches cannot guarantee that instruction will be organized consistent with elite economic and social interests in preparing productive workers and docile citizens; so that the return to the decentralized cycle of control may well be brief and undermined by contradictions, as it was last time around.

Through both the end of ideology thesis and the notion of a vicious cycle of bureaucratic control, Weberian theorists have presumed that a better management of existing social and institutional problems, associated with the contradiction of bureaucracy and democracy, is our inevitable lot. While Weber generally treated bureaucratization and rationalization as a progressive force, in his most pessimistic works

Introduction

he talked of the modern capitalist society of rationalization and instrumentalism negatively, as an "iron cage" that had trapped modern culture, and from which there was no escape. He talked of a social order "bound to the technical and economic conditions of machine production which today determine the lives of all the individuals who are born into this mechanism... [F]ate decreed that the cloak [of instrumentalism] should become an iron cage."[15] Early critical theorists of the Frankfurt school tended to take this despairing attitude for granted in their critiques of the one-dimensionality of modern life.[16] However, Habermas provides the basis for a critical rereading of Weber that moves beyond this stance of despair. He does this by defining instrumental or purposive rationality as a particular form of rationality, associated with the functional imperatives of the capitalist state and economy, that is undermined by crisis tendencies and may be transcended by a more democratic, discursive rationality—what he terms "communicative rationality." Such a rationalization of society would mean that practical questions of public interest are submitted to broad discussion and decided on the basis of discursive consensus, and that democratic values and purposes guide discourse rather than instrumental, means-ends considerations.[17] A critical theory must rest on the presumptions that we can (although not necessarily will) reason and struggle our way out of the iron cage in constructing a more humane, democratic, and juste society, and that rationality need not always serve its current imperatives.

Phenomenological and "Game" Theories

Marxist and Weberian constructs and themes provide important insights in a structuralist account of how modern, advanced capitalist societies are organized, how they operate, and what historical dynamics drive them. However, in conducting research in schools and in describing concrete institutional beliefs and practices, we must link this structural or systems theory of advanced capitalist society to a theory which focuses our attention upon the active production of culture by individuals and groups as they "make" history in their everyday lives. Such a constitutive, strategic theory of cultural production is needed in order to "see" how meanings and structures are both reproduced and struggled over in specific institutional sites. One way I link a substantive discussion of the crisis of urban schooling and teachers' work culture to the everyday construction of social reality is by drawing upon

Introduction

concepts and themes from neo-rational, phenomenological, "negotiated order", and game theories in the social sciences. In these various discourses of strategic action, the focus is upon situational rationality, pragmatic interests, and the constitutive rules of the game that actors employ to structure their everyday relations.

In this study, for example, I examine the situational negotiation of order in urban schools and classrooms and the "gaming" or strategic character of teacher union response to the crisis in Urbanville schools. Most directly, game theory is useful in the analysis of teacher-administration relations, which have been organized during the collective bargaining and basic skills era consistent with a "them versus us" orientation. The research questions that emerge from this perspective include: How did teachers play the wage-labor contract game? What strategic thinking did they employ? and How effective were they in playing the game to their advantage? Of course, neo-rationalist theories of situational reality and the negotiation of order in everyday life are limited if they do not move beyond an analysis of the situational rules of the game to see the historical and cultural embeddedness of these rules and their dynamic and contested character. In an extreme form associated with methodological individualism, this tradition recognizes no reality beyond the situational and limits itself to an analysis of the constitutive rules that operate in particular social situations.[18] As such, its usefulness in formulating a cultural and historical account of institutional rules and dynamics is fundamentally limited. In its most critical form, associated with phenomenology, this theoretical tradition helps focus our attention on the arbitrariness of situational rules and meanings, which implies that they could just as well be otherwise and that the current rules of the game enjoy no privileged status as representative of a "rational" order.

One way of contextualizing a game theory of teachers' interests in the schools within a broader study of teachers' work culture is to recognize that the construction of teachers' interests in terms of instrumental payoffs in a contract game is itself ideological and cultural. That is, game theory and a gaming orientation towards individual and group interests are expressive of the economic worldview of advanced capitalism. As the instrumentality of the economic sphere increasingly has pervaded all social spheres in the 20th century, behavior has become less explainable in terms of adherence to traditional mores such as respect for authority, hard work, and pride in craftsmanship, and more in terms of instrumental motivations in which actors negotiate with what power they possess to increase their instrumental payoffs within the situation. An instrumental orientation among subordinates

Introduction

implies that their compliance with institutional routines must be secured through a negotiation process and is not, therefore, assured in advance. This, consequently, relates instrumentalism and a gaming orientation to crisis tendencies within the culture. Superordinate groups must continuously resecure the support of subordinates through a better mix of inducements, and they must seek new and better ways to make subordinates comply with managerial expectations in the face of a tendency among subordinates to do only what is minimally required in the wage-labor contract. Much of the current crisis in urban education is explainable in terms of these consequences of an accepted gaming orientation among school staff and between teachers and students.

Poststructuralist Perspectives

Neo-rationalist and phenomenological theories of strategic conduct provide one way of studying the active construction of social reality at institutional sites such as schools. However, they need to be integrated within a poststructural theory of the discursive construction of power relations and dynamics which links situational or site-based discourse and practice to broader discourses in the culture. Poststructuralism already has moved critical educational analysis into a new era and opened up new fields of inquiry, and new ways of doing research and analysis, that were not possible within a strictly class-based, structuralist discourse. It may well be the case, as Cleo Cherryholmes has claimed, that a "paradigm shift" in educational research has occurred with the increasing use of poststructuralist language and perspectives over the past decade.[19]

One central poststructuralist concept is that of *discourse*—what gets talked about or said within cultural, historical, and situational contexts, along with the linguistic rules and presumptions that govern what can be said or talked about. From a poststructuralist perspective, discourse (and hence meanings, worldviews, or ideologies) is not separable from the practices that it describes, informs, and ultimately constitutes, or from the individuals (or subjectivities) that constitute themselves through discourse. This implies that discourse is always involved in a field of action and struggle, and that it serves strategic purposes within discursive (and hence cultural) struggles. To use Michel Foucault's terminology, discourse is '"deployed" strategically within a

Introduction

pragmatic, developing field of action. Consequently, language cannot be studied in terms of its idealized, abstract, or "objective" meaning, but rather must be understood in terms of its uses by particular individuals and groups in advancing particular sets of interests within particular, developing situations. The central task in research, according to Foucault is ". . .to account for the fact that it [a topic or issue] is spoken about, to discover who does the speaking, the positions and viewpoints from which they speak, [and] the institutions which prompt people to speak about it and which store and distribute the things that are said." Discourse is, at the level of concrete practice, no more than the "polymorphous techniques of power," engaged in the discursive production of power through the propagation of knowledge.[20]

However, if discourse is always strategically employed within developing situations, discourse is a product of a culture as well, which also implies that discourse has a certain stability since meanings are sedimented or deposited in tradition. In a crude or vulgar form of poststructuralism, this means that individuals are limited in the last instance by the language they have available to articulate a discourse on a given topic. Discourse constitutes subjectivities and hence all practice. While we need to reject this extreme position, it is important that we trace major clusters of meaning in educational discourse, link them with dominant discourses in the culture, and thus reveal more of what they signify. For example, in analyzing the discourse on effective urban schools I am interested in the uses to which this discourse is put in advancing a particular elite managerial line of reasoning in the schools. I am also interested in embedding the "basic skills" and "effective schools" discourse within a broader mainstream discourse in educational research and curriculum theory, beyond that to a corporate industrial discourse that emerged early in the 20th century in America, and beyond that to an historically emergent capitalist worldview. As another example, basic skills reforms in urban education may be defined in terms of an *apparatus* of discourse-practice designed to constitute power along with knowledge. Foucault defines an apparatus as an ensemble of discourses, procedures, instruments, juridical regulations, rituals, and so on which control subjects, in this case teachers and students. Together, the various elements in the basic skills apparatus participate in a common discursive project which calls them into concrete existence.[21] The discourse of basic skills and effective schools constructs particular bureaucratic state forms of institutional organization and control that empower bureaucratic and corporate elites and disempower teachers, students, and parents. One cannot but artificially separate a discussion of basic skills and effective schools from an

Introduction

analysis of these power relations it has been involved in constituting in the schools and the broader culture.

Poststructuralism also focuses our attention on the discursive formations and meanings individuals and groups draw upon to "construct" their identities. In this regard, particular attention is placed upon the notion that identities typically are constructed in terms of "difference" and "otherness." That is, individuals in particular institutional sites and role positions (such as teachers, students, and administrators in urban schools) construct identities based on a number of taken for granted bipolar oppositions, including: *masculine/feminine, black/white, working class/middle class, management/labor, them/us,* etc.[22] While generally taken as "natural" categories in everyday life, critical poststructuralists have argued that these oppositions are in fact humanly constructed, serve particular interests within the culture, and may be reconstructed in more democratic, emancipatory, and nonoppressive ways. The challenging of bipolar oppositions is thus one of the central poststructuralist projects. In this study I am particularly interested in the formation of teachers' interests with regard to several bipolar oppositions and hence several "others." I argue that urban teachers' view of students as the other is grounded in the problem of classroom order and the need for teachers to assume adversarial and authoritarian control over resistant students, and that it is reinforced by racial and class "otherness." Teachers' view of administrators as the other is reinforced by bureaucratic power inequalities between teachers and administrators, the legal collective bargaining process that defines teachers as labor and administrators as management, and gender differences between administrators and teachers, particularly in elementary education. Other structural factors, however, may serve to counter oppositions. Teachers, students, and parents, for example, have common interests in resisting elite managerial models of curriculum and instruction that exclude them from the educational decision-making process, and teachers and building-level administrators share common interests in the education of students in their schools. How all of these factors enter into the process of identity formation among teachers is, in the last instance, an empirical question.

Poststructuralism is also associated with the notion that discourses *deconstruct*. This term, as Jacques Derrida uses it, implies that all discourses fail to sustain their claims, reveal logical contradictions, or do not deliver on all their promises.[23] When a discursive practice fails on one of these counts, we may say that it deconstructs (or falls apart conceptually) and must be reconstructed in order to offer an adequate account of, or response to, the situation at hand. Its usefulness in the

Introduction

meantime as a conceptual guide to practice is impaired. Discourses that constitute power relations of domination and subordination more easily deconstruct when evaluated in terms of democratic values; and it is this level of deconstructive analysis that has directed much poststructuralist research. In applying this notion to the substantive issues raised in this book, we can say, for example, that the state-sponsored discourse on effective schools fails to deliver on its claims that it can effectively manage the crisis tendencies that confront urban schooling, fails to explain why urban schools are in a state of crisis in the first place, fails to account for a social phenomenon (urban school crisis) as anything beyond a problem of mismanagement at the school building level, fails on its claims to be politically disinterested, and in all of these ways fails as a democratic discourse on educational change.

The liberal discourse on urban school reform is more complex and represents the results of conflicts and contradictions between humanistic, democratic, and social justice commitments and concerns on the one hand, and corporate concerns with an ever-expanding economy, cheaper labor costs, and increased profit-making on the other. That is, liberalism in America has been forged and discursively organized out of the pursuit of human rights within the context of a society deeply divided by class, gender, and race. Its essential limitation has been its failure to account for the contradiction between social justice and the continuation of such extreme power inequalities. I do not mean to suggest that because of these limitations liberalism has played no progressive role in American politics. Particularly in the 1960s, liberalism played an important role in advancing a civil rights agenda for African-Americans; and since then it has helped advance the civil rights projects of women, gays and lesbians, the physically handicapped, and senior citizens. As Herbert Gintis observes, "the demand for distributional equity, the demand for the extension of the spheres of social life in which rights are vested in persons rather than property, and the demand for the extension of regions of social decision-making governed by formally democratic practices" have been progressive demands; and the struggle to secure and extend civil and human rights in the face of authoritarian and oppressive tendencies in American society is an important one that must continue.[24] Specifically in education the liberal discourse has focused attention on the need to promote both "excellence" and "equity," for teachers to be granted more control of their profession and craft, and for power to be decentralized to the local school site.[25] Adoption of the liberal reform program would go a long way towards overcoming some of the obvious manifestations of crisis in urban schools.

Introduction

Nevertheless, while liberal discourse embodies democratic or emancipatory potential, as Gintis remarks: "Liberalism puts forth a promise it cannot make good. The promise it extends is that of democracy, equality, liberty, and personal fulfillment for all, within the context of capitalism, in the here and now."[26] Liberalism deconstructs to the extent that it lacks a sufficient or comprehensive analysis of the roots of crisis and what must be done to promote excellence in urban schools; and the limitations of the liberal discourse are at least partially responsible for the "conservative restoration" of the 1970s and 1980s.[27] Much of this study, consequently, can be read as an attempt to address these problems in liberal discourse so that it may be better linked to a democratic project capable of challenging the status quo in urban education and formulating a reform agenda that addresses the roots of crisis.

Finally, poststructuralist theory, because it challenges all binary oppositions, including the primary opposition between theory and practice, directs our attention to social and cultural movements, in much the same way that the neo-Marxist notion of hegemony directs our attention towards struggles over meaning.[28] Social movements involve the active rearticulation of cultural themes, values, and agendas in a new "collective discursive practice."[29] This concern with struggle and the possibilities of rearticulating cultural themes in new, more emancipatory ways, returns hope to the democratic project—a hope that had almost been smothered by the determinism of Marxist reproductive theory.[30] Individuals and groups shape their identities or "self-definitions" around struggles of meaning and signification, as they respond to concrete, historically emergent situations. My ultimate concern, then, is in the articulation of an alternative, democratic-progressive discourse in education that draws upon categories from a number of traditions of social theory, and that is linked to democratic, counter-hegemonic movements and struggles. Only through the development of a new "public philosophy" of education, based on a rearticulation of democratic themes and values within concrete situations of educational practice and struggle, can the Left offer a viable way of moving beyond the basic skills era and beyond the crisis that grips America's urban schools.[31] To that end, this book is dedicated.

Organization of the Book

The organization of the book is as follows. Chapter One explores crisis tendencies in urban education from a very broad perspective. My

Introduction

objective here is to provide the general context for the specific discussion of teachers' work culture that follows in subsequent chapters. To do so, I examine four interrelated crisis tendencies in urban education that have motivated crisis management efforts by elite groups during the basic skills era. The first and most publicized crisis tendency in urban education is associated with a failure to effectively teach students the literacy skills and work dispositions workers are expected to possess in the new high-tech, semi-skilled work force. Legitimation crisis tendencies result from a failure to effectively explain the continuation of gross inequalities of achievement between urban and suburban schools and the tendency for urban schools to specialize in preparing students for second-class status. Fiscal crisis tendencies in urban education have continued to threaten system reform efforts, and could lead to the collapse of public education in the years ahead and the privatization of schooling. Finally, crisis tendencies in urban education are related to the "problem of order" in urban schools and classrooms and the failure to effectively contain or defuse student discontent, resistance, and rage. I indicate how basic skills restructuring represents a response to each of these crisis tendencies in urban education, and I point to some of the contradictions and dilemmas of basic skills approaches to crisis management.

Chapter Two places teachers within the context of these various and interrelated crisis tendencies in urban education and analyzes teachers' historically emergent work culture, with a particular focus upon teacher union discourse and practice during the collective bargaining era. Mainstream educational analysis has tended to associate teacher unionism with "role formalization" or narrow adherence to contract language that impedes efforts at "innovation" in the system; while critical analysis has tended to support an "incorporation thesis" that suggests teacher unions serve to accommodate teachers to the existing oppressive system of schooling. Neither the political Right nor the Left, consequently, has looked to teacher unionism as a force for change in the schools. I critique both of these perspectives and suggest elements of teacher union discourse and practice that challenge elite models of institutional organization and control either directly or indirectly.

In Chapter Three I introduce the case study by describing developments in Midstate since the late 1960s associated with state support of basic skills curricular and instructional reorganization in urban schools. These developments culminated in the institutionalization of a minimum competency test for high school graduation and a growing emphasis in urban schools on teaching to the test in order to raise student test scores. I also document the role of the state teacher union

Introduction

in responding to, and attempting to influence, these developments. Ironically, teachers supported an increased state role in education and increased state funding of urban schools throughout the study period, yet the rise of the educational state in the 1970s and 1980s resulted in institutionalization of basic skills reforms that rigidly subordinated and further disempowered teachers. This also points to the dilemmas of liberal reform proposals based on increasing state or federal funding to equalize spending between suburban and urban districts. Recent state supreme court decisions across the nation have pushed states, including Midstate, to assume a much greater share of the urban school budget; and while the equalization of funding is a desirable development, it is hardly progressive if it results in a further transference of power in education to bureaucratic state elites.

Chapter Four begins with a description of the organization and operation of the Urbanville Education Association (UEA), the local teacher union. I point to several factors that impeded the effectiveness and limited the power of the local teacher union in countering central office reform initatives, including: rank-and-file apathy and a small leadership cadre, patriarchal tendencies within a union that represented primarily women, and an inability to link up with black and Hispanic groups in the community that had common interests in challenging bureaucratic elite domination of the system. I then focus upon an examination of specific basic skills reforms in Urbanville between 1968–69 (the first year of collective bargaining for teachers in the state, and the year the state began deliberations on the growing fiscal crisis that gripped urban schools) and 1985–86, based on data from the files of the Urbanville Education Association (UEA). I argue that in the face of new reforms designed to make them teach the basics in a more efficient and effective manner, teachers followed a largely reactive pattern of seeking to slow down and water down central office reforms. Ultimately, teachers were not very successful in countering the slow erosion of their control over classroom work processes that followed from basic skills restructuring and an increasing emphasis upon a "one best way" of teaching the basics, although they were able to impede the effectiveness of central office reforms.

In Chapter Five I analyze a "contract orientation" among Urbanville teachers and the game character of relations between teachers and administrators in more detail. Playing the game absorbed a good deal of time and energy on the part of both teachers and administrators in Urbanville and it undermined the achievement of institutional goals, yet there seemed no clear way out of playing the game without being taken advantage of by the other side. I document conflicts between the

Introduction

local teacher union and the administration over preparation periods, after school meetings and events, school transfers, teacher evaluations, the physical conditions of the schools, etc. This chapter also takes up theoretical issues in more detail that relate to the end of ideology thesis in labor-management relations. I provide a brief history of this thesis in both mainstream and leftist theory and point out some of its limitations and inadequacies in explaining labor-management relations in the era of collective bargaining.

Chapter Six is concerned with classroom management and the problem of order in the basic skills classroom. For this chapter I draw upon data on incidents of teacher-student conflict in Urbanville schools, along with ethnographic data from a middle school in a nearby school district (which I call McKinley School) with a largely Hispanic student population, where I conducted a research project in cooperation with a particant-observer teacher. In both Urbanville schools and McKinley Middle School, basic skills restructuring was associated with promotion of a managerial model of depersonalized, businesslike control of students. The objective, in approaches to classroom management such as "assertive discipline," is to avoid disruptions in the smooth flow of classroom work processes and reduce the level of overt teacher-student conflict so that students spend more time on task and are thus more "productive." I argue that while such attempts to manage the problem of order in urban schools may help defuse some of the conflict potential, the underlying problem is not resolved through the depersonalization of authority relations. Consequently, at some point most urban school teachers almost inevitably fall back upon more directly repressive forms of control in order to maintain their fragile authority in the classroom, which further delegitimizes the school in the eyes of students and lowers both teacher and student morale.

In the concluding chapter I review and summarize major conclusions of the case study data. I then describe and critique the conservative and liberal perspectives on urban school reform at this point in time. Finally, I suggest some of the factors that need to be considered in articulating a democratic discourse on the urban school crisis and school restructuring. Specifically, I discuss critical literacy and critical pedagogy as a foundation for the reconstitution of teachers' and students' work together, the implications of workplace democratization in urban schools, teacher unionism as a potential base in articulating a democratic discourse in education, and the need to integrate class, race, and gender analysis in building a democratic discourse that can effectively move us beyond persistent crisis tendencies in urban schools and in American culture.

1

Crisis Tendencies in Urban Education

> Here then is our conclusion: America must confront, with urgency, the crisis in urban schools. Bold, aggressive action is needed now to avoid leaving a huge and growing segment of the nation's youth civically unprepared and economically unempowered. This nation must see the urban school crisis for what it is: a major failure of social policy, a piecemeal approach to a problem that requires a unified solution.
> Carnegie Foundation for the Advancement of Teaching, *An Imperiled Generation; Saving Urban Schools* (1988).[1]

The Carnegie Foundation's conclusion, while accurate, is hardly new; nor, for all of its impassioned rhetoric, does it suggest a viable way out of the current crisis in urban education. Urban school reform since the early years of the century has been initiated in reaction to persistent crisis tendencies; and these same basic tendencies continue to undermine the system in the waning years of the century. Political and educational leaders in early 20th century America, for example, looked with alarm at the illiteracy of the new southern European immigrants, suggested that they were probably of inferior genetic stock, and decried the disintegration of the traditional family in the new urban slums. They also argued in support of various reforms that were designed to raise students achievement levels, lower drop-out rates,

Chapter One

and attract and hold more good teachers in urban schools. Finally, they all complained that urban schools were not adequately funded, and that this partially accounted for the failure of urban schools to achieve their democratic mission.[2] Of course, while things remain the same in American education, they also change. We are currently witnessing an intensification of a number of interrelated crisis tendencies in urban education as industrial America rapidly becomes post-industrial America, and as society is restructured along even more inequitable lines. Because urban schools are primary sites in which class and race identities are constructed and power relations reproduced and resisted, latent crisis tendencies in urban education have become more manifest over the past several decades as class and race inequalities (in isolation and in combination) have been heightened in the culture. The basic skills reform movement of the past several decades may be viewed as a response by the state to this intensification of crisis tendencies. However, while basic skills curricular and instructional reform may have helped contain or manage crisis tendencies, at least temporarily, it has generated its own contradictions and dilemmas which undermine reform effectiveness, and thus it has failed to resolve or overcome the basic problems that confront urban schools in late 20th century America. Whether or not the corporate and state sponsors of basic skills reforms will be able to patch over these problems indefinitely remains to be seen, for the problems run very deep and crisis tendencies confront system managers and policy-makers on a number of fronts simultaneously. In what follows I examine four crisis tendencies in urban education, suggest how basic skills curricular and instructional reform has been a response to these crisis tendencies, and point to some of the contradictory ways that the basic skills restructuring of the urban school curriculum has also contributed to current crisis tendencies.

Crisis Tendencies and Crisis "Management": A Theoretical Grounding

Before embarking on a discussion of the particular, interrelated crisis tendencies that shape urban school reform, we need a general conceptual model of crisis, crisis tendencies, and crisis management, along with a sociohistorically specific theory of crisis tendencies in contemporary Western democratic society. We may begin by observing that the notion of "crisis" implies, of necessity, some notion of a "system" that is in crisis. "System" implies an analysis of discursive practices that is

Crisis in Urban Education

structural and that emphasizes the reproduction of dominant power relations, although in its less reductionistic form, systems theory also emphasizes the analysis of dynamics within cultural systems that lead them to change and transformation. Systems theories are limited by their structural-functional view of social reality, in which discursive practices get abstracted and reified. Nevertheless, a systemic theory of discursive practices can prove useful, and is in fact essential to a comprehensive appreciation of the current situation. In what follows in this chapter, and through this book, I employ a theory of crisis tendencies in urban schooling to provide a broad conceptual picture of how various developments are linked in discourse and practice and how they participate in "producing" a culture which is more than a collection of individual beliefs and actions. Systems theory focuses our attention on the societal forest rather than its individual or constituent trees, and upon the ecological forces that impact upon that forest and shape its development. "Urban schooling" as a systemic notion implies that individual urban schools participate in broader structures of discourse and practice that have identifiable effects and consequences within cultural formations. It is important to bear in mind, however, that the image of the system is always a constructed one, created to aid in the clarification of concrete social phenomena. As some point, abstract notions of system and crisis tendencies need to be deconstructed and analyzed as historical and situationally specific discursive practices.

In general terms, all critical theories of crisis presume that crisis tendencies are the more or less inevitable outgrowth of contradictions in the discursive governing principles or imperatives by which social formations and relations of domination are organized and maintained within a culture. Of contradictions in the economic governing principles of advanced capitalism, for example, Marxist economics points to the tendency for the rate of profit to fall, the tendency for markets to become "saturated," and the tendency for an economic system that depends upon competition and decentralized decision-making to become increasingly centralized and monopolistic. Environmentally, capitalism as a discursive practice is organized around the imperative for unrestricted growth, which leads to the progressive despoilment of the environment, decline in the quality of life, and ultimately an environmental crisis—the proportions and implications of which we are just beginning to comprehend. That is, definite limits exist within the ecosphere which make unrestricted exploitation of resourses and markets impossible.

Of course, the basic contradiction of capitalist society as Marx saw

Chapter One

it was that the technical and social relations of production generate conflicts that lead to the formation of classes—self-constituting and antagonistic social groups organized around competing discursive practices. Individuals' class affiliations and positions within the material productive processes place them in the position of either dominating subordinate groups, being dominated, or participating in a combination of both options. This structures "objective" conflicts of interests between those who dominate and those who are being dominated, which at some point *may* lead to conflicts which can no longer be contained within the constraints of existing power relations. In "crude" (reductionist and deterministic) Marxism, class conflict and crisis is believed to be inevitable, so that intervention in the scientific progress of history towards socialism is unnecessary or futile (depending upon one's perspective). The system collapses on its own accord, based on its own contradictions.[3] Lenin and the Bolsheviks revised this deterministic Marxism by arguing that a revolutionary cadre was needed (at least in some cases) to bring about the revolution and impose socialism.

Within the Western democratic socialist and neo-Marxist traditions crisis tendencies have been understood much more complexly, and the analysis has focused on sociocultural and political crisis and struggle. That is, belief in the inevitability of the transformation to a post-capitalist, democratic socialist society has been rejected. Among the most well-developed critical analyses of crisis tendencies in advanced capitalism over the past several decades has been that provided by Jürgen Habermas, writing out of the Frankfurt tradition of critical theory.[4] Habermas and others in the Frankfurt School have argued that elite groups, with the assistance of an interventionist state, may be able to avoid crisis situations altogether through the proper fine-tuning of the economic system, the co-optation of opposition, and a general fragmentation and instrumentalization of interests in the culture. Furthermore, when crisis situations develop, they have no inevitable path. They may just as likely result in conservative or reactionary political change as transformative and democratic change, which is to say the politics of crisis remain open. Crisis tendencies, consequently, must be understood in their historical and cultural specificity, not through the application of some scientific model of progressive development.

To Habermas, the end of liberal, 19th century capitalism and the emergence of advanced, 20th century capitalism in the West is signaled by heightened concentration of power and monopolistic tendencies in the economic sphere, and state intervention in the regulation and subsidization of markets to create and improve the conditions for utilizing excess capital and "heightening the productivity of human labor."[5] This role, performed by the state administrative apparatus, is in turn made dependent upon the securing of public support and the belief that state policy serves democratic values and ensures equality under the law. In formal democratic societies, this legitimation of state policy must be secured and resecured against tendencies for state policy to be revealed in the mass media and popular culture as interested rather than "neutral." To the extent that state policy that serves elite more than democratic interests is legitimated, it is through the widespread promotion of an ideology which depoliticizes civic life. Habermas talks of a "civic privatism of the civil public" in advanced capitalist society, which orients individuals towards "career, leisure, and consumption." The ideology of advanced capitalism also seeks to instrumentalize all discursive practice by emphasizing a narrow means-ends or "purposive rational" approach to policy-making and a calculative, economistic conception of individual interests.

According to Habermas, while the ideology of advanced capitalism has been fairly successful in depoliticizing the role of the state, and state officials have become quite effective in managing crisis situations, crisis tendencies threaten on a number of fronts. First, mass loyalty is maintained only so long as governmental policies are rationalized as serving the interests of the democratic majority. But if state policy is presented as the end product of a rational decision-making process based on broad public interests, it lays itself open to rational analysis and questioning in the public, which may reveal its contradictions and hidden interests. Habermas uses state educational planning, especially curriculum planning, as a case in point. "Whereas school administrations formerly merely had to codify a canon that had taken shape in an unplanned, nature-like manner, present curriculum *planning* is based on the premise that traditional patterns could as well be otherwise."[6] That is, the ideology of purposive rational decision-making generates pressure to rationally justify a curriculum that was previously largely taken for granted; and this may be quite difficult to do. Second, as the instrumental orientation towards life that characterizes the capitalist worldview spreads throughout society and as traditional cultural values regarding respect for authority and deference are eroded, policians and state officials must increasingly buy public support by promising what they cannot always deliver. "Advanced capitalism creates 'new' needs it cannot satisfy."[7] Finally, to maintain the stability of a system of power relations, the dominant values of the sociocultural

Chapter One

system must be sufficient to motivate individuals to perform at peak levels in schools, at the workplace, and in the home—beyond what is minimally required. Advanced capitalist society, according to Habermas, "does not generate the requisite quantity of action-motivating meaning" to induce individuals to perform at such peak levels.[8] Motivation crisis tendencies in this regard are related to the failure of bourgeois privatism and competitiveness to permit access to "relations of solidarity within groups or between individuals" or to offer support or consolation "in the face of the basic risks of existence."[9]

Since these crisis tendencies identified by Habermas are not the result of random or idiosyncratic forces, but rather are imminent within the discursive practice of advanced capitalist power relations, "the possibilities of dealing with these crises are specifically limited to the system."[10] Furthermore, each response by elite groups to institutional crisis involves some revision in the social contract and some sharing of power. While Habermas portrays Western culture as riddled with contradictions and crisis tendencies, it would be wrong to give the impression that he views the collapse of the current system as inevitable, or even likely in the near future. In fact, Habermas tends to presume—wrongly, I think—that the current form of crisis management by elite groups works pretty well to maintain their domination. Consistent with the generally pessimistic appraisal of mass culture by the Frankfurt School of critical theorists, Habermas concludes that "a system crisis is not to be expected in advanced capitalism.... This does not exclude constellations in which crisis management fails, with far-reaching consequences. But the appearance of such constellations can no longer be systematically predicted."[11] While I would be less pessimistic than Habermas about the prospect for a radical democratic response to crisis in advanced capitalist society, one important point here is that nothing is assured regarding either a crisis in bourgeois culture or the response to that crisis.

On a surface level, Habermas's view of state policy-making as a form of "muddying through" from one crisis to the next is similar to that advanced by various inherently conservative theorists of political science and administrative management, although Habermas carries the analysis much further and politicizes a purposive-rational worldview that is taken for granted in the neo-rationalist forms of administrative theory and political science.[12] For example, in a classic mid-1950s text on administrative rationality, Herbert Simon argued that effective management involved a continual need to respond to rapidly changing situations, which implied a strategy of adopting satisfactory rather than optimal solutions to particular problems at hand—what he called

Crisis in Urban Education

a "satisficing" strategy. Of the modern "administrative man" Simon noted: "Whereas economic man maximizes—selects the best alternative from among all those available to him, his cousin, administrative man, satisfices—looks for a course of action that is satisfactory or 'good enough.'"[13] Simon viewed this satisficing policy on the part of administrators as resulting from a "limited rationality." That is, they lack complete information on all possible options and the consequences of given courses of action. However, consistent with Habermas, we may recognize a satisficing strategy as primarily necessitated by systemic contradictions and crisis tendencies that prevent a full resolution of conflicts, rather than from a mere lack of complete information. Even if bureaucratic administrators had all the information they could possibly want in deciding on a given course of action, they could not choose a course of action that would not generate its own contradictions—at least so long as their options are limited by the imperative to maintain elite bureaucratic domination. This implies that dominant groups are not able to maximize their interests within situations, even if they are able to ensure that the current institutional structure remains basically intact. Furthermore, "satisficing" approaches may only succeed in putting off resolution of systemic conflicts and thereby increase the likelihood of a major crisis at some point.

All of this has important implications when applied to the analysis of developments in urban schools and the basic skills reform movement. This movement represents a response by bureaucratic and political elites to a cluster of crisis tendencies in urban education that, over the past several decades, have threatened the effectiveness of urban schools in meeting their assigned goals and mandates. To the extent that these crisis tendencies have become more manifest in recent years, we may speak of a crisis in urban schooling that is composed of four interrelated sub-crises. These crises include: a crisis of work skills in the semi-skilled labor force, a legitimation crisis, a fiscal crisis, and a crisis of control. Let me now discuss each of these in turn and suggest how basic skills restructuring has been both a response to crisis and (ironically) a contributing factor in the perpetuation and extension of crisis tendencies in urban schools.

Curriculum and the Crisis of Work Skills in the Economy

While curriculum and the educative process are obviously about much more than preparing young people for the job market, throughout

Chapter One

much of this century (and particularly since the mid-1950s) curriculum reform has been heavily influenced by a "human capital" rationale which suggests that economic progress and increased productivity can be engineered through a greater investment in the pre-skilling of future workers in schools.[14] Somewhat ironically, while neo-Marxists are often accused of advancing a deterministic and functionalistic "correspondence principle" which explains what goes on in schools in terms of economic needs and interests, the conservative state discourse on school reform has done far more to advance an economically determinist and functional analysis.[15] Much of the conservative criticism of American education in recent years has been directed at the failure of the schools to prepare students with the requisite skills and knowledge base expected of workers in an increasingly high-tech and high-skill labor market. More specifically, the high-tech critics of the schools have argued that in the post-industrial information age of sophisticated microelectronics and computer advances, the schools have failed to train enough qualified young people in the various disciplines that underlie the design, application, and management of new production technologies. Secondary mathematics and science are cited in particular as curricular areas that have been severely weakened by teacher shortages, a lack of attention to critical thinking skills, a watered down or dumbed down curriculum, and too much student freedom to choose easy electives and "frill" classes rather than more demanding and rigorous advanced math, science, and foreign language classes. Teachers have been urged to promote higher order critical thinking and decision-making skills among their students rather than memory and recall of factual information. The overall social and economic aim, of course, is for America to regain its competitive edge in the development and marketing of new products and the application of new technologies in an increasingly global economy.[16] While low-paid, semi-skilled Third World workers use the technologies we design to produce the commodities we consume, American jobs, we are told, should be professional, technical, and managerial in nature. The problem is then understood in terms of public education's failure to supply enough new high-tech workers to meet the growing demand.[17]

I do not wish to downplay the significance of the economic restructuring that has occurred over the past several decades or its impact on the movement to reform the curriculum to produce more high-tech workers. The high-tech, high-skill labor force is growing in America, and industry has trouble recruiting enough candidates with the general intellectual, technical, and decision-making skills it looks for in employees; and this is one reason American industry must import so much

Crisis in Urban Education

brainpower. In suburban schools, where most future workers of this type are being educated (in advance of post-secondary education), student thinking skills are often limited to outlining lectures and reducing course content to lists and "facts."[18] Nevertheless, this problem is less extreme, and more manageable, than the crisis that grips urban schooling in America, where most of the new semi-skilled workers are being educated. For example, there is an oversupply of college graduates on the job market vying for high-tech, professional, and managerial jobs but an undersupply of high school graduates in the semi-skilled job market.[19] In spite of all the talk about changes in the structure of the economy consistent with the growth of high-tech industries and a new professional-managerial class, America in the late 20th century is not becoming a primarily middle-class country.[20]

The number of traditional assembly line factory jobs has plummeted in America over the past several decades as production has shifted to the Third World, but few of the new jobs being created to replace them call for a significantly higher skill level.[21] Instead, most are what we might call high-tech/low-skill jobs. This is the case, for example, even in California's much-heralded Silicon Valley and along Boston's Route 128 corridor. The majority of jobs call for no more than a high school diploma, and workers are expected to perform relatively routine and menial operations. They assemble micro chips and monitor quality control checks on assembled chips, and they enter and retrieve data using simple computer programs. The video display terminal, in cases such as this, is used to control the worker more effectively and completely by standardizing and regimenting work processes. Even in the service industry, the fastest growing segment of the job market, the video display terminal has made significant inroads in rationalizing and regimenting work processes. In one sense these new entry-level jobs *are* more high-skilled than the old manual labor jobs in industry. The new technologies require an understanding of symbols, codes, and written directions far more than did the old technologies. Now, workers must be able to read and interpret gauges, printouts and graphs to monitor job processes.[22] More than specific manual job training, semi-skilled workers are now expected to have transferable or generalizable literacy and computation skills.[23] While the literacy standards for this fast-growing segment of the labor force may be higher than for the old manual working class, they are still low, and literacy gets defined in a way that promotes direction-following rather than decision-making and autonomy.

The problem, as business sees it, of course, is that urban schools have not been able to guarantee that their graduates are functionally

Chapter One

literate even in these narrow terms. Not only is student achievement low, but half or more of the students in most urban school districts drop out before the twelfth grade. The direct economic costs of this literacy crisis are enormous and well-documented. According to a recent press report, one medium-sized corporation estimated that it could save over one billion dollars each year if its employees had stronger basic reading and math skills. Because some employees had trouble taking measurements, material was wasted unnecessarily in the production process; because other workers misread job orders and computer instructions, the plant had to redo many orders and pay more overtime.[24] Aside from these obvious inefficiencies, the remedial education of employees on the job represents yet another cost that is routinely absorbed by the employer and passed on to the consumer. The bottom line, then, has been a prime motivating factor in corporate support of the state-sponsored "war on illiteracy."

The mismatch between the literacy skills of high school graduates and the literacy requirements of the semi-skilled job market was a serious problem by the mid-1960s and partially accounts for the Johnson administration's heavy investment in remedial or compensatory education and job training programs for disadvantaged youth. The Nixon administration continued to focus attention on the declining literacy skills of American workers; and in early 1970, shortly after American astronauts first landed on the moon, the U. S. Commissioner of Education proclaimed that the achievement of universal literacy was to be the "moon shot for the seventies."[25] In fact, more time and effort (and federal money) went into studying the literacy problem and defining "functional literacy" than in fighting illiteracy in the schools. Literacy skills, federal officials argued, first needed to be identified through task analysis so that these skills could then be taught to students through performance-based "instructional delivery systems." One of the most influential examples of such a task analysis was conducted at the University of Texas as part of an Adult Proficiency Level (APL) study, the results of which were released in 1975. Research focused on identifying the everyday literacy needs of a minimally functional American worker, citizen, and consumer through interviews and observations. Based on this task analysis research, the study team identified 65 separate reading and writing skills that all Americans supposedly needed, including such things as reading job notices, filling out job applications, addressing envelopes, and reading road and street signs.[26] These skills subsequently served as a basis for constructing standardized minimum competency tests to evaluate whether or not students had mastered them following exposure to a skill-based curriculum. An official of the U. S. Office of Education, using the APL study, inferred that 57 million Americans did not then have the skills needed to perform basic entry-level job tasks, a figure far higher than previous official estimates.[27] This alarming figure promoted a sense that urban schools were failing in their mission and that they needed to be drastically reorganized to teach the basics. By the end of the decade, most states were considering some form of minimum competency test, generally set at the ninth-grade reading and writing level, as a requirement for those seeking to obtain a state-certified high school diploma.[28] As W. Winterowd observes, from such a definition of basic skills a vision emerges of the "functionally literate" citizen "who should not aspire beyond the modest rounds of getting a job, going to work, and coming home in the evening to read the newspaper (briefly, before watching television)."[29]

As a result of increased pressure from the state, throughout the 1970s and 1980s urban schools underwent a systematic streamlining of the curriculum to eliminate those classes, topics, and activities not directly related to basic skills mastery. Many students were enrolled in up to three or four "communication skills" or "developmental math" classes each day, with instruction tailored to the particular skills students were identified as lacking in diagnostic pre-tests; and teachers were expected to teach the basics in all other courses as well, so that students would score well on standardized state achievement tests. By the mid-1980s, little room remained for a liberal arts curriculum, such as that once available in urban schools for the college-bound. Nor was there room for a progressive curriculum and the project method, that appealed to students' intrinsic desire to work cooperatively on practical, hands-on activities. Nor was there much room left for the traditional vocational-technical curriculum that once enrolled so many students in urban high schools, since businesses had found that in most cases it is more cost-effective to provide training on the job to workers with general literacy skills. All of these curricular domains, along with many of the extracurricular activities that were long a hallmark of public schools in the inner city, largely had been jettisoned as school officials sought to concentrate and focus attention on mastery of basic skills.

In spite of all the attention given to the crisis of literacy by state and federal officials and all the changes in the urban school curriculum, there was no sign that the situation was improving by the mid-1980s. In fact, it seemed to be getting worse. When Jonothan Kozol published his best-seller, *Illiterate America*, in 1985, he concluded that "Sixteen percent of white adults, 44 percent of blacks, and 56 percent of His-

Chapter One

panic citizens are functional or marginal illiterates. Figures for the younger generation of blacks are increasing. Forty-seven percent of all black seventeen-year-olds are functionally illiterate. That figure is expected to climb to 50 percent by 1990."[30] In 1987, one researcher on the topic was led to conclude: "Reports that tens of millions of Americans are illiterate excite waves of indignation, excoriations of the school system, and demands for prompt redress and rectification. Hundreds of millions of dollars are spent annually on the teaching of reading, on research, on the production of textooks, and on the training of teachers—and the problem persists."[31] And in 1989, it was possible for the *New York Times* to warn of an "impending U.S. Jobs 'disaster'" with a "work force unqualified to work" and with "schools lagging far behind needs of employees."[32] Like the earlier war on poverty, the war on illiteracy had become bogged down as it began to confront the magnitude of the problem and its resistance to quick fixes.

Why is it that urban schools have not been able to ensure that disadvantaged students learn the functional literacy skills they need for gainful employment? One simplistic (if also partially accurate) response is that students come to school with more skill deficits than in previous eras, so that schools must spend more time on remedial education. A related presumption is that students come to school with severe psychological and emotional problems which result from growing up within a culture of poverty. While these may be signicant contributing factors in explaining the functional literacy crisis, they tend to end up blaming the victim.[33] For one thing, such "skill deficit" and "culture of poverty" rationales fail to recognize that because inequalities in the socioeconomic sphere account for many of the learning deficiencies and psychosocial problems students bring with them to school, these inequalities will need to be reduced in order to make significant progress in responding to the functional literacy crisis.

Secondly, the functional literacy crisis has more to do with a failure to motivate students than with any deficits or deficiencies on the part of students. Urban schools have presented students with a basic skills curriculum and a mode of instruction geared to preparing them for the semi-skilled labor force; and this limits the intrinsic motivation students can derive from their learning experiences. Furthermore, skill-based workbooks and drill sheets may provide a logical basis for organizing the learning process to maximize basic skills mastery, but they structure student work processes in a routinized manner which is minimally engaging and offers few learning surprises or variation in learning activities. Basic skills supporters argue that motivation can be supplied through an extrinsic system of student rewards and incentives

Crisis in Urban Education

for good work and high achievement on standardized tests. But as the curriculum becomes increasingly devoid of intrinsic motivation, it seems doubtful that a few rewards and incentives will adequately motivate most students to excel. So long as students feel estranged from the school world, and view their school work as a form of alienated labor, they will merely go through the motions of learning or actively resist the learning process. Consequently, a basic skills curriculum generates a crisis of motivation related to a lack of meaning or purpose in work. Schoolwork does not provide a discourse or practice that helps students form identities around personal empowerment, community, or social justice. Work constituted around a basic skills curriculum ceases to be an arena for the objectification of experience in self-enhancing ways; it fails to produce anything of value that students can "own" or identify with.[34] Furthermore, because the school's knowledge and discourse of instruction represents to disadvantaged students the knowledge and discourse of the dominant culture, in opposition to which their own identities are constructed, they resist learning it or valuing it. This is partly because the bearers of this knowledge are often middle-class, white teachers. To adopt the discourse and values of the teacher and the school is to side with the "other."[35] Finally, as getting ahead becomes a less realistic option for most urban students, and as school credentials fail to provide a means for getting ahead, it is more difficult to convince students they should work hard and stay in school.

An emphasis upon skill mastery and passage of minimum competency tests may also be expected to encourage a calculative teach-to-the-test orientation among urban school teachers that is counterproductive to the acquisition of transferable or usable literacy skills by students. Preparing students to pass specific tests, rather than ensuring that they understand or can apply what they are learning in real life situations, becomes the direct object of instruction. Since administrators, teachers, and students are all urged to focus upon raising test scores, a form of institutional goal displacement is encouraged in which means become ends. Teachers are rewarded for going to almost any means (short of giving students the test in advance) in order to ensure that target test pass rates are attained, so that the superintendent can demonstrate to state officials that the district is making progress in the battle against illiteracy. In fact, recent rises in state competency test scores reported in some states may be attributed largely to the success of teachers in teaching to the test; and these gains may not even be transferable to other standardized achievement tests for which students are not explicitly prepared.[36] Basic skills restructuring may, conse-

Chapter One

quently, become increasingly difficult to sell to the public in the decade ahead as test scores are demystified as indicators of student achievement, and this poses the possibility of a legitimation crisis.

Up to this point, I have limited my comments to a crisis of functional literacy in the post-industrial labor force. But literacy skills are not the only economically functional skills students are expected to learn through exposure to discursive and ritualistic practices in schools and classrooms. Students are also expected to learn certain work norms, attitudes, dispositions, and habits which make them good workers and able to adapt to modern institutional (i.e., bureaucratic and hierarchical) structures. Philip Jackson coined the term "hidden curriculum" in 1968 to refer to the tacit level of meaning conveyed to students through the overall organization of classroom life, a meaning that, Jackson presumed, must help young people learn to negotiate adult roles successfully.[37] For example, learning how to work on your own, compete with others for advancement, value neatness and form over content, wait in lines, be evaluated impersonally, deny immediate desires, and so forth, were all important lessons, according to Jackson, although they tended to become the most important curriculum, and conflicted with the educative goals of the institution in that they encouraged docility and conformity more than creativity and critical thinking.

While Jackson adopted a basically noncritical, functionalist stance towards this hidden curriculum of classroom life, preferring to view it as the inevitable consequence of progress, leftist analysts have appropriated the notion of hidden curriculum to refer to the process whereby students learn alienated modes of labor through the organization of the social and technical relations of classroom work. For example, in Michael Apple's and Nancy King's mid-1970s study of the hidden curriculum of work in a kindergarten classroom, the authors demonstrated that at a very early age, children were already learning to view work as alienated labor. Within the context of the kindergarten classroom, work came to be defined in a number of concrete ways. Among them: "Work includes any and all teacher-directed activities;" "all work activities, and only work activities were compulsory;" "every child had to start at the designated time;" and "work activities also involved the children with the same materials and produced similar or identical products or attainments."[38]

The most elaborate and well-developed critical analysis of the hidden curriculum of work norms is to be found in Samuel Bowles' and Herbert Gintis' *Schooling in Capitalist America,* which was published in 1976.[39] The authors' analysis of schooling pointed to the fact that

Crisis in Urban Education

major elements of school organization and practice roughly correspond to, or replicate in important ways, the social and technical relations of production and the hierarchical division of labor typical of capitalist society. Schooling helps meet the needs of the capitalist economy for different types of workers not only through tracking but through a differentiated hidden curriculum. Bowles and Gintis remark: "The structure of social relations in education not only inures the student to the discipline of the work place, but develops the types of personal demeanor, modes of self-presentation, self-image, and social-class identifications which are the crucial ingredients of job adequacy."[40] Furthermore, the authors argued that differences in the social backgrounds of students, combined with expectations regarding their likely future economic positions, accounted for the fact that poor, minority students "are concentrated in schools whose repressive, arbitrary, generally chaotic internal order, coercive authority structures, and minimal possibilities for advancement mirror the characteristics of inferior job situations. Similarly, predominantly working-class schools tend to emphasize behavioral control and rule-following, while schools in well-to-do suburbs employ relatively open systems that favor greater student participation."[41]

Despite being limited by a functionalistic and deterministic analytic perspective, the hidden curriculum and correspondence principle literature pointed to important general *effects* of the schooling process in maintaining relations of domination. Corporate leaders certainly understand the importance of the hidden curriculum and have sought to make it a more explicit element of the curriculum. For example, a 1984 report released by the Conference Board (a nonprofit business think tank) which examined what personnel officers in major companies think about the work habits and attitudes of current high school graduates, concluded that employers are even more distressed by a lack of discipline and direction-following skills among workers than they are about inadequate literacy skills. The report noted that while functional literacy is important, "so also is a willingness to show up, to take directions, to work together, and to be responsible for your job."[42] To the extent that work attitudes and dispositions such as these have been made a more explicit concern in curricular and instructional reform in recent years, the term "hidden curriculum" becomes less appropriate as a descriptor for the transmission of these attitudes and dispositions through the learning process.

A basic skills curriculum is designed to address the crisis of work norms and attitudes in several ways. Most significantly perhaps, it elevates direction-following and listening skills to the status of formal

Chapter One

curricular topics. Students, for example, may be assigned a drill sheet which asks them to follow a set of detailed directions to find their way out of a maze or solve a mystery puzzle. Similarly, skill kits may include cassette tape recordings of someone reading directions, and students are expected to listen carefully, keep up with the pace, and not fall behind or get lost. In these cases, work norms are the primary curriculum students are learning. In a more general sense, and as I have already noted, the form of the basic skills curriculum (irregardless of the explicit curricular content) promotes certain adaptations to work routine. Self-guided and self-paced workbooks and other curricular materials teach self-disciplined direction-following along with the curricular content, as students learn how to pace their work to complete piecework expectations within the established time frame. The contradictions of a basic skills curriculum in this regard have to do with a tendency for students to go through the motions of completing learning activities without much awareness of, or concern for, the topic being studied. Students learn to follow directions at a low level of engagement, do the minimum expected, and in other ways adapt to routine in ways that result in a minimalization of learning. Since these adaptations to work are widespread in the lower rungs of the labor hierarchy, a basic skills curriculum appears to socialize students well to fit into the working world that awaits them. Nevertheless, since this work ethic is responsible for many of the problems faced by American industry as it strives to compete around the world, the hidden curriculum of basic skills instruction may actually exacerbate rather than ameliorate the crisis of work skills in the economy.

I have suggested that in organizing the curriculum and instructional process in ways that better prepare young people with the literacy skills and work dispositions appropriate for their expected occupational destinations, urban schools further alienate students and generate a crisis of motivation that is irresolvable within the parameters of existing basic skills curricular reform models. This problem is exacerbated by the current stretching out of the labor hierarchy in post-industrial America, which produces greater inequalities and conflicts between socioeconomic groups. Between 1979 and 1987, the income of the poorest fifth of the American population fell by nine percent, while that of the top fifth rose 19 percent.[43] If these disparities increase, as they are expected to, and as the opportunity for social advancement declines in a society in which there are fewer good jobs, it seems likely that it will become even more difficult to motivate urban students to stay in school, learn the basics, graduate, and become "good" semi-skilled workers. At the same time, urban schools will be pressured to focus more on basic skills instruction, to overcome the skill deficits associated with a culture of poverty, and to better prepare urban youth for gainful employment in jobs that are available. The contradictions of basic skills instruction are, consequently, likely to become even more visible in the years ahead.

Legitimation Crisis Tendencies and "Effective" Urban Schools

Max Weber's classic treatment of the problem of legitimation in *Economy and Society* pointed to "the generally observable need of any power to justify itself."[44] In the modern era, Weber argued, authority was increasingly legal, formal, rational, and procedural in nature, and legitimacy was grounded in the appeal to the bureaucratic rational manner in which a decision is made. Domination within a formally democratic society could no longer be legitimated through appeals to traditional norms of deferrence to authority and belief in a natural order. Those who dominate must stake their claims upon merit, which implies several things. First, bureaucratic decisions are supposedly based on rational procedures, which ensure that they maximize the public good rather than serve the more narrow interests of a power elite. Second, to sustain the claim that those who make decisions do so because of their special merit and expertise rather than privilege, the state is charged with ensuring that all persons and groups in society have an equal opportunity to advance themselves. In the Weberian tradition, consequently, public education is typically presented as an essential legitimating institution in modern society, and it is presumed to perform (albeit imperfectly) its assigned role of actually providing for equality of opportunity.[45] Critical theorists, on the other hand, see the legitimation claims of the state as an ideological distortion, designed to mask the fact that public institutions serve some interests more than others.[46]

The public schools in America have obviously played a central role in legitimating the existence of inequalities in American society through claims to the universalistic and impartial evaluation of all students according to a common standard. However, once the schools are shown to primarily reproduce existing class and race power relations rather than provide equality of opportunity, the stabilization of validity claims is brought into question, and this further politicizes the role of the schools. Legitimation problems may be particularly severe when competition for scarce "good" jobs increases and as these jobs become

Chapter One

even more tied to the possession of credentials. Of course, even when urban schools served a largely ethnic European student population early in this century, when students supposedly pulled themselves up by their own bootstraps and took their education seriously as a means of social mobility, urban public schools still prepared many more students for the semi-skilled industrial labor force than for middle-class status, and resistance to the schooling process and credentialing was strong among many young people and their parents.[47] But as urban schools have served more poor African-American and Hispanic students, and as opportunities for socioeconomic advancement have declined in recent years, urban schooling—in its effects—has become even less a vehicle of advancement for urban youth and more a restricter of opportunities. That is, for most students it confers a relative disadvantage rather than advantage in the competitive, hierarchically structured socioeconomic world that awaits them after they leave school.

How, then, have urban schools legitimated their role in the construction of dominant power relations, particularly those organized around class and race? How have they sold the public a package of basic skills reforms, and through what significations and validity claims? Traditionally, legitimation problems in urban education have been contained and criticism of the schools deflected by pointing to exceptional individuals from disadvantaged backgrounds who did well in school and left the community to "become somebody" in the mainstream (i.e., white, middle class) society. In an ironic fashion, this emphasis upon those who "made it" against the odds also serves to blame the victim—in this case the majority of socioeconomically disadvantaged students who are presumed to be deficient in some way.[48] Similarly, school administrators in the inner city have pointed with pride to their small college preparatory programs as signs that some of their students are "salvagable" and "have futures" while ignoring the great majority of students who are failing or entering the job market with very limited options. An example is provided by Michelle Fine in her ethnographic study of a New York City high school. She reports: "At the first Parents' Association meeting, Mr. Stein, the principal, boasted an 80 percent 'college-bound' rate. Almost all graduates of this inner-city high school head for college: a comforting claim oft repeated by urban school administrators in the 1980s. Although accurate, this pronouncement masked the fact that in this school, as in other comprehensive city high schools, only 20 percent of incoming ninth-graders *ever* graduate. . . . Not named, and therefore not problematized, was the substantial issue of low retention rates."[49]

While conservative educational critics have pointed to the exceptional students who get ahead to prove that the system can work for disadvantaged students, and have explicitly or implictly placed the blame for lack of achievement and a failure to get ahead squarely upon individual students and their families, liberal critics have been more inclined to place blame with the culture of poverty which presumably leaves many students emotionally disturbed, lacking in proper motivation, and prone to delinquency. Cameron McCarthy observes that, "while rejecting conservative emphasis on the defective innate capacities of children from minority and low socioeconomic groups," liberal educators have "sought to explain minority failure by an equally damning theory, ... that minority youth [are] 'culturally deprived'.... Children are culturally deprived when they come from home environments that do not provide the kind of organized stimulation that fosters 'normal' development."[50] Liberals have advocated a therapeutic approach to helping individual disadvantaged students overcome their particular cultural and academic deficiencies so that they (as individuals) can get ahead within the dominant culture. The professional educational discourse has drawn heavily, in this case, upon a medical anology. Student learning "disorders" and "pathologies" are diagnosed using standardized tests developed by professional experts, and individualized curricular programs are presribed for each student, tailored to their particular learning needs. If an emotional disturbance is interfering with the student's ability to learn effectively, an Individualized Educational Plan is designed, and the student is categorized for special treatment in a "resource room." The public is encouraged to view teachers, administrators, and other professional staff members in the school as specialized technicians, with access to a highly esoteric body of knowlege derived from the "science of education" that allows them to "prescribe" a curricular remedy for student learning problems. In this way, a process of schooling which is laden with political implications is presented in a depoliticized manner, and a system to bring the individual student under more complete control and domination is constituted through professional discourse as a means of "normalizing" deviants and "helping" the disadvantaged.[51]

These legitimating themes in urban education—a blame-the-victim ideology, a medical-prescriptive view of student learning "needs," and claims to "scientific" expertise and neutrality—have all been reasserted in somewhat revised but not essentially different form in the basic skills era. This time, however, the individual student or the culture of poverty is not blamed exclusively for student failure. The individual school and/or local school district staff are also (and more directly) blamed for failing to reorganize to effectively teach basic skills. This is the

Chapter One

primary message of the so-called effective schools movement in urban educational policy-making and research that was advanced with the support of the Reagan administration and a number of state departments of education during the 1980s. Effective schools research was aimed at revealing the attributes of effective urban schools, those in which students' test scores were significantly higher than would be expected given the socioeconomic mix of the student body.[52] Supposedly, once these attributes of effective schools were revealed through organizational studies and statistical multivariate analysis of school differences, principles of effective school management could be derived. In fact, although the more respected researchers in effective schools research have downplayed the significance of the differences revealed through research, many researchers and state officials have pointed to the effectiveness literature as proof that urban schools can be effective without fundamental changes in the organization of the schools.

In the Reagan-Bush era, effective schools research has provided support for arguing that urban schools can heal themselves without a massive infusion of new funds. All local administrators need to do, according to this perspective, is to study the principles derived from research on effective schools and replicate them in their schools. The problem is identified as one of poor management at the local level based on inadequate information about what works to raise test scores. For example, in the introduction to a 1987 report on the findings of effective schools research distributed to local educators by the U.S. Department of Education, entitled simply *What Works*, Secretary of Education William Bennett wrote: "The first and most fundamental responsibility of the federal government in the field of education is to supply accurate and reliable information about education to the American people. The information in this volume is a distillation of a large body of scholarly research in the field of education. . . . [We] now *know* certain things about teaching and learning as a result of the labors of the scholarly community."[53] What is being invoked here is a technical-rational or purposive-rational model of curricular decision-making that, as I have already argued, legitimates state educational policy as the end product of a rational or scientific rather than political or interpretive process of assessing problems and possible responses. The state, effective schools supporters claim, is merely interested in finding out what works so that all schools can be more effective. Yet behind this mask of benign neutrality lies an implicit set of educational goals, paradigms of curriculum and instruction, and models of teaching and learning that are never questioned, yet have political origins and implications.

Crisis in Urban Education

What, then, are the principles of effective schools endorsed in reports such as *What Works* and supported in "effective schools" research? Among those principles generally associated with effectiveness are: a clear school mission that focuses on basic skills mastery, agreement among the staff as to the importance of basic skills, selective recruitment of teachers who accept the basic skills philosophy of the school, and clear guidelines for the achievement of instructional goals with everyone assigned a specific role, so that all know what is expected of them. School principals are depicted as assuming a particularly important role in setting "explicit operational goals regarding students' academic performance, which are clearly communicated to their staff members."[54] The managerial ideology of school effectiveness that lies behind these various principles is one borrowed directly from industry, with a powerful but caring plant manager setting clearly defined production goals and assigning roles to workers. It calls to mind the image of the harmonious "company family," where everyone works together to increase productivity, and in which workers prefer to be told what to do rather than be bothered with making decisions. To the extent that individual urban schools fall short of this ideal image, they may be blamed for their own ineffectiveness, and the state is absolved of responsibility.

Along with the legitimation of a business managerial model of school organization, the effective schools discourse has promoted the notion that the learning styles and needs of socioeconomically disadvantaged students in urban schools are significantly different from those of middle class students in predominantly suburban schools, and it thus has contributed to the legitimation of a dual system of education based on class and race differences. I am not suggesting that this has been the explicit or deliberate intent of effective schools researchers or their supporters in the state; but it has been one of the presuppositions that define this discourse on urban school reform. For example, in a mid-1980s study of effective schools for students of differing socioeconomic status (SES), Philip Hallinger and Joseph Murphy concluded that teachers in high SES schools are most effective when they encourage "attainment of broader intellectual and social goals," and that "teachers in the high-SES schools were more likely than their low-SES counterparts to talk in terms of meeting the needs of the whole child. In the low-SES schools, teachers and administrators felt a keen responsibility to focus on the mastery of cognitively oriented basic reading and math skills."[55] The authors also suggest that urban students are more likely to develop positive self concepts and feel better about themselves when the focus is on the basics and when extrinsic rewards are used to

Chapter One

motivate. They note, for example, that "instruction that focuses on mastery of basic skills... is structured to promote a high level of success results and higher self-expectations among [disadvantaged] students." Consequently, "It may be that schools that serve low-SES students must focus on a limited set of learning objectives in order to achieve a high level of instructional effectiveness."[56] The "success" of disadvantaged students is thereby presented as a paramount concern even if success comes by lowering expectations for students.

Finally, the effective schools discourse has supported the contention that socioeconomically disadvantaged students should be motivated primarily through extrinsic means. Hallinger and Murphy, for example, noted that middle class students, who possess the "proper foundations of readiness skills, tend to find learning tasks more interesting and rewarding in and of themselves."[57] On the other hand: "Studies of effective schools for the urban poor indicate that widespread systems of reward and recognition for academic and behavioral accomplishments contribute to the development of positive learning norms among students."[58] Urban students supposedly will conform and achieve as expected in return for citations, small prizes, and recognition. What gets legitimated here is a hidden curriculum of work motivation. School work for urban students, like the work most of them will perform later in the labor force, is not designed to be intrinsically motivating. Consequently, student workers must be motivated to cooperate through means external to the curriculum and the process of learning. The "science" of behavioralism, with its emphasis upon positive reinforcement, takes for granted the bifurcation of work and human motivation that characterizes alienated labor. But none of these issues are raised in the literature; and the effect is to tie a conservative educational policy to scientific research findings.

While the effective schools movement in urban education is generally viewed as a fairly recent phenomenon, in fact it is a recent manifestation of a quite long research tradition in education, concerned with uncovering the attributes of effective teaching or instruction. Literally thousands of studies have been conducted within this tradition, generally multivariate statistical studies linking particular instructional practices and organizational variables with significantly higher or lower student test scores. By 1964, when Bruce Biddle and William Ellena reviewed the field in their introduction to *Contemporary Research on Teacher Effectiveness,* a study sponsored by the American Association of School Administrators, the National School Boards Association, and the Department of Classroom Teachers of the National Education Association, they concluded on a pessimistic note: "[W]ith all this research

Crisis in Urban Education

activity, results have been modest and often contradictory. Few, if any, facts are now deemed established about teacher effectiveness, and many former 'findings' have been repudiated. . . . Many educational researchers have abandoned the field of competence research as a simple-minded approach to a vastly more complex topic. . . ."[59] J. M. Stephens, at about the same time, argued that effectiveness research was flawed by a myopic concern with differences between schools of equal socioeconomic status. Most of the research reported "no significant differences" or only minor significant differences between effective and ineffective teaching or administrative styles because they were looking at schools which were more similar than dissimilar. He concluded that "in the typical comparison of two administrative devices, we have two groups which are comparable in the forces responsible for (say) 95 percent of the growth [in student achievement] to be had and which differ only in the force that, at best, can affect only a small fraction of the growth."[60]

Finally, in the early 1970s, Christopher Jencks and his associates at Harvard, in their influential reassessment of the Coleman Report's statistical data on equality of opportunity in education, sought to lay the effectiveness research tradition to rest. They reported: "We can say that if all high schools were equally effective (or ineffective) inequality between twelfth graders would fall less than one percent."[61] Differences between schools, they found, tended to "wash out" or become almost trivial in accounting for student achievement when compared to the much more powerful influence of the socioeconomic mix of the student body, or the socioeconomic status of students' parents. The effective schools movement is, of course, right in affirming that schools can make a difference and, in a few cases, do. But by emphasizing the often slight or questionable statistical differences between effective and ineffective urban schools, the broader and more decisive uniformities are deemphasized. Furthermore, while minor statistical differences between urban schools may tell us something about how to better organize a school as a basic skills factory engaged in the routine production of test score outputs, these differences tell us little about how to change urban schools in ways that empower students and actively engage them in the pursuit of educational excellence. The urban school crisis cannot be reduced to a series of individual school, teacher, or student failures but must be seen as the result of contradictions and dilemmas that lead outward from the schools into the culture.

How successful has the effective schools movement been in legitimating a basic skills focus for the urban school curriculum and in shifting responsibility for the urban school crisis to individual students, teach-

Chapter One

ers, and local administrators? That is a difficult question to answer. There has been no major resurgence of delegitimating crisis tendencies in urban education since the 1960s, when America's inner cities exploded and radical community groups accused public educators of perpetuating a racist tracking system and curriculum and refusing to dismiss racist teachers and administrators. Over the past several decades, African-American, Hispanic, and other disenfranchised groups have devoted much of their energy to working within and with the public school system to ensure that the schools are made accountable for raising student achievement levels, that overt racism and the brutalization and intimidation of students stop, and that students leave school with marketable skills. While these concerns have been important ones, they have led many urban community and civil rights groups to support a strong basic skills focus for the curriculum based on the belief that without basic skills urban students will not stand a chance on the job market once they leave school. The alternative to basic skills instruction, from this viewpoint, is a return to the irrelevant, watered down curriculum and dead-end vocational programs of the pre-basic skills era. Test scores have also been accepted by many African-American, Hispanic, and other urban community groups (as they have by a broad spectrum of the American middle class) as indicators of achievement; so that when state officials assert that they are committed to raising student test scores and have a plan to do it, it is understandable that these groups may rally around the state reform agenda rather than oppose it.

At the same time, it is important to keep in mind that the legitimation of the current structure and operation of urban schools must be continuously rewon by dominant groups in the face of destabilizing, delegitimating tendencies which are not fully containable or resolvable without dramatically changing the role that urban schools have come to assume within the culture. Many community groups and parents in the inner city view the public school system with a good deal of mistrust, as a basically middle-class, white institution designed to keep "our kind" at the bottom. Whether or not legitimation crisis tendencies will soon lead to another crisis similar to that of the 1960s, or will be more or less successfully managed indefinitely, remains impossible to predict. However, it would seem that at some point in the not-to-distant future, when the basic skills reform agenda has clearly failed to deliver on its promise of providing urban youth with the real-life skills they need to get ahead, and as the cost of not getting ahead increases in post-industrial America, major legitimation problems are likely to surface again in urban education.

Crisis in Urban Education

Fiscal Crisis and a "Cost-Effective" Curriculum

In the mid- to late 1970s, local governments in America's blighted urban areas were hit with a severe fiscal crisis at the same time that the nation's economy began to sink into recession. New York City, for example, after years of living beyond its means and with a declining tax base, found itself barred from the municipal credit market in 1975, and municipal bankruptcy loomed. The infrastructure of the city—its roads, sewer systems, subways, and bridges—could not adequately be maintained, and essential social services were threatened. Under the auspices of state and federal officials, New York City was allowed to avoid bankrupcy by embarking on an austerity budget that involved cutbacks in essential city services, higher fares and taxes, widespread dismissal of city employees (even some with a good deal of seniority, or in the case of teachers, tenure), and tighter systems of fiscal oversight by state and federal officials. The city laid off 60,000 employees between 1975 and 1978 as part of the bail-out plan.[62] The New York City fiscal crisis sent shock waves through the financial and educational communities and underscored the fragility of local urban government in America. For at the same time that New York City was experiencing fiscal crisis, most other major urban governments were experiencing a similar if less severe phenomenon.

Public schools in particular were among the most hard hit of local urban governmental agencies by fiscal crisis. Throughout the 1960s, the urban landscape in America changed, as the white working class and middle class moved out of urban neighborhoods and poor black and Hispanic families replaced them. Many of the whites who remained in the inner city enrolled their children in parochial and private schools; so that urban schools became increasingly institutions which served the urban working class and underclass. At the same time, property taxes had plummeted in urban areas as industry relocated to the suburbs along with the middle class; and urban schools, which were dependent upon local property taxes, faced a situation of rapidly declining fiscal resources and increased need for special student services and programs. The federal government, through the Johnson era "war on poverty," and more particularly through passage of the Elementary and Secondary Education Act (ESEA) in 1965, stepped in to compensate somewhat for the inability of urban school districts to go it on their own. Through categorical funding for special programs for the disadvantaged under Title I of the ESEA, local urban districts were able to establish more remedial programs, hire more teacher aides, purchase instructional materials, etc. At its height in the late 1970s,

Chapter One

the federal share of the educational budget was less than ten percent; but it was two to three times as high in urban districts, which had quickly become dependent upon the new federal monies.[63]

With the monies also came new performance-based program funding and evaluation requirements, which began basic skills restructuring. Only by adopting skill-based, teach-to-the-test approaches to curriculum and instruction could urban districts generate the kinds of hard data federal officials required.[64] However, the federal education budget was facing significant cutbacks by the early 1970s as the "war on poverty" spurted to a halt, and state funding was also increasingly restricted. In response to renewed fiscal crisis tendencies in the 1970s, and under court pressure in many cases, state government moved to assume more funding responsibility for urban schools. By 1985, the major source of school revenues was state government, which contributed 50 percent of the total, a rise of ten percent or more in most states within one decade, while the federal government contributed six percent.[65] As with federal monies, most state monies have been categorical, and require quantitative output data on student achievement. The rise of the educational state has thus encouraged local urban school districts to restructure curriculum and instruction around basic skills mastery and test passing. By the early 1980s, with the nation's economy beginning to recover from recession, with austerity measures beginning to have an effect, and with state funding on the rise, the threat of an immediate fiscal crisis subsided somewhat. But the underlying crisis tendencies remain in most urban areas, ready to erupt again when recession hits. In 1990, for example, 9,000 teachers in Massachusetts—a full one fifth of the public school teaching staff—received layoff notices because of insufficient state funds; and in New York City schools faced cuts in funding that threatened an ambitious new program of reform. In a number of states, a shortfall in state funding threatened to close public schools until the legislature could find a way to fund them.[66]

The fiscal crisis of the state, and of urban public schools more particularly, was a hard new reality by the early 1970s and it remains with us in the 1990s. On the broadest level, fiscal crisis tendencies in urban school districts are an outgrowth of contradictions in American society. As James O'Connor argued in his influential 1973 study of *The Fiscal Crisis of the State*, the state in advanced capitalist societies "must try to fulfill two basic and often contradictory functions— *accumulation* and *legitimization*." By accumulation, O'Connor meant that "the state must try to maintain or create the conditions in which profitable capital accumulation is possible." Through tax policies, court rulings, state-sanctioned collective bargaining, a military policy designed to open up Third World resources and markets, and an educational policy designed to prepare skilled and disciplined workers, the state works to increase profit margins. Legitimation involves the attempt "to maintain or create the conditions for social harmony" within the context of an economy which benefits some much more than others.[67] Specifically, this entails convincing people that state policy serves the interests of the democratic majority more than the interests of economic power brokers. In order to do this, some effort must be made to "meet various demands of those who suffer the 'costs' of economic growth, primarily in terms of welfare payments, unemployment compensation, and social security."[68] O'Connor's argument regarding fiscal crisis was that although the state increasingly pays the bill to maintain the conditions necessary for profit accumulation, profit is appropriated privately. "The socialization of costs and the private appropriation of profits creates a fiscal crisis, or 'structural gap' between state expenditures and state revenues. The result is a tendency for state expenditures to increase more rapidly than the means of financing them." Secondly, fiscal crisis results from the "private appropriation of state power for particularistic ends."[69] That is, various special interest groups—including corporations, organized labor, the military lobby, etc.—make claims on the state budget which are not easily satisfied.

Fiscal crisis creates contradictory pressures upon the state. On the one hand, the state must invest in essential social and educational services since these are not provided for in the free market economy but are essential to its survival; and on the other hand, the state faces economic pressure to reduce state expenditures because they represent a diversion of capital from the "productive" private sector and the generation of profit. Consequently, powerful economic forces pressure the state to cut taxes and further reduce spending on essential social services, which ultimately impacts adversely on the economy. The fiscal crisis, O'Connor argued, is also fueled by middle- and working-class cynicism and distrust of government, because they believe it does not serve their interests. That is, the very recognition that the state serves elite rather than democratic interests (a legitimation crisis) discourages the average citizen from investing financially in the state, and this leads to a deterioration of public services that increases public cynicism and distrust. The tax revolts of the 1970s were visible signs of this disaffection by a broad spectrum of the American public. O'Conner viewed these tax revolts as forms of resistance against a state which did not serve the public. "Voting 'big spenders' out of office, organizing

Chapter One

political movements, refusing to pay taxes as an act of political conscience—these are a few of the many forms of political noncompliance." But because these are depoliticized resistances, that is, resistances that fail to relate specific reform agendas to a general critique of the cultural system and a vision of a better society, O'Connor argued that they are also limited and contradictory, that "in the last analysis, tax resistance is likely to fail. . . ." For its part, he argued, the Left had not exploited the issue of the fiscal crisis of the state "because it had been wedded to the modern liberal tradition that has sought an enlarged government role in the economy and has paid little or no attention to the structure or the burden of taxation."[70]

While fiscal crisis tendencies threaten to destabilize the current system of public education in urban areas, in some ways fiscal problems have also helped elite groups assert more top-down bureaucratic control over the schools. For example, when funding is tight, it is easier to rationalize institutionalization of cost-effective basic skills delivery systems, which are compatible with top-down control. Basic skills curriculum materials, such as workbooks, mimeographed drill sheets, and skill kits are also cheaper than investing in textbook series, the price of which has risen dramatically over the past decade or so. As the fast food industry has learned that disposable food containers and utensils are more cost-effective (even if less environmentally sound) than reusable containers and utensils, so urban schools have learned that a disposable or throw-away curriculum, which students use once and then discard, is more cost effective than using reusable textbooks—especially when textbooks tend to get trashed quickly. Aside from the fact that basic skills curricular materials are cheaper than textbook series to begin with, they also represent a discursively leaner curriculum, since they specifically target the skills students are expected to know on standardized achievement and competency tests.

Basic skills restructuring has also allowed urban school districts to keep their labor costs within tight budgetary restrictions, since the more rationalized and self-guided the instructional process becomes, the more teacher assistants, aides, and permanent substitutes can be employed to replace experienced teachers when they retire or leave the system.[71] Classroom management, more than pedagogic skills, is required. I am not suggesting here that such making do with less-qualified and lower-waged teachers has been the intent of either those who support basic skills curricular reform or those who manage urban schools. To a large extent, urban school administrators have had to make do in these ways because it is hard to attract and hold highly qualified and experienced teachers in the system. Nevertheless, the effect has been to lower the cost of teacher labor within the educational process and the quality of instruction in the classroom.

In a related way, the basic skills curriculum has facilitated a policy of maintaining relatively large classes in urban schools, a policy made necessary by fiscal crisis. Because curricular materials are largely self-guided by students and students are kept busy at their seats in the routine production of "piecework," they can be supervised by one teacher who scans up and down the rows of students working on their own. While "excellence" in education may require a highly *personalized* approach to instruction, in which the teacher negotiates the curriculum and helps students construct meaning and significance within the context of individual and small group projects, such an approach to education would also be more expensive since it would require a significant lowering of the student to teacher ratio. Individualized instruction, in which a standardized and technologically-rationalized curriculum is prescribed to all students, has allowed fiscally starved districts to continue to get by with larger classes in an attempt to cut costs. While such a policy was not the intent of state reformers and works against goals for raising achievement levels in urban schools, it has proved to be a policy that makes sense in responding to an immediate fiscal crisis situation in urban schools in which highly-personalized, small-class approaches to instruction are out of the question. This suggests the need to better address the continuing fiscal crisis of the state before significant advancement can be made in hiring more teachers and dramatically lowering class sizes.

While urban school districts have somehow found a way to get by financially during the basic skills era, the costs have been significant. Financially starved schools, no matter how cost-effective they are, cannot hope to fulfill the role they are expected to perform by various interest groups. Furthermore, the reduction in labor costs achieved by relying upon basic skills curricular systems and materials must be offset by the fact that highly-qualifed and experienced teachers are an absolute prerequisite to achieving excellence in education. This is probably so even if we define excellence in the narrow sense of higher test scores on minimum competency tests. In the long run, labor-intensive approaches to organizing instruction in urban schools—with more teachers working in a highly personalized manner with fewer students—seem a much better and even more cost effective response to the urban school crisis. Yet, with fiscal crisis tendencies threatening, such a response is not seriously considered as a realistic option. Of the

Chapter One

various crisis tendencies that undermine the system of urban schooling, fiscal crisis looms as a real possibility in the years ahead and is one of the most tangible and pressing manifestations of systemic crisis.

Basic Skills and the Crisis of Order

Since discourses are always constituted in concrete social practice, they are always strategic and have transformative capacity as well as ideational content.[72] Because they are always about power relations, and are always involved in constituting and reconstituting power relations, discourses always address in some way the problem of order within situations that is an inherent aspect of the constitution of power relations of domination and subordination. Discourse-practice constitutes (and is constituted by) power, which Cleo Cherryholmes defines as "relations among individuals or groups based on social, political, and material *asymmetries* by which some people are indulged and rewarded and others negatively sanctioned and deprived."[73] If urban schooling is implicated in the construction of particular sets of power relations whereby inner-city youth are negatively sanctioned and deprived relative to their suburban counterparts, who are indulged and rewarded, then these power relations must be constituted in concrete discourse-practice. The final crisis tendency in urban education, consequently, is this problem of order at the classroom and school building level as teachers and students resist the imposition of dominative sets of power relations and attempt to reconstitute power relations in ways that increase their sense of control over their everyday working lives.

Poststructuralist theory helps us appreciate the dualities of power and knowledge and theory and practice in analysing the problem of order in urban schools. But in the critique of traditional and modern approaches to constituting power relations within the culture, Max Weber remains a primary source. Weber distinquished between three "ideal typical" forms of authority used to maintain relationships of domination and subordination: traditional, charismatic, and bureaucratic rational.[74] Each of these may also be understood as an ideal typical form of managing the problem of order in schools and classrooms and thus as a way of organizing curriculum and instruction. Traditional domination relies on a belief within the public that authority is to be respected, and that authority does not need to answer to the public. It is the right of traditional leaders to grant privileges or decree punishments at whim, and their judgements are not to be

Crisis in Urban Education

questioned. Psychologically, despotic authority is maintained at least partially by an orientation towards obedience and submissiveness within the culture. Nevertheless, traditional authority must also rely on the power of coercion and censorship when the public begins to doubt that authority represents its interests. Power relations may be maintained through a rein of terror, fear, and intimidation.

Certainly in education, the image of the traditional teacher is most associated with the stern, disciplinarian approach to instruction favored in 19th century Victorian British grammar and "public" schools, where the emphasis was on disciplining both the mind and the body and corporal punishment and humiliation were primary mechanisms for control. This type of traditional teacher was long favored by administrators in urban schools in the early decades of this century, since such teachers were presumably best able to maintain classroom order and student discipline. But traditional teaching was already under attack during the progressive era for being undemocratic. Early progressives such as William Heard Kilpatrick viewed traditional approaches to teaching the immigrant working class as too Prussian or disciplined for American tastes, since they glorified obedience rather than initiative. Kilpatrick wrote in his classic *Foundations of Method* (1925): "I have heard certain persons talking a great deal about 'instinctual obedience,' as if they wanted some of our people to grow up especially strong in obedience while others perhaps should grow up especially strong in commanding those more obedient ones. It doesn't sound like democracy to me."[75] It was not until the late 1960s, however, that traditional authoritarian approaches to instruction in urban schools began to be seriously challenged. The civil rights movement made the public and public officials more sensitive about charges of institutional racism, and created a public climate in which repressive forms of control in urban schools could no longer widely be legitimated or were no longer politically viable. Finally, traditional forms of control in urban schools were associated with heightened conflict and hostility between teachers and students, and this encouraged bureaucratic and state elites to search for ways of lowering the conflict potential of the classroom through new approaches to classroom management.

In an effort to move beyond traditional approaches to teaching in urban schools, a number of leftist and humanist critics of the schools began in the late 1960s to celebrate charismatic urban school teaching. According to Weber, charismatic leaders arise precisely because they are able to appeal to people's desires and hopes and articulate their discontents. Charismatic leaders emphasize the virtues of duty, loyalty, and trust among the people; and they maintain authority precisely so

Chapter One

long as the people believe that their leader or leaders embody these virtues. Charismatic leaders also are presumed to possess highly unusual or extraordinary capacities which set them apart from the ordinary, so that people are willing to invest trust in them.[76] When applied to teaching, the charismatic model is associated with an ideal that has been very influential both within the profession and popular culture. The force of teachers' convictions, their appealing personalities, and their success in grabbing and holding student attention are often depicted as the primary means by which effective teachers' teach. Cooperation rather than conflict between teachers and students characterizes these idealized depictions of teaching, with the teacher serving as a primary role model for eager students who are motivated to "please the teacher" by working hard and succeeding. From *Goodbye Mister Chips,* to *Welcome Back Kotter,* to *The Prime of Miss Jean Brodie,* to *Head of the Class,* to *Stand and Deliver,* the mass media has equated good teaching with charismatic teaching. One problem with charismatic teaching, however, is that it depends upon the exceptional personality. According to Weber, charisma is a "purely personal gift of grace." This means that "one can neither teach nor train for charisma. Either it exists *in nuce,* or it is infiltrated through a miracle of magical rebirth—otherwise it cannot be attained."[77] Furthermore, while charismatic teaching may be valorized and may appeal to teachers' professional ideals and commitments, it is difficult to carry off consistently, from day to day and class to class. Finally, the impositional character of urban schooling works against charismatic teaching, since charismatic leadership tends to lose its appeal when students lose faith in the institution of schooling as serving their interests.

As Weber saw it, traditional and charismatic forms of domination tend to deteriorate into despotism since they cannot be legitimated adequately as consistent with the interests of the majority. They may also evolve progressively into a third, distinctively modern form of authority, in which control by social elites is grounded in meritocracy—a meritocracy of trained specialists working for various state agencies, applying scientific research and purposive-rational analysis to various social problems, and held accountable to the public through formal democratic controls. This third type of authority Weber called "legal," and its characteristic modern Western form was bureaucracy. To the extent that they approached the ideal type, officials in modern state bureaucratic agencies exercised authority through the application of universalistic rules and procedures to all specific cases. Power became impersonal and neutral in its application, and upon this basis (along

Crisis in Urban Education

with formal democratic controls) the state legitimated the exercise of power. For Weber, social progress could be measured by "irresistibly expanding bureaucratization of all public and private relations of authority and by the ever-increasing importance of expert and specialized knowledge."[78] Supposedly, bureaucratic control lowered the conflict potential within society, since authority was exercised impersonally. Bureaucratic officials merely "followed the book" in making decisions, so that they could not personally be blamed for dominating subordinate groups. Furthermore, because the rules were rationally grounded, it became harder to criticize them. For Weber, then, bureaucratic control within the context of formal democratic oversight provided the soundest basis for legitimating dominative power relations in society.

Weber focused on the description and critique of purposive-rational thinking as expressed in the modern bureaucratic organization. However, the purposive-rational worldview of 19th century capitalism also gave rise to technical control of work processes through the mechanization of production. Unlike bureaucrartic controls, which are found in their most ideal typical form in various bureaus and agencies of the 20th century state (whether bureaucratic socialist or democratic capitalist), technical controls have been most fully developed in industry, and the critique of the technical relations of production is associated with the Marxist rather than Weberian tradition. The study of technical controls has been associated in recent years with Harry Braverman's influential book, *Labor and Monopoly Capital*, the main theme of which is the deskilling of labor through "scientific management" at the turn of the century.[79] Braverman shows how Frederick Taylor and other early pioneers of scientific management, through the process of time and motion studies and task analysis, were able to break complex craft skills into a series of discrete, sequenced performances which could be taught to semi-skilled workers. Henry Ford, of course, added the technical control of a moving assembly line, with stationary workers performing assembly line-paced tasks in a routine, repetitive manner. Since the technology of production is the controlling factor, the worker is conceptualized as an extension of the machine, controlled by it. Technical control represented a powerful new means of holding subordinated workers accountable to the central office plan, and while technical controls were first developed in industry they have slowly been extended to clerical office work in this century.[80] Most recently, the computer keyboard and video display terminal, computer software, and the clerical workstation all represent efforts to guide employees through a predictable work sequence using primarily technical con-

Chapter One

trols. Like bureaucratic controls, technical controls are also impersonal, and thus may be expected to lower the potential for conflict on the shop or office floor.

Bureaucratic and technical controls may be viewed as manifestations of a common transubstantiation of power relations in modern, industrial society. Both also embody similar contradictions. Although Weber viewed bureaucracy as a progressive phenomenon, he also agreed that it was prone to red tape and sometimes placed upholding a rule above the just resolution of a dispute or service to the client.[81] By the mid-20th century, as the term bureaucracy had come to be synonymous in the public mind with inefficiency and undemocratic control, a generation of liberal and leftist neo-Weberians in America began to focus on the issue of inherent "bureaucratic irrationalities," or "dysfunctions." One of these irrationalities is encapsulated by the term "vicious cycle of control," the notion that modern hierarchically organized institutions go through a cycle of control in an attempt to resolve the problem of order. For example, Alvin Gouldner, in his 1950s study of bureaucratic control in American industry, argued that central office managers are motivated to impose more bureaucratic rules over shop floor production in an effort to ease the workplace conflict and tensions resulting from close, personalized supervision and direction of workers.[82] However, the proliferation of bureaucratic roles and job rationalization, accompanied by an "indulgency pattern" of supervision, leads to worker slowdowns and a decline in productivity as workers meet only minimum job requirements. This situation, in turn, motivates central office managers to reassert a "stringency pattern" of close and personalized supervision of workers to increase productivity, which sets the vicious cycle in motion once more. Neither "indulgency" nor "stringency" patterns of supervision adequately resolve the problem of order. This means that attempts to depersonalize relations of domination and subordination through bureaucratic rationality always confront a dilemma; at some point, top-down control must be reimposed in a personal, authoritarian manner, especially during certain periods of increased resistance by subordinates.

The contradictions of technical control are similar to those of bureaucratic control, as one might expect, since they both involve a rationalization of power relations. Marx argued that the technical relations of production in capitalist societies alienated individuals from both the process and the product of their labor, and even when this alienation remains depoliticized and fragmented, it clearly generates motivation problems that are not easily resolved. Furthermore, the logic of capitalism is based solely on the maximization of individual

Crisis in Urban Education

self-interest in the achievement of desires, and this leads to an instrumentalism among workers that fails to support high levels of productivity. That is, since work is not perceived as a pleasant or fulfilling experience, workers seek to lower time and effort expended at work in exchange for a given wage, and they devote their attention to family, leisure activities, and consumption. As I noted earlier, Habermas argues that traditional values (such as deferrence to authority, an achievement orientation, and pride in work) are essential to motivate individuals in advanced capitalist societies, since capitalism cannot provide the necessary motivational values on its own. Yet these traditional values have been progressively and "non-renewably dismantled" during the modern era.[83] Disengaged, apathetic, and vaguely discontented workers may appear to pose no obvious threat to the continuation of elite domination, but their disengagement generates motivational crises that resist treatment by more bureaucratic and technical control.

To this point I have indicated the general theoretical and conceptual framework for an examination of the problem of order in urban schools, and I now want to apply this framework to the specific case of basic skills restructuring. We may begin by observing that basic skills restructuring represents one phase of a vicious cycle of control in urban education. The 1960s had been a time of empowerment for urban teachers. They won the right to organize and engage in collective bargaining (even if bargaining was severely restricted), and in schools and classrooms across the country, individual teachers and groups of teachers, often with the active support of principals but sometimes without it, began to experiment with a radical new pedagogy and curriculum. It was, to a large extent, a curriculum constructed in practice by individual teachers and students, organized around the project method rather than traditional subject areas, with textbooks abandoned or used only as one resource. What came to be known as the "open classroom" or "alternative education" movement in American public education represented a grassroots attempt by teachers, in collusion with students, to take over the classroom from the bureaucratic institution within which it was located. They were allowed to get away with such a radical decentralization of power because bureaucratic elites hoped to cool out much of the discontent from below and coopt critical teachers by allowing them space within the system to "do their own thing." This represented a phase of de-bureaucratization and an indulgency pattern of control in an attempt to overcome growing teacher and student resistance to the stifling bureaucratic, top-heavy structure of urban schooling, and growing resistance more generally in the culture to bureaucratic and hierarchical forms of control. There

Chapter One

was also evidence that a radically decentralized and student-centered approach to curriculum and instruction was working, to remotivate students, and this partially accounts for early support of "informal education" by liberal foundations such as the Carnegie Foundation for the Advancement of Teaching.

In Charles Silberman's widely influential 1970 book, released by the Carnegie Foundation and entitled *Crisis in the Classroom*, the author argued that the real crisis in urban education was the failure of the old system to properly educate some students for anything other than docility as workers, consumers, and citizens. The new approaches that Silberman found teachers were experimenting with in his travels across the country seemed to offer real hope of actively engaging students and helping them gain control over their lives. Of such programs in urban schools, he noted: "They are showing that alienated, hostile, bitter, semiliterate or illiterate young people who have been living off the streets can become articulate, sensitive, highly motivated learners—that many of them not only can finish high school but can go on to college."[84] The trouble was that such a decentralized system of control allowed teachers and students to use their newfound freedom to reconstruct curriculum and instruction in ways that were inconsistent with preparing individuals to fit into the existing economic, political, and sociocultural order; corporate and state leaders began calling for a return to the basics, which also implied more top-down bureaucratic control over what went on in classrooms. This bureaucratic control is constituted as: standardized testing schedules and procedures, performance-based lesson and unit planning requirements, individualized educational plans (IEPs) for classified students, and other reporting and record-keeping requirements designed to hold local administrators and teachers accountable to the basic skills instructional goals of the school. Basic skills restructuring, consequently, may be viewed as the most recent bureaucratization phase of a vicious cycle of control in urban education that has a long history.

However, basic skills reforms represent more than a reimposition of bureaucratic controls over classroom work processes, for bureaucratic controls are now tied to new *technical* controls over instruction, which had not been available in an earlier era. Basic skills technical controls include: self-guiding curricular skill kits, skill-based pre-tests and post-tests, workbooks and drill sheets, and other prescriptive curricular materials. On the most obvious level, such prescriptive curricular materials place rigid parameters around what gets taken for legitimative knowledge in urban schools. But on a more pragmatic if less obvious level, prescriptive curricular materials control students, since they are

Crisis in Urban Education

kept occupied with their self-guided "seatwork." Furthermore, because the curricular materials are self-guided by students, teachers do not assume a central role in directing work tasks and focusing students' attention on their work, and this helps defuse some of the conflict potential between teachers and students that characterize more traditional forms of dominative teaching. Students are also less prone to challenge the teacher's authority or disrupt work processes if they are allowed to socialize or work together quietly with a partner while they complete assignments.[85] So long as students continue to progress at the expected pace in the curriculum and pass criteria-referenced post-tests, even if they seem a bit bored in the process, central office administrators have cause to view basic skills restructuring as a success.

The bureaucratization and technicalization phase of the vicious cycle, however, is undermined by its own contradiction. As the curriculum becomes more highly rationalized, and as teachers no longer direct and oversee student work as much as monitor the classroom work routine, students tend to respond by minimizing their effort and slowing down the pace of work as much as possible, which encourages teachers to use personalized, authoritarian control tactics to reestablish the work routine and expected work pace. This is where the current situation presents special problems. For although authoritarian control of students was a viable option in the past, it has become less viable in recent years, for both legal and political reasons, which means that the system may have to continue to rely upon bureaucratization and technicalization of control, and pay the increasingly high costs of such control. One of these costs, for example, is the high level of "wasted" time in the classroom—wasted, that is, in terms of productive engagement with the curriculum to generate expected learning outcomes. The "effective schools" movement has emphasized the importance of increasing "time on task" as a means of raising student achievement levels. However, as teachers prod students to waste less time socializing, devote more attention to their assigned work, and speed up the pace of work, students are likely to respond with increasing hostility and resistance. In response, as Linda McNeil observes, teachers may "choose to simplify content and reduce demands on students in return for classroom order and minimal student compliance on assignments."[86] Bureaucratic and state officials are consequently left with a limited set of reform alternatives in responding to the "time on task" problem in urban schools.

Another sign of the dilemma of control in urban education is the unofficial tolerance of high class-cutting and truancy rates. According to a 1988 study by the New York City Board of Education, class-

Chapter One

cutting and truancy reduces the total classroom attendance in the system by up to 20 percent on any given day; and since the school system is funded by the state on the basis of average daily class attendance, the system loses substantial money because of this problem. In the worst schools, according to the study, up to half of all students were typically missing from any given class on any given day. Some students cut so many classes—three or more out of a seven period school day—that school officials referred to them as "in-school truants." One central office administrator was quoted as saying: "Years ago, cutting was considered something akin to a high crime or jail break. But social attitudes have changed. Today, cutting is much more rampant in some schools."[87] My point here is that administrators cannot successfully resolve the problem of class-cutting and truancy in urban schools so long as they cannot offer urban students a more motivating and less alienating curriculum; and because they cannot crack down on students without further alienating them and encouraging them to drop out, the system puts up with intolerably high levels of student disengagement. Consequently, as with other crisis tendencies, the crisis of control in urban schools is managed at a very substantial cost.

Conclusion

In this chapter I have sought to describe the basic skills restructuring of the urban school curriculum as a response to various crisis tendencies that afflict urban education. These crisis tendencies generate certain perennial problems. Curricular reform, in these terms, may be understood as a strategic response, by dominant interest groups in public education, to a set of destablilizing tendencies in institutional steerage that continuously threaten to deteriorate into crisis. The objective of reform is the amelioration or containment of unanticipated consequences and conflicts resulting from contradictions in the governing principles and imperatives of the institution. I have also argued that, while basic skills reform initiatives over the past several decades may have helped manage or contain some crisis tendencies, this has been at the cost of exacerbating other crisis tendencies.

The state has been remarkably successful in promoting the restructuring of the urban school curriculum consistent with a basic skills orientation; but success in implementing reforms should not be confused with successful reforms, that is, reforms that effect the changes for

Crisis in Urban Education

which they are designed and sponsored. In 1989, incoming Education Secretary Lauro Cavazos released the latest federal report on student performance in the nation's schools and acknowledged that, since 1983, when *A Nation at Risk* was issued, the schools have failed to stem the "rising tide of mediocrity" to which that report called attention. According to information released in the federal report, the nation's schools are becoming more "urban" each year as white and middle class student enrollment continues to drop; approximately 60 percent of students currently enrolled in public schools come from single-parent families, with the parent most often the mother and living on public welfare. Drop-out and truancy rates continue to rise in the inner city and test scores remain stagnant at an unacceptably low level.[88] Although federal and state education officials talk about the need to turn around the worsening situation in urban schools, it remains unclear how they intend to do it. As socioeconomic inequalities increase and the new semi-skilled work force grows in size (along with the underclass), as the root causes of fiscal crisis tendencies remain unresolved, and as new technological developments continue to transform the curriculum in ways that allow for the further standardization and regimentation of teachers' and students' work, things may get worse in the years ahead. The current state-sponsored reform initiatives in education have not been very effective, and at this point they face a contradiction of diminishing returns: each new reform that further centralizes institutional decision-making in the name of greater efficiency and accountability further alienates teachers and students from both the process and product of their labor. While many current problems in urban schools are at least partially attributable to the widespread adoption of basic skills reform models, it seems doubtful that a return to more repressive, authoritarian forms of control in urban schools is a viable political option. Whether or when this might lead to crisis which can no longer be managed without major structural changes cannot be predicted with any accuracy.

2

Teachers and Crisis: Teachers' Work Culture in Sociohistorical Perspective

Teachers are employed in schools, which have the primary ideological function of constituting biological individuals into individual ideological subjects who will freely enter the labour market as willing bearers of labour power. Insofar as teachers assist in, or are the agents of these processes... then to that degree are they agents of capital (almost certainly unwitting ones) serving the ideological function of capital by contributing to the formation of consciousness conducive to maintaining and reproducing capitalist social relations. (Kevin Harris, 1982)[1]

Instead of defining teachers as clerks or technicians, we should reconceive the role of teachers as engaged and transformative intellectuals. This means viewing teachers as professionals who are able and willing to reflect upon the ideological principles that inform their practice, who connect pedagogical theory and practice to wider social issues, and who work together to share ideas, exercise power over the conditions of their labor, and embody in their teaching a vision of a better and more humane life. (Henry Giroux and Peter McLaren, 1989)[2]

The critical theory of education that emerged in the 1970s and early 1980s in America suffered from one major dilemma regarding its

Chapter Two

treatment of teachers and teaching: it provided little if any basis for viewing teachers as part of the solution rather than the problem. The image of the teacher that Harris expressed was a functionalist, abstract one that defined teachers by their role within a schooling process that reproduces relations of domination and subordination, and in such an analysis teaching is generally understood to be unproductive labor. Any suggestion that public school teachers could be "transformative intellectuals" in the sense that Giroux and McLaren use the term must be dismissed if we adopt a strict structural-functional analysis, and the effect is to promote cynicism and retreatism on the part of progressive-minded teachers and other educators. This does not mean, however, that nothing stands in the way of transforming the public schools by turning teachers into transformative intellectuals, as Giroux and McLaren would be the first to acknowledge. The schools *do* perform important, perhaps essential, work in preparing young people with the skills and dispositions that are compatible with their expected roles as disciplined workers and passive citizens, and the bureaucratic organization and elite control of public education place real barriers in the way of urban teachers who attempt to do other than "teach to the test."

Transformative teaching or critical pedagogy is particularly difficult in urban schools, where it is arguably needed the most, since bureaucratic and technical constraints on teachers are greater. Consequently, while the ideal of the transformative intellectual teacher is a potent one in the formulation of an alternative democratic-progressive model of teaching, powerful interests and ideologies work against its realization at present. Any attempt to realize it would have to be part of a much broader movement to redirect the schools and to redefine work in the culture. Equally important, critical pedagogy as a form of teaching will have to emerge out of teachers' work culture and involve a reconceptualization and rearticulation of teachers' interests in the schools. Since teachers are the only ones who constitute pedagogy as both discourse and practice, any new pedagogy that hopes to widely influence educational practice in the public schools must be articulated, at some point, by teachers.

My concern, consequently, in this chapter is with an analysis of teachers' work culture to indicate how it has shaped teachers' interests and entered into the dynamic of change in the schools. In general terms, I argue that teachers' craft and professional movements have supported forms of curriculum and instruction that are more consistent with critical pedagogy than teaching the basics, although these job control interests remain largely depoliticized and unlinked to a movement with a broader agenda. I also argue that, during the basic skills and collective

Teachers and Crisis

bargaining era in urban education, teachers' interest in resisting changes in the terms and conditions of the wage-labor contract has been associated with crisis tendencies involving teacher resistance to "innovation." Finally, I suggest that, so long as the current model of labor relations continues to dominate in urban schools, these crisis tendencies cannot be effectively managed. While teachers have not typically politicized or broadened their professional or trade union work culture consistent with democratic conceptions of critical pedagogy and school restructuring, many of the elements of a potentially radical challenge to conservative, bureaucratic reform agendas currently exist in teachers' work culture.

Teachers as Political Actors: A Conceptual and Theoretical Grounding

In order to take up these various issues I have alluded to, I want to begin by examining teachers as political actors in the everyday life of the school. Within the context of everyday institutional life, of course, individuals typically do not interpret their discursive practice as political. When individuals *do* speak of the "politics" involved in everyday life, they typically mean that personal bias guides decision-making when only "rational" considerations are supposed to prevail. The cynical belief among many workers that "everything is politics" when it comes to making decisions at the office or plant is in fact insightful to the extent it recognizes that formal and rational decision-making procedures often hide the arbitrary and capricious exercise of power, and also that power serves some interests more than others.

However, this politics of everyday life is still depoliticized in that it fails to move beyond the individual level of analysis, to see the situation as embedded in an emergent cultural and historical context, to see patterns of power within the institution and the culture which are immanent in everyday life, and to recognize that conflicts of interests and values underlie all social life. When I say that everyday life (that is, discourse-practice within specific institutional sites) is political, I mean that it is inextricably implicated in the constitution of institutional structures and power relations that have broad political implications. Relevant research questions thus become: How do power relations get constituted within specific institutional sites? What ideological worldviews or discursive formations are used and appropriated by participants to generate these power relations? How is power contested

Chapter Two

and negotiated in institutional sites in ways that threaten the stability of the current negotiated order? The "politics of everyday life" in this sense refers to the realm of conflict over the constitution of power relations and to the negotiation of order in concrete institutional sites, and also to the realization that the power relations and struggles of everyday institutional life are ultimately inseparable from the power relations and struggles in the overtly political and sociocultural realms. Since all power relations and struggles within a culture are constituted in concrete institutional sites by real individuals, the belief that one's everyday beliefs and practices are apolitical deconstructs upon analysis.

Given that all institutional actors participate in discourses and practices that have political import, what is the "politics" of teachers' everyday work culture? I have already indicated that urban schools are important institutional sites in which power relations are constituted that have far-reaching implications. They are also sites of deep-rooted conflicts and crisis tendencies that constantly threaten to become overtly politicized. In assessing teachers' historical involvement in, and response to, this politics of urban schooling, I draw upon a number of critical theoretical concepts and principles from several quite distinct schools of theory and research. In general terms, these traditions of critical research and theory include: (1) a structuralist theory of schooling and social and economic reproduction, (2) a structuralist theory of the "proletarianization" and de-skilling of the "new middle class," (3) a cultural theory of resistance, and (4) a post-structural theory of identity construction and the "other." I explore the usefulness of each of these discursive traditions in the following, and I also point out some of the major conceptual inadequacies or limitations that characterize each.

The Reproductive Theory of Teaching

Neo-Marxist structuralist accounts of the advanced capitalist state and state schooling as an apparatus of dominant group interests provided critical theorists of education in the 1970s with a highly usable conceptual and theoretical framework for examining what gets constituted in schools, to what ends, and in whose interests. The most influential structural theorist in this regard was Louis Althusser, probably because he made the connections between schooling and the reproduction of capitalist hegemony a central concern in his 1971 essay, "Ideology and Ideological State Apparatuses."[3] His theory of how the social relations

Teachers and Crisis

of production are reproduced represents a significant advancement over earlier, mechanistic base/superstructure models, in which various institutional discourses and practices are viewed as unilaterally determined by the economic base. Consistent with other French structuralists, Althusser understood structure as a totality of "objective levels" of discourse-practice, with all levels relatively autonomous from the others but also inescapably interconnected, so that each reciprocally influences all others in the totality. The economic infrastructure is presented, nevertheless, as a "structure of dominance" that has an asymmetrical relationship with other institutional structures. This means, according to Althusser, not only that the economic infrastructure has more relative power within the social formation, but also that its ideology is present in all non-economic institutions. In the last instance, it is this ideology, this structure of meanings that reproduce a system of domination, that is determinate to Althusser. His notion of "structural causality" makes human subjectivities into occupants of roles within the structure of dominance, "supporters" and "bearers" of structure who are constituted by ideology.

In his oft-cited essay on ideological state apparatuses, Althusser narrows his focus to education and its role in constituting subjectivities who have certain economically functional competencies. Education is about providing students with the ideologies that are suited to their expected roles in class society, and this requires a differentiated, class-specific system of schooling. Labor power must be diversely skilled "according to the requirements of the socio-technical division of labor, its different 'jobs' and 'posts.'"[4] Schooling represents a form of "apprenticeship in a variety of know-how wrapped up in the massive inculcation of the ideology of the ruling class. . . [in which] the relations of exploited to exploiters, and exploiters to exploited, are largely reproduced."[5]

While this structuralist theory of schooling provided a general grounding for a theory of teaching, Althusser never developed a more specific analysis of the role of the teacher, since he understood teaching only as an element in the educative process. To provide some basis for a more complex and specific analysis of teaching, critical theorists of education also looked to the theory of the "new middle class" that was advanced by a group of structural neo-Marxists in Europe in the mid-1970s. According to that theory, advanced or monopoly capitalism is differentiated from earlier forms of capitalism by (among other things) the emergence of a new class (or sub-class), which develops out of the last great consolidation of power in industry near the beginning of the 20th century. This "new middle class," "professional-managerial

Chapter Two

class," or "new petite bourgeoisie" (as it was variously labeled), was defined as an intermediary class between the two great camps in capitalist society: capital and labor.[6] Its collective political functions were understood to include: supervision of the process by which surplus value is extracted from workers during the production process; technical improvement of the production process to extract more surplus value from workers; and ideological indoctrination of workers (and future workers) regarding the importance of hard work, discipline, authority, etc.

Included in this new class were supervisors and middle-level managers, efficiency experts and accountants, planners and other technicians, engineers, bureaucratic functionaries, *and* teachers. Teachers supervise and dominate future workers, oversee their sorting and differentiation, and uphold the dominant ideology of equality of opportunity and advancement on the basis of merit. They also "skill" students with the minimum linguistic competencies they will need to be productive workers in the economy. As Harris remarks: "Teachers are the effective agents in schools. . . . Their political function *qua* teachers, then, parallels the political function of schooling. . . . Just as schooling is a direct form of political control over children, teaching is a direct political struggle with children, especially working-class children."[7] Members of the new middle class are *not* generally considered productive workers from this perspective since they do not contribute anything directly to the production of commodities and hence the generation of use value. Along with capital, the new middle class lives off the surplus value created by labor. Supposedly, there would be no need for the services of these intermediary workers under socialism, since labor would no longer need to be dominated ideologically or through new forms of bureaucratic and technical control. Some "unproductive" jobs would disappear; others, such as teaching presumably, would serve new, productive roles. Teachers' work would become productive to the extent that it contributed to the capacity of young people to engage in non-alienating labor and socially useful production. Since preparation for non-alienating labor and socially useful production would not require indoctrination or domination of students, teachers could focus on developing the full intellectual and creative potential of students. However, if the structuralist theory of the new middle class held up some hope that teaching might be productive in an ideal socialist society, the overwhelming message was that teaching in public schools was unproductive, that one could not help, as a teacher, dominating and socializing working-class students in ways that prepared them to be exploited on the labor market.

Teachers and Crisis

The primary problem with the reproductive theory of teaching, conceptually speaking, was that by invoking a structuralist theory *only*, no provision was made for system dynamics, contradictions, and conflicts. Attention was focused on how the structure of advanced capitalist society was maintained and reproduced as an everyday accomplishment, as if a fixed social structure was being mechanically imprinted on every social situation. Structuralist analysis also implies some level of functional analysis, that is, an analysis of how various levels of discourse-practice operate within the overall cultural system to uphold a fixed social order. Much of the critical educational discourse of the 1980s may be appreciated as an attempt to move beyond this overly deterministic and pessimistic appraisal of teaching in urban schools by arguing that "space" exists within the institution for counter-hegemonic work, that the schools enjoy "relative autonomy" and thus are not fully determined, etc. But these efforts only qualified the determinism of the structuralist model, and in the end structuralist analysis always reinforced an image of teaching as domination and ideological control that left little hope that teachers might serve as critical pedagogues and that relegated most, if not all, teachers to the status of agents of ideological hegemony.

As I have argued elsewhere, the structuralist model is not so much wrong as one-sided and limited. It is a good starting point for a critique of urban school teaching, so long as we do not stop there. For example, it is important to recognize that urban school teachers *are* working in a system that has the overwhelming effect of dominating students and preparing them for alienated labor. The schools are not autonomous institutions and efforts to reconstruct teaching in non-dominative ways face stiff resistance on a number of fronts. The basic problem with the structuralist account of social and economic reproduction is that it does not provide a basis for changing the existing system. That is, it lacks an account of cultural dynamics and contradictions that drive the system towards crisis and it fails to see schools as sites of ideological stuggle as well as reproduction. By stopping at a structuralist account, we *always* overdetermine the possibilities for action within situations, and we promote either a conservative position that the social order is "natural" and unchanging and thus should not be radically challenged, or a radical pessimism that presumes that ideological hegemony is so all-pervasive and the role of schooling so determined, that working within the system seems a futile gesture. Philip Wexler has observed in this regard that by enhancing political apathy, structuralist terms such as "reproduction" may actually contribute in a paradoxical way to reproductive forces.[8]

Chapter Two

Teacher Deskilling and the "Proletarianization" Thesis

A second structuralist theory that widely influenced critical analysts of education in the 1970s was that of the proletarianization of the new middle class, and in this theory at least some effort is made to account for system dynamics and contradictions. Not only are teachers agents of capital and the oppressors of working-class children, according to this thesis, they also are exploited by capital and increasingly disempowered.[9] *De-skilling* is one aspect of proletarianization, involving the fragmentation of complex craft skills into a series of relatively routine and thus simple skills which can be taught to semi-skilled workers. This not only makes possible greater predictability of product quality and quantity, it also removes control of the actual production process from craft workers and relocates control within the highly rationalized production process. Workers become attachments to machines and perform routine operations in harmony with the cyclic rhythms of the machine; and only central office planners and managers oversee the entire production process. The de-skilling of industrial labor in America began around the turn of the century, but according to the proletarianization thesis, the new middle class is also subjected to many of the same kinds of job rationalization pressures and will (at some unforeseen point) become as de-skilled as the industrial working class and create a new super-class of "collective labor."

A second aspect or aim of proletarianization is the *cheapening* of the cost of labor in the production process. By lowering the skill requirements needed for a job, management is able to buy more low-priced labor on the job market. Experienced and well-paid union craftspersons in industry, for example, were replaced by semi-literate, non-union workers as "scientific management" replaced craft production techniques early in the century. So long as no special expertise was required to perform a job, the pool of potential workers was also dramatically increased; and this helped keep wages low.

Related to the above, proletarianization is associated with the *substitutability* of workers. Rather than treat workers as a long-term investment, job rationalization encouraged management to treat workers as interchangeable units of labor power, "plugged into" various activity points in the production process. When workers quit, for whatever reasons, they could easily be replaced. In fact, the increased job stress and alienation from labor that is associated with job routinization discourages worker integration with the firm and encourages a high turnover rate. This high turnover rate presents no problem to management so long as one worker can be substituted for another.

Teachers and Crisis

Supposedly, then, all of these elements of proletarianization are to be found in rapidly developing form within the new middle class, a situation which places that class in an objectively contradictory position. On the one hand, it continues to serve the interests of the dominant culture; and on the other, it is exploited by the interests it serves. How this contradiction will be resolved remains uncertain; but the theorists of the new middle class generally supported the notion that the new middle class might be expected to take a contradictory and vacillating position in the years ahead in the conflict between labor and capital.

The proletarianization thesis provided some obvious advantages in understanding urban school teachers as bureaucratized professionals who are also increasingly treated as labor, and critical educators saw in it a powerful conceptual tool for approaching the analysis of teachers. Michael Apple, for example, pointed out in an influential essay on the logic of technical controls over the curriculum that teachers have been de-skilled in both content and pedagogic knowledge as new skill-based curricular technologies and self-guided curricular materials have taken over more of the task of organizing and presenting a lesson. "Skills that teachers used to need, that were deemed essential to the craft of working with children—such as curriculum deliberation and planning, and the ability to design teaching and curricular strategies for specific groups and individuals based on intimate knowledge of them—are no longer as necessary. With the large scale influx of prepackaged material, planning is separated from execution."[10]

Teachers have been *reskilled* during the basic skills era as monitors and supervisors of a largely self-guided instructional process, and as test-givers and record-keepers. Their work becomes more regimented and less expressive, and it is overdetermined by those who design the curricular materials and tests. As supervisors of an overdetermined instructional process, their job is defined as keeping students "on task" and preventing any disruptions in the smooth flow of the classroom work routine. Harris remarks that if present trends continue, "the proletarianized teacher will control children more and instruct them less."[11]

The *cheapening* of teachers' labor has been a century-long phenomenon; however, the real wages of teachers continue to fall, especially in urban school districts, and especially when we take into consideration the increased use of low-paid substitutes and uncertified teachers. While teachers made some initial gains during the early collective bargaining period of the mid- to late 1960s, the ongoing fiscal crisis of local and state government has kept teachers from making wage gains

Chapter Two

since. In the worst years of the fiscal crisis that hit American cities in the mid- to late 1970s, teachers actually had to negotiate wage rollbacks, and in many cases these rollbacks have not been restored. While many observers have pointed to the fact that low wages drive good teachers out of the profession and make it impossible to attract the best and the brightest to teaching, the cheapening of teachers' labor has continued unabated; and this may be considered another contradiction of the current system of education.

Finally, basic skills restructuring has been associated with an increase in the *substitutability* of instructional labor. Teachers can be shifted from school to school and program to progam according to shifts in student enrollment, they can fill in classes for other teachers who are absent, and when they quit they can be replaced from the pool of permanent substitutes—all of this without (theoretically, at least) interfering with the overall operation of the skill-based instructional program. Furthermore, should teachers go on strike, they can more easily be replaced when the curricular and instructional program is highly rationalized.

While the proletarianization of teaching may serve dominant interests in most ways, it too works in contradictory ways since it may draw teachers into closer alignment with the rest of organized labor in understanding their workplace interests and their broader social and political interests. As with other members of the new middle class, teachers' position within class conflicts and dynamics must be considered ambiguous, contradictory, and open to realignment and repositioning.

The Resistance Theory of Teaching

By the mid-1970s, in spite of some important conceptual advances and contributions, critical educational discourse had boxed itself into a conceptual corner through almost exclusive reliance on a structuralist and functionalist account of the schooling process, the roles of teachers and students, the form and content of the curriculum, the "hidden curriculum," the proletarianization of the labor process, etc. Probably no single book did more to move the discourse forward again than did Paul Willis' *Learning to Labour*, published in 1977.[12] Willis was associated with the Centre for Cultural Studies at the University of Birmingham in England, and at that time researchers and theorists at the Centre were interested in the question of how working-class culture

Teachers and Crisis

had been encapsulated or contained within the parameters of continued capitalist domination. They were also working within a discursive tradition in the British sociology of education that went back to the 1950s and that was associated with the *incorporation thesis*: the notion that the industrial working class had incorporated itself within, or accommodated itself to, the structure of the very system that dominated it. In return for a decent wage and enough time off from work to enjoy a private life of family, friends, and consumption, the industrial worker (presumed to be a male) had supposedly accepted the drudgery of alienated factory labor. David Lockwood, a leader in this tradition of research, wrote of the privatized, instrumental industrial worker of the 1950s: "[H]is involvement in work is too low to allow for strong feelings of any kind, except perhaps the desire to escape from it altogether. He is neither deeply involved with his workmates nor deeply antagonistic to his employer; on the whole his attitude to both more nearly approximates one of indifference."[13] Since work was no longer a "central life interest," the privatized worker supposedly sought only a better trade-off between leisure and wages.[14]

The incorporation thesis was also associated with the notion that informal shop floor resistances by workers, such the "goldbricking" and "soldiering" that were designed to slow down the production process, were largely contained within the existing system of labor-management relations, since they did not directly challenge managerial prerogatives or politicize worker discontent. In fact, in a paradoxical fashion, such resistances seemed to invite repressive control tactics by management and affirmed the managerial conviction that workers could not be trusted and that they needed firm guidance and direction from management. Resistances could, then, be accounted for in one of two ways: either they did not threaten the central structures and the processes that reproduced these structures, or they actually contributed to the reproduction of hierarchical institutional structures that subordinated workers. In either case, resistances, like other forms of accommodation by subordinates, could be explained in terms of the incorporation thesis. Domination was not imposed through some impersonal structure; it was constituted with the active participation of those dominated and in the face of their active resistance.

A final element in the incorporation thesis was that trade unionism served to accommodate workers to the existing social and technical relations of production by fostering a contract mentality. This position, in turn, was grounded in a tradition of Marxist discourse which viewed the industrial trade union movement as of limited potential in building a radical working-class movement. Marx observed that: "Trade

Chapter Two

Unions work well as centers of resistance against the encroachments of capital," however, ". . . they fail generally from limiting themselves to a guerrilla war against the effects of the existing system, instead of simultaneously trying to change it."[15] The incorporation thesis, then, provided the foundation for a theory of social reproduction that was much more historicized and culturally specific than mechanistic structural models and that was grounded in the analysis of working-class culture. Furthermore, class culture is not presented as having a simplistically functional relationship to the needs of capital and is treated as a somewhat autonomous force, actively involved in and partially resisting the reproduction process.

It was within this discursive context that Willis set about to study working-class culture in the making, to test out the incorporation thesis one step removed from the shop floor—in the classrooom. Since his study is so well known, and so much has been written already on it, let me limit my comments here to a brief treatment of Willis's major categories to suggest how they take for granted an incorporation thesis. Willis showed in his study how a group of rather delinquent adolescent boys, "the lads" as they called themselves, actively constructed a counter-school culture with strong parallels to working class culture, and that in doing so they carved out some measure of autonomy and some room for expressivity in opposition to the irrelevant curriculum and the oppressive authority relations of schooling. He used the term *penetration* "to designate impulses within a cultural form towards the penetration of the conditions of existence of its members and their position within the social whole."[16] For example, the lads' rejection of the belief that school credentials signaled special expertise or knowledge, their refusal to compete among one another for high grades and promotion, and their attempt to have some "laffs" and recapture spontaneity in an institutional context that seemed overly repressive could all be considered as penetrations of the dominant ideology of schooling. To use a less sexually laden terminology, and one more consistent with poststructuralism, we may say that the dominant ideology *deconstructed* under analysis by the lads.[17] That is, it failed to live up to its claims and revealed itself to be full of contradictions and half-truths. Resistances are then understood by Willis as practices that are linked to these penetrations or this deconstruction of the dominant ideology.

But this is where Willis structurally balances the situation by proposing that penetrations are kept from threatening the dominant discourse-practice by certain ideological *limitations*. Willis defines limitations as "blocks, diversions, and ideological effects which confuse and impede the full development and expression of working class discontents."[18] Among the lads, ideological limitations include a devaluing of all intellectual activity with the devaluing of school work, a sexist belief that only manual labor is masculine, and a grumbling form of acceptance of their subordinated status. Willis' theory of penetrations and limitations, of active resistances and ideological blocks, is an important one; and it extends reproductive theory to its limits.

How does such a theory of cultural production and reproduction help us in the explication of teachers' response to urban school crisis? Although this theory has more often been applied to an analysis of students than teachers, the most direct applications in analyzing teachers appear to be in two areas: (1) an analysis of teacher resistances to the social and technical relations of production in the schools which keep them subordinated to school administrators, and the containment of teacher resistances at the everyday shop floor (i.e., classroom and school building) level; and (2) an analysis of teacher unionism as it operates to shape teacher interests in ways that incorporate them within the dominant structure. An example of the first area of analysis is provided by Harry Wolcott in his ethnographic study of teachers in one school district and their resistances to a new PPBS (planning-programming-budgeting system) program for organizing instruction in the district.[19] Wolcott's study is particularly important in the context of a discussion of basic skills reforms, since basic skills systems of curriculum and instruction are grounded in quantitative output approaches to organizing the learning process such as PPBS. The new system in the district called for more standardized testing, more use of performance objectives in lesson and unit planning, and more paperwork and record-keeping for teachers in general. Wolcott identified a range of responses by teachers to the innovations, from resistance to compliance, with active and passive forms of each. These responses included: *routine acceptance*—"I don't like it, but I use it," or "I'm going through the motions;" *antagonistic acceptance*—complaining loudly but in the end swallowing the "bitter medicine;" *innovative acceptance*—modifying the form or intent of the innovation so that "we're still doing what we've always done;" *a wait-and-see attitude*— which allows the teacher to either go along or resist at a later date; *dropping out*—leaving the system or quietly doing the minimum; *heel dragging*—"Just drag your heals a little bit and wait. It will all pass;" *dialogue management* (with administrators explaining the new systems)—involving "playing dumb" or "playing silent;" and *consciously subverting the system*—by, for example, reporting false test data. Wolcott identified a good deal of ongoing resistance by teachers on a

Chapter Two

number of levels as the implementation of reforms continued. These resistances, Wolcott concluded, did not threaten the immediate plans of administrators and coordinators in charge of implementing the new PPBS system, but they did impede the system's effectiveness once it was in place. Thus, while Wolcott basically endorses the incorporation thesis, he does recognize that teacher resistances have an impact at some level.

The second possible application of the cultural reproduction theory, involving an analysis of teacher unionism, has been less developed than the analysis of individual teacher resistances. We have no good studies such as Wolcott's which focus on teacher unionism as a form of collective resistance and accommodation, at least not in an American context. In Britain, however, Gerald Grace's study of an urban teacher union stands out as an example of research that generally falls within this tradition.[20] One of the findings to emerge from Grace's ethnographic study of a group of teachers working in ten inner-London comprehensive schools and the union that represented them, was that teachers cannot be treated as a homogeneous whole. Some teachers, particularly union stewards, politicized their conception of teacher interests in opposition to the "dominant order" and "controlling apparatus." However, the vast majority of teachers, according to Grace, did not politicize their teaching and looked to the teacher union only to protect their job autonomy and bargain for higher wages. Of these teachers, Grace wrote: "[T]heir ability to formulate radical alternatives is very circumscribed and controlled in the sense that 'being professional' inhibits the considerations of the relations between education and the socio-political structure."[21] Even though this liberal majority of teachers supported their union, they did not link teacher unionism to a broader trade union or working-class political movement. For teachers to become "fraternally united with working-class pupils and parents," Grace observes, would have been "inappropriate to their autonomous and impartial position as educators."[22] Thus, teachers tended to limit themselves to a struggle for more autonomy and better treatment within the existing structure of the school system. As I said, no ethnographic studies along these lines have been conducted in America, although the Urbanville case study in this book and historical data discussed in the next section of this chapter do provide some examples of how this class culture tradition can inform an analysis of teacher unionism.

The class cultural theory of resistance and accommodation extends our analysis of teachers in important ways. It particularizes analysis, emphasizes the human construction of order, and shows how power relations are contested and subverted during the process of cultural reproduction. Nevertheless, it too is limited by conceptual problems and a form of structural determinism. It remains structural in that its emphasis is on how the system is maintained or reproduced, and since it begins with the presumption that a relatively stable system of power relations exists within institutional sites. The issue, then, is how individuals actively play parts in reproducing this systemic structure as they pursue their interests, which implies a functional explanation. Furthermore, this tradition continues to rely on the notion of ideology as a form of "false consciousness" that keeps individuals from recognizing their *real* or *true* political interests in opposition to dominant power relations. Similarly, resistance is treated as either "emancipatory," "oppositional," "countervailing," or "liberatory" (on the one hand), or as "reactionary," "depoliticized," or "accommodating" (on the other); and most resistance is categorized in the latter grouping. Poststructuralist theory suggests that we should be wary of these bipolar oppositions, for they rarely reflect the complexity of the situation and tend to be constructs imposed by the researcher to make concrete beliefs and practices fit within a structural-functional model. Even in Willis' sophisticated analysis, he effectively cancels out each ideological *penetration* with a corresponding ideological *limitation*; and the overall effect is to reinforce an image of a stable cultural system of domination.

Class cultural research has also tended to take for granted a materialist conception of social reality, grounded in Marxism, which presumes that ideologies or worldviews are, in the final instance explainable in terms of the technical relations of work. Willis, for example, argues that "all locations at the same level in a class society share similar basic structural properties, and the working-class people there face similar problems and are subject to similar ideological constructions."[23] Rather than arguing that the economic base itself determines consciousness, Willis supports the contention that working-class culture is the prime determiner, since class culture "not only set[s] particular 'choices' and 'decisions' at particular times, but also structure[s]. . . how these 'choices' come about and are defined in the first place."[24] Thus, the basic structural qualities of the workplace determine working class culture, and that culture in turn constitutes individual subjectivities.

The result is that Willis looks for correspondences between working class culture and the demands of the workplace, and this implies an analysis of how individuals adjust (more or less) to the working world. In this regard, Willis notes that "the lads" become incorporated quite

Chapter Two

well into social relations of shop floor life once they leave school, and pose no real threat to managerial authority. The study ends up revealing how the dominant ideology is reproduced and power relations maintained through a form of self-oppression by those being dominated. This also means that Willis takes for granted many of the assumptions of the blaming-the-victim ideology, with its conservative political implications.

Finally, the class cultural tradition has been limited by its narrow definition of class, and by its tendency to ignore other axes of struggle. The incorporation thesis developed out of the study of the "traditional" working class, which was defined as men who did manual labor on shop floors. This explains why Willis studied the "lads." He was interested in understanding how this manual, male working class was being prepared in the schools. While this is a productive line of analysis, it does not tell us much specifically about how other groups of workers in different types of jobs adapt to work and other roles. Furthermore, the particularity of the analysis becomes more and more outdated as we move into a post-industrial age where most working class students are being prepared for data processing, clerical, and service industry work. The fact that this tradition has largely limited its concern to the traditional male working class also means that it has less applicability in understanding the adaptations of workers in a highly femininized, intellectual occupation such as teaching.[25]

Teacher Identity Formation and Teachers' Occupational Movement

It should be apparent at this point that in order to overcome the limitations of the reproductive model of teaching, we must at some point move beyond a structuralist analysis. As I have previously argued, this does not mean abandoning structuralist models and replacing them with non-structural or poststructural models, but rather using structuralist models as snapshots of a system under constant construction and reconstuction. It does imply, however, abandoning the conceptual neatness of the structuralist model, with everything accounted for within the parameters of the given system. Rather than depicting resistances and oppositions as incorporated or non-incorporated, relying upon a bipolar opposition, a poststructuralist or post-modern perspective emphasizes that each action within a cultural system sends ripples throughout the system that ultimately affect every other element in the system. Nothing, from this perspective, is ever "incorporated" in

Teachers and Crisis

the sense of being sealed off or contained so that it does not undermine system structure. To adequately account for teachers' work culture, that culture must be treated as historically and culturally developing rather than static, and as entering into the conflicts and contradictions that continuously drive the system towards crisis and change. Current discourse-practice is emergent; that is, it has developed over time, and consequently must be understood by tracing discourse and practice back to their roots within the culture

Teachers' work culture must also be seen as an aspect of teachers' identity formation, since teachers assume an identity as an occupational group through the act of articulating and defending particular interests in particular concrete situations. In this regard, poststructural discourse points us toward an analysis of teachers' identity construction in terms of difference and the "other." In the basic skills era, the primary "other" for urban school teachers has been the administration. The them-versus-us orientation that currently organizes relations between teachers and administrators is, of course, part of a larger discursive formation that is used to organize relations between managers and workers in industry, which in turn is part of a broader discursive formation that organizes power relations in major institutional spheres. Basic skills reforms, collective bargaining in the schools, accountability models of teaching, and a them-versus-us orientation among teachers are all discursively related, for they all have common discursive origins and all presuppose the bureaucratic subordination of teachers to administrators. Basic skills reforms have reproduced and also extended this bipolar opposition in the schools. Such a bifurcation becomes contradictory in that it fails to provide for the requisite level of cooperation necessary to sustain an effective educational program and encourages teachers and administrators to undermine each others' efforts. It thus deconstructs as an effective way of organizing schools and generates crisis tendencies that cannot be resolved without rejecting the rigid bipolar opposition between management and labor roles in urban schools.

Although much is to be gained through a poststructural reading of teachers' work culture, its limitations have to do with a privileging of discourse as the determining force in the construction of work culture. Along with this, it lacks a sufficient account of the material infrastructure of the schooling, and thus teaching, process which constrains role formation and identity construction. The point is that we need both structural and poststructural theory, and abstract and concrete analysis, to adequately account for teachers as political actors within the context of urban school reform. In the following section, consequently,

Chapter Two

I suggest how all of the various discourses discussed in this section can contribute to a comprehensive analysis of teacher unionism as an historically emergent institutional phenomenon involved in institutional dynamics and crisis tendencies.

Teacher Unionism and Urban School Crisis

We may view teacher unionism as consisting of discourse-practices associated with different models of teaching as work. In this century, three distinct but also interwoven models of worker organization, worker interests, and labor relations have influenced teachers' work culture and shaped teacher unionism: (1) a craft and professional model of work culture, (2) a "company family" model of work culture, and (3) an industrial model of work culture. These may be related, in turn, to three ideal typical forms of teacher unionism: craft and professional unionism, company unionism, and industrial unionism. Although these forms of teacher unionism developed during different historical periods, and some have been more influential than others, each in its own way has continued to influence teachers' work culture in the 1990s. However, it is also clear that the industrial model of teacher unionism has become increasingly influential during the basic skills era and the the two earlier forms appear to have less and less direct influence over teacher union policy and practice.

Craft Unionism, Professionalism, and Teacher Job Control

In the late 19th century in America, factories were rapidly replacing cottage industry forms of production, which had been controlled by the early craft guilds and unions of the various manual skilled trades. However, the craft union movement, which was grounded on the presumption that work should be controlled by independent workers and teams of workers who contracted with businesses for the delivery of services, still represented a significant threat to managerial efforts to introduce new innovations in mass production and scientific management designed to bring the point of production, and thus workers, under much tighter top-down control.[26] The early craft unions, organized first as the Knights of Labor and later as the American Federation of Labor (AFL), exercised significant control over the point of production in many shops and factories through an elaborate system of negotiated rights that management had agreed to over the years. The first of these was that new members could enter the trade only through an extended apprenticeship process, during which they would be closely supervised and instructed by experienced craftspersons of various rankings. Through apprenticeship, new workers were initiated into the secrets of the craft—secrets not known by management or non-union workers. A second right won by the early craft union movement was to establish the guidelines for work performance and evaluation, and also to set the pay scale for union labor. Finally, union stewards in each factory had the right to enforce work rules and production standards. All of this was designed to enforce a good deal of autonomy for individual workers and work groups, and to ensure that workers as a group controlled the actual production process.

By the early 20th century, however, although craft unionism appeared to be stronger than ever, it was already being undermined by scientific management and mass production technologies. By systematically studying workers at their jobs, and then rationalizing their tasks into a sequence of discrete tasks, managerial systems such as those developed by Frederick Taylor (the so-called father of scientific management and efficiency in industry) and Henry Ford (who developed the first fully integrated assembly line) led to the rapid decline of craft unionism in the first several decades of the new century. "Taylorism" and "Fordism" allowed management to replace craft union workers in the new industrial factories with semi-skilled, non-union workers; and central office management seemed once more to have gained the upper hand on labor. It had won back control of the point of production from workers through administrative rationality and scientific management, and in doing so it seemed to have resolved the "labor problem" that had stood in the way of consolidation of control.

While the heyday of craft unionism was over by World War I, vestiges of the movement have continued to influence American working class culture, especially in those fields where the work, by its very nature, requires a good deal of worker discretion and where job rationalization is therefore more difficult and only partially realizable. Such fields include police, firefighters, electricians, plumbers, and *teachers*. Workers within each of these occupational areas have continued to assert job control rights and have upheld the ideals of craft control organization and control of work tasks, although in the face of continuing job rationalization pressure.

Teachers' claims that they should enjoy professional autonomy draw upon this tradition of craft unionism in some obvious ways, although

Chapter Two

19th century American teachers never developed autonomous craft or professional guilds similar to those of the skilled trades. From the start, teachers were bureaucratically subordinated public employees and granted no special job control rights. As Dan Lortie observed in his classic study *Schoolteacher*: "Teachers never did gain control of any area of practice where they were clearly in charge and most expert; day-to-day operations, pedagogical theory, and substantive expertise have been dominated by persons in other roles."[27] State and local bureaucratic officals controlled teacher training from the outset. In late19th and early 20th century America, prospective teachers were trained in two-year "normal schools" that specialized in training teachers for the new mass education system. Later, many of these normal schools became four-year teacher training colleges and still later began offering degrees in other fields. However, throughout this historical development, these state-supported colleges have taught an education curriculum that is closely linked to state teacher certification guidelines and mandates, and that does not reflect much teacher input.

Although teachers lack a strong tradition of craft union or guild control and have not controlled their own professional education, the image of the teacher as a semi-autonomous practitioner of a skilled trade or profession continues to influence teachers' work culture. To some extent, collegial forms of decision-making and governance at the college and university levels serve as models for public school teachers, particularly secondary teachers, to emulate. Teachers' unions have also drawn upon a model of professional occuational and practitioner autonomy borrowed from the medical and legal professions in asserting job control rights. For example, Albert Shanker, president of the American Federation of Teachers, in a special 1985 position paper issued by the AFT entitled *A Call for Professionalism*, proposed that professional teacher boards be established in each school to develop standards for evaluating teaching, handle parental complaints, and evaluate curricular materials. Shanker argued that: "The only thing that's going to turn the schools around is to start turning the decision making as to what works and what doesn't work over to the people who are actually doing the work and know what's happening in classrooms. We ought to have the power to make the decisions because we know more— more about... all of the issues in education."[28]

A craft unionist or professional conception of teachers' interests is *oppositional*, using the analytic framework of cultural reproduction theory, to the extent that it advances demands for direct control by teachers over curriculum, instruction, and the evaluation of instruction that are incompatible with the imperative to maintain elite managerial

Teachers and Crisis

control of the system. In fact, craft union and professional models of teaching are generally more consistent with democratic approaches to work organization than elite managerial and bureaucratic approaches, in that they emphasize worker control of actual processes and worker involvement in "shop floor" decision-making. Craft unionism also implies a commitment to personalized, non-regimented, and non-standardized approaches to curriculum and instruction over highly rationalized, standardized approaches. Teachers' continuing identification with craft and professional work culture would thus seem to mitigate against efforts by bureaucratic elites to reconstitute teaching as a merely technical process of preparing students for basic skills tests.

In this regard, two crisis tendencies are associated with a strong professional and craft orientation among teachers. The most direct of these is a *control* crisis tendency associated with teacher resistance (individually and collectively) to highly prescriptive, top-down models of organizing the learning process and to close supervision by administrators. The more teachers assert professional claims, the more they resist relinquishing power over specific curricular and instructional decisions that call for their unique knowledge of students and their learning difficulties. One way teachers assert such professional autonomy is to maintain a strong commitment to the self-contained classroom. Once the door to the classroom is shut, outsiders (including the principal) are not made to feel welcome. Teachers may still be effectively controlled in their self-contained classrooms by holding them accountable to "teach to the test," but during any given class period or school day, teachers may decide to make room for other learning activities of their own design, or may temporarily abandon the scheduled lesson to explore something in which students are particularly interested. Of the spatial power relations of schooling, Dan Lortie remarks: "[Teachers] erect the shield of territorial jurisdiction, granting the principal the hegemony over corridors and assemblies and all other areas save their classrooms. . . . One is reminded of the established craftsman [sic] who insists on his [sic] right to arrange space and tools and fashion his [sic] product as he [sic] wishes."[29] Centralized steerage of the educational process is thus always threatened and undermined by the degree of professional and craft autonomy that teachers have been able to maintain through the spatial construction of the school.

Legitimation crisis tendencies are also exacerbated when teachers attempt to assume greater professional control over their work, and confront powerful interest groups that attempt to block or subvert such efforts. Whenever teachers are granted a degree of autonomy by school officials, it is always with the stipulation that teachers will

Chapter Two

continue to uphold managerial goals for the schools. Teachers, consequently, cannot use their limited job control rights in ways which significantly empower them or their students, since to do so would invite school administrators to take these rights away. But by pushing the system to its limits and revealing the impediments that stand in the way of a significant occupational re-empowerment of teachers, the struggle for job control may undermine the belief among teachers that the system as it is now structured can adequately serve their interests.

Having said this, it also must be added that legitimation crisis tendencies associated with a craft or professional orientation towards work may remain primarily latent for long periods of time. American craft unionism, after all, has historically disassociated the struggle for job control from wider political objectives. For example, within working class culture, a craft and professional orientation has been associated with the belief that some workers deserve more rights over their everyday working lives than others because of their special expertise, training, or education. This so-called "labor aristocracy" perspective was influential among AFL leadership in the early decades of this century, and kept the AFL from identifying with the struggles of the new industrial working class being organized by the Congress of Industrial Workers (CIO).

Among teachers, a belief that they deserve special job control rights and privileges to which other groups of workers are not entitled obviously impedes the development of linkages with other workers in the school and the community, and promotes occupational conservatism. Even today, while the National Education Association (NEA) consistently sides with organized labor on most political issues and works actively with the labor lobby in Washington, it prefers to call itself a professional association rather than a teachers' union, and much of the adherance to this distinction is attributable to the belief that, as middle-class professionals, teachers should disdain working-class identification. Finally, a craft or professional orientation among teachers may be associated with belief in *exclusionary* rights for teachers. Teachers who follow this logic often argue that community groups, parents, and students should have little involvement in curriculum and instructional decision-making or teacher evaluation since only teachers, as experienced and knowledgable professionals, have the expertise to decide these matters. As practioners of a craft, teachers should have special rights in curricular and instructional decision-making, especially when it comes to personalizing instruction to the particular needs of children. Nevertheless, within public education, almost no decision-making rights can be called exclusionary, for so many parties in the schools, the

Teachers and Crisis

community, and the society are affected by curricular and instructional choices.

By emphasizing the special rights of educational "experts," teacher professionalism has also encouraged teachers to accept an ideology of bureaucratic state professionalism that treats educational issues as primarily technical and scientific rather than political or ethical, and this has aligned teachers' interests with those of the "transpolitical" state, in which specialized experts, employing scientific data, supposedly manage the state in the interests of the democratic majority.[30] From this perspective, public education should stand above politics to ensure that it does not serve any special interests and that decisions are made rationally rather than in a biased manner. Professionalism in this sense is consistent with an end-of-ideology perspective on society; and to the extent that teachers have accepted such a depoliticization of an educational process that is deeply involved in constituting power relations of class, race, and gender, this depoliticization has served to encapsulate teachers' discontent and limit their course of action to one of making appeals to bureaucratic superiors to look after teachers' interests.

The challenge, then, is to work for the professional and craft empowerment of teachers within the context of a broader democratic empowerment, based on a recognition that the former is dependent upon the latter. Examples of such a progressive perspective on teachers' work culture are to be found throughout the 20th century, among both teachers' union leaders and rank-and-file teachers, though efforts have been made to repress them. For example, in the first decade of the century, Margaret Haley led the Chicago Teachers' Federation, composed primarily of elementary women teachers, to link up with the women's movement and the anti-racist and trade unionist movements in Chicago. The intention was to build a new coalition of interests to fight a City Hall dominated by moneyed interests and political patronage. Haley warned the 1904 convention of the National Education Association of "the increased tendency toward 'factoryizing' education,' making the teacher an automaton, a mere factory hand, whose duty is to carry out mechanically and unquestioningly the ideas and orders of those clothed with the authority of position."[31] The CTF, however, ultimately fell victim to a refusal by City Hall to recognize its legitimacy or follow through on the concessions the union had won through its militancy.

Similarly, throughout much of the first half of this century, the most powerful teachers' association in New York City, the New York City Teachers' Union, also sought to link up teachers' interests with broader

Chapter Two

political struggles. It opposed, for example, the racist tracking system in the city (Harlem schools had only vocational tracks and no academic tracks for much of the first half of the century), it worked with African-American groups in pushing for a curriculum that recognized the contributions of minorities in America, and it called for a political challenge to the business domination of the public schools. However, the union was a victim of socialist witch-hunting by various state legislative committees and city commissions during that era, that succeeded in demoralizing its leadership and undermining rank-and-file support.[32] These examples from the pre-collective bargaining era in education indicate that progressive traditions of craft unionism and professionalism have influenced teachers in shaping their occupational interests. Although it remains questionable whether these progressive traditions in teachers' work culture have exerted much influence in recent years, they might be rekindled should educational issues be drawn further into the political arena.

Company Unionism and the Professional Educational "Family"

The second distinctive strain of trade unionist discursive practice in American working class culture was what came to be called "company unionism".[33] Company unionism was the progressive solution to the labor problem in American industry, and it was most influential in the first three decades of the century. Both labor and business leaders gave at least formal support to the notion that the company is or should be a family, with management and various types and levels of workers cooperatively performing their specialized roles to achieve organizational goals (generally understood as increased profitability or efficiency). Labor, from this perspective, was depicted as an associate rather than as a natural adversary of management and business interests, and trade unions were expected to devote themselves to achieving organizational goals, since they supposedly would share in the benefits of increased productivity and profitability. Groups such as the powerful National Civic Federation (NCF) promoted company unionism as a solution to industrial relations in the new progressive era by bringing business and labor leaders together in support of one overarching principle: "The only solidarity natural in industry is the solidarity which unities all those in the same business establishment, whether employer or employed."[34] The new partnership between business and labor was heralded as the "American answer" to industrial conflict.

Teachers and Crisis

Like good parents or guardians, business leaders were expected to look after the interests of their children (the workers) and listen to their grievances before making decisions that affected them. In return, labor was expected to abandon and condemn the use of militant work stoppage tactics.

The dominant force for the promotion of a company family ideology in public education during the first half of this century was the NEA. Each specialized professional role in the schools had its own division within the united NEA, and all divisions were, in theory, equal. Dan Lortie refers to this as the "inclusiveness era" in public education: "State associations... included 'all ranks' within the membership and inclusiveness was the practice of local associations. There was talk of an 'integrated profession' and of 'strength through unity'; all who worked in schools were presumed to benefit from such coordinated activity."[35] In their recent study of the changing idea of teacher unionism in the 20th century, Charles Kerchner and Douglas Mitchell characterize this ideology in terms of a meet-and-confer form of labor relations: "[T]he profession of education is viewed as a unitary one. School administrators are distinquished from teachers by status and job role, but their interests are seen as fundamentally the same. Both teachers and administrators are supposed to express a selfless and univeral interest in 'what's good for kids,' and open displays of self-interest are socially illegitimate. It is the *duty* of the institution to look after teachers' welfare."[36]

In reality, the NEA always reflected in its organizational structure, and in the power relations between divisions, the considerable power inequalities between teachers, building administrators, and superintendents and their staffs. All key leadership and power positions were controlled by administrators. Anthony Cresswell and Michael Murphy report that "the NEA was an integral part of the control mechanism of American public education.... It urged school boards and citizens to trust in their professional superintendent and his staff."[37] As late as 1964, on the eve of collective bargaining in education, the NEA excluded teachers from positions of influence, even though teachers comprised 85 percent of total NEA membership. In that year the NEA executive committee of eleven members included only two teachers; its six-member board of trustees had only one teacher; and its 75-member board of directors included only 22 teachers.[38]

On the local level, NEA affiliates served as teachers' "company unions" throughout the pre-collective bargaining era. Teachers had no legal rights to bargain with local school boards. Instead, the NEA supported a system whereby teachers were limited to making requests

Chapter Two

and pleas to the school board and hoping they were listened to—which they most often were not. Like good children within the professional educational family, teachers were expected to subordinate their own interests to the larger purposes and interests that educational administrators, planners, and policymakers (the father figures in education) supposedly represented. When teachers complained that their concerns were largley ignored by their professional superiors, that their grievances were not seriously considered, or that they still had not received the pay raise they had been promised, they were accused of acting unprofessional by placing their own self-interest before the interests of the children. Stephen Cole notes in this regard: "For the NEA, professions differed from other occupations in one major respect: the primary goal of professionals was to provide service to clients and the community. . . . If the members of an occupational group showed too great a concern with financial rewards, their status as professionals would be weakened; hence, early in its history, the NEA claimed that discussions of teacher salaries were 'unprofessional.' "[39]

The ideology of the company family has its appeals, both in industry and education; and much of the recent interest in Japanese models of industrial relations in America bears witness to this continuing appeal. Leftists have also generally endorsed as an ideal a model of workplace cooperation in which the divisions and conflicts between management and labor are overcome. In fact, both the political Left and Right tend to accept the notion that institutional productivity and efficiency would increase dramatically if some variation of the company family ideal were realizable. However, it is not realizable without a drastic redistribution of power in institutions and society; and support of the company family ideology by groups such as the early National Civic Federation consequently served primarily to legitimate the continuation of existent power inequalities. Workers were called upon to commit themselves to organizational goals which were presented as broadly consensual and in the interests of all, when in fact those goals were based on the further exploitation of labor.

By the early 1930s, the company family ideology had pretty well *deconstructed* as a viable framework for articulating workers' interests in the organization, since it so obviously failed to deliver on what it claimed, and the new industrial trade union movement, organized under the banner of the CIO, disdained any suggestion that management and labor could cooperate out of a common sense of purposes and interests. However, the ideology of company unionism and the professional educational family continued to hold sway in public education for three more decades, partly because the ideal of educational professionals working together for the common educational good has been such a powerful one within the occupation of teaching, and partly because teachers had not been granted the same legal rights as industrial workers to engage in collective bargaining with management. Nevertheless, it proved increasingly difficult to sustain the company family ideology in public education, and by the early 1960s, it had begun to collapse. Its influence among urban teachers during the basic skills era has been neglibible. It may enjoy somewhat of a comeback, however, as educational policy-makers search for new ways of overcoming the roadblocks to reform imposed by an adversarial relationship between teachers and administrators. For example, the current interest in school-based management presupposes that teachers and administrators in local schools can govern cooperatively. But as I have argued elsewhere, real school-based management with teachers and administrators working on the same side, making major curriculum and instructional decisons, would be inconsistent with the imperative to maintain elite bureaucratic control of the schools. At some point, then, all efforts to return to a company family approach to school management risk increasing legitimation problems by raising teachers' hopes unrealistically. When teachers find that their participation in curricular and instructional decisions at the building level is limited to questions about how to more effectively raise student test scores, or how to increase time on task, then school-based management is revealed as a mangement "trick" to win teachers' cooperation in carrying out a predetermined managerial plan.

Industrial Unionism and the "Great Bargain" in the Schools

The third major strand of trade unionism to emerge in American work culture developed first among the ranks of the semi-skilled assembly line workers, the rapidly expanding stratum of the labor force that was virtually created by the technological transformation of production through scientific management and mass production techniques. Industrial unionism has its roots in the1920s, when shop floor workers in the new mass production industries (automotive manufacturing, steel production, home appliance manufacturing, garment industry, and so forth) began to organize their own, independent unions outside of the company unions. It was not until the early 1930s, however that industrial unionism became a powerful and unpredictable force to be reckoned with by both the business community and the state. In the

Chapter Two

face of rapidly deteriorating economic conditions, the new Congress of Industrial Workers (CIO) drew together the various independent industrial unions behind a common set of objectives and strategies for achieving them.[40] Among these objectives were better wages and working conditions, a seniority system for laying off and rehiring workers and for granting pay increases so that management could not make such decisions either arbitrarily or capriciously, and some form of workplace democracy so that shop floor workers could participate in decisions affecting the overall operation of the plant or firm.

The strategies endorsed by the early CIO to achieve these objectives were all, in one way or another, grounded in the basic recognition that while factory workers, as individuals, exercised less and less control over their work, they had considerable potential power, if they acted collectively, to stop the production process. That is, while they lacked the power to initiate work changes themselves, they could exercise a *reactive* power, effectively preventing management from achieving its goals until it conceded some of the demands of labor. The sit-down strike ultimately proved how effectively this power could be used, although the costs were high both in jobs lost and in repressive and brutal retaliation against striking workers by police and paid stooges. As the depression continued, the consensus among enlightened business and political leadership was that the industrial union movement and business were heading into a period of intense struggle, and there were no assurances that industrial unionism could be prevented from moving in radical political directions. In the meantime, American industry was slowing grinding to a halt as sit-down strikes spread from coast to coast, factory to factory. John Commons had argued in his classic 1921 study of trade unionism and the "labor problem" that capitalism would have to change if it wanted to survive. "Capitalism," he wrote, "is threatened because it has not furnished the working people a similar security to that which it has furnished to the investors. . . . They [working people] have tried to get security by rough methods. Trade-unionism, closed shop, union shop, and so on are their methods of obtaining security on the job. Not until the capitalistic system, not until the great financial interests that control this system, have learned that it is just as important to furnish security for the job as it is to furnish security for the investment will we have a permanent provision for industrial peace."[41] By the mid-1930s, Commons' argument, that workers had to be guaranteed some formal rights if capitalism was to survive, finally began to be accepted by a broad spectrum of the business community.

The crisis of business-labor conflict was resolved in the so-called "Great Bargain" struck between the two warring camps, with the

Teachers and Crisis

Roosevelt administration as the mediator and overseer of the accord. Industry agreed "to accept an enlarged role for the government and to share power with other organized interest groups as a way of ensuring economic stability and the long-term political hegemony of business."[42] Labor was formally recognized by business as possessing certain rights, including the rights to organize and to be represented by a bargaining agent (a union) in collective negotiations with management over the "terms and conditions of employment." For its part, organized labor had to agree to limit the scope of bargaining to wages, benefits, and a narrow definition of working conditions (safety in the workplace, number of breaks in the work routine, and so on). It also agreed not to engage in militant actions such as the sit-down strike. Strikes would technically be allowed, but only if all other avenues of bargaining had failed to resolve differences; and the state was granted the right to intervene in the public interest to order workers back on the job. Through this bargain, formalized in the Wagner Act and overseen by the National Labor Relations Board, the state came to play a much more direct role in ensuring the conditions for the survival of a corporate-dominated economy, while at the same time it recognized that workers had rights in the workplace.

The Great Bargain between labor and capital marked the beginning of a new phase in the management of crisis tendencies related to industrial relations and the "labor problem" in advanced capitalist societies. Collective bargaining was perceived by almost everyone as a major victory for organized labor, and in some ways it was. Particularly during the long post-World War II era of an expanding economy, collective bargaining did provide a framework within which many workers could advance their economic interests far more than they ever had before. But as industrial unionism gained legitimacy and a certain type of power, its leadership became increasingly accommodative to the current form of corporate management. So long as they could continue to keep the rank and file happy with bigger and bigger wage contracts, union leadership and corporate management could get along without major conflict, and the basic hierarchical structure of authority in industry was accepted. By the mid 1950s, following the merger of the old and declining AFL with the now much bigger and more powerful CIO, organized labor focused much of its efforts on realizing for workers a very consumer-oriented conception of the good life. Work itself was not to be overly debilitating and workers were to get plenty of time off. Overtime work was to be available at a much higher hourly rate for those workers who chose to make more money. Workers' interests were reduced to an instrumental calculus based on

Chapter Two

the maximization of work remuneration and the minimalization of work time and effort. The payoff for the drudgery of industrial labor was to be an ever-expanding standard of living, based on an ever-expanding economy, all made possible by unlimited power resources.

To the extent that workers accepted the conservative industrial union perspective on workers' interests, they made peace with the system that kept them subordinated and disempowered. But it was always a conditional peace, grounded on the premise that business could deliver on its promise of an ever-expanding standard of living, something business has not been able to deliver on for several decades. When the system cannot deliver, motivation crisis tendencies are brought to the surface, manifested in a general malaise among workers and a lowering of commitment to the organization. Furthermore, by emphasizing the adversarial nature of labor and management interests, the collective bargaining ideology encouraged a them-versus-us orientation at the workplace that made it hard for management to win labor agreement to any changes in the terms and conditions of employment.

To effectively manage these crisis tendencies, elite groups have sought ways of moving beyond the collective bargaining era, to reintegrate the worker into the company family. However, it is not yet clear whether labor is ready to give the company family idea another go-round. Crisis tendencies consequently remain unresolved at this point. Finally, history demonstrates that trade unionism may, under crisis conditions, politicize workers' interests in ways that directly challenge dominant power relations in the institution and society. Events in Poland during the 1980s indicate how powerful trade unionism can be in building an oppositional political movement; and in this country, labor unions (and more particularly rank-and-file union members) were among the strongest supporters of Jesse Jackson's Rainbow Coalition during the 1988 presidential campaign. That campaign demonstrated not only that workers were disaffected from the traditional Democratic party, but also that they were not becoming part of a new Republican majority. They were moving leftward in their politics, engaged in articulating a new political movement in America.

While the collective bargaining and industrial union model of industrial relations has come under increasing attack from business leaders and state officials in the past decade or so, it appeared to be working well (in that it had contained workers' discontent by redirecting their interests around consumerism, leisure, and the family) in the post-World War II economic boom years. The merger of the AFL and CIO in the mid-1950s reflected the growing consensus among trade union and business leaders that all workers shared the same basic economic

Teachers and Crisis

interests, and that they had no interests in the actual organization and evaluation of their work or in broader political struggles. Since the state has always looked to corporate models of organization and control, it is not surprising to find that this apparently successful model of managing workplace conflict was soon advanced by state bureaucratic and political leaders and by AFL-CIO leadership as a basis for formalizing relations between public employees and the management of state agencies. When John Kennedy became president, with the help of the AFL-CIO, he quickly signed an executive order extending collective bargaining rights to federal employees. The Kennedy executive order was then used as a model for states to adopt similar policies, either through executive order or legislative action. By the end of the 1960s, most public employees, including teachers as the single largest group, had become unionized and were busy learning the rules of the game of collective bargaining.

Much of the direct impetus for these changes, particularly in the public schools, may be attributed to the efforts of organized labor, which was perhaps the most interested of all interested parties in support of extending collective bargaining to the public schools. The reason for this was simple: between 1950 and 1960, the number of workers engaged in factory labor in America had declined from 13 milllion workers to 11.5 million. Simultaneously, the number of white-collar and professional-managerial workers had jumped dramatically, from 29 million to 37 million. Although this latter group of workers represented a full 43 percent of the labor force by 1960, only three percent were unionized.[43] If these trends continued, as they were expected to, labor would have to be content to represent a shrinking power base.

Consequently, the AFL-CIO leadership begin a campaign to organize public sector employees. Teachers were identified as a target group whose unionization would greatly strengthen the unionization movement among public employees in general. Walter Reuther, then president of the powerful United Automotive Workers, declared that "the importance of a growing, active teachers' union to all of organized labor cannot be too greatly stressed." Another union official involved in the effort to organize public employees asked, "How long will a file clerk go on thinking a union is below her dignity, when the teacher next door belongs?"[44] When the AFL-CIO finally assigned Walter Reuther, as head of the Industrial Union Department (IUD), to begin the organization of teachers, he picked New York City as the first city to be organized. The IUD funneled money and organizing assistance to the then-new United Federation of Teachers (UFT), which was

Chapter Two

committed to the AFL-CIO's brand of industrial unionism. The UFT quickly moved to stage a one-day walkout by teachers throughout the city in 1960 in support of teachers' rights to unionize and engage in collective bargaining. When state courts ultimately granted New York City teachers that right, the UFT easily won a follow-up election to decide who among the various teacher organizations should represent the city's teachers as a sole collective bargaining agent. Within a few short years, most public school teachers in America were organized.

The efforts of the AFl-CIO in organizing teachers were aimed at bringing teachers within the fold of organized labor through the American Federation of Teachers, which was an AFL-CIO member; this had been accomplished in New York City and in many other big city school districts in the country. However, the AFT was not successful in organizing the majority of teachers who taught in small and medium-sized urban areas, in suburbs, and in rural areas. Perhaps it would have been more broadly successful in its aims if it had not draw the larger NEA into the battle to organize teachers. NEA leadership was initially confused and hesitant in the face of rapid developments towards collective bargaining in the schools. That leadership was still primarily from the ranks of school administrators rather than teachers, and it was still officially committed to the idea of the professional educational family, with all the members of the family standing together and speaking as one voice. In reality, as I indicated earlier, the NEA represented the interests of an educational elite, and it served to contain teachers' grievances within a company union ideology. By the early 1960s, however, there were stirrings within the NEA classroom teachers' division, particularly among a group of urban teacher activists who became enthusiastic supporters of teacher unionism and who were encouraged by developments in New York City.

These teachers managed to get the classroom teachers' division to invite James Carey, the secretary-treasurer of the Industrial Union Department of the AFL-CIO, a man who had been intimately involved in organizing New York City teachers for the UFT, to speak at the 1962 NEA national convention in a symposium on "Public Education Tomorrow." When Carey delivered his speech, he minced few words in challenging teachers to abandon the pursuit of the "Holy Grail" of professional status and to accept trade unionism. He argued: "One of the prime troubles—if not the chief curse of the teaching *industry* [emphasis mine] is precisely that word 'profession.' That term, as it is used so frequently here, implies that your craft is somewhat above this world of ours; it implies a detachment, a remoteness from the daily

Teachers and Crisis

battle of the streets, in the neighborhoods and cities." He concluded with this comparison: "If the charwomen of the schools have sense enough to band together and organize and negotiate contracts, and the teachers do not, I wonder sometimes who should have the degrees."[45]

Carey had appealed to teachers' sense of reality and received a rousing response from his audience. Public education had become an industry, and teachers had become industrial workers. To refuse to recognize that fact and act as if school administrators could be trusted to look out for teachers' interests was naive. From that point on, the NEA would never be the same. By the mid-1960s, the NEA was a professional family being split apart, with much bitterness and hostility on all sides. The administrative leadership of the NEA struggled to manage the rising tide of discontent from below without driving teachers out of the NEA to the rival AFT. To do so, it decided to authorize local NEA affiliates to serve as collective bargaining agents for teachers. But this only fueled the fires of change, since courts ruled that local affiliates could not represent both educational management (administrators) and labor (teachers). This led all administrative divisions within the NEA to sever their ties with the professional educational family, a process that was completed by 1972, effectively allowing the NEA to become a teachers' union in practice if not name.

Collective bargaining in public education was generally heralded as a major victory for teachers, much as it had been for industrial workers in the 1930s. It *was* a victory in that it mobilized teachers around a cause, and it demonstrated that teachers could use their collective power to make the system respond to their interests. In the first several years of collective bargaining in New York City, for example, the UFT was able to increase the average pay of a city teacher by over $1,000.[46] Unfortunately, these gains did not continue very long, and the sense of teachers' empowerment fostered in the 1960s by the militant teachers' union movement gave way to a mood of cynicism and frustration by the mid-1970s. In the fiscal crisis of the mid-1970s, which hit urban school districts particularly hard, teachers' unions had to accept negotiated wage rollbacks and staff cutbacks, and in most cases wages did not rise significantly after the immediate fiscal crisis subsided since urban schools were placed under severe budget restrictions to avoid another crisis situation from developing.[47] As the funding burden in urban education has shifted more to the state, state education officials have also placed restrictions on the local school budget, and in most cases the school board has little room to negotiate. Finally, the courts and state legislatures have increasingly restricted strike actions by

Chapter Two

teachers through binding arbitration requirements and through stiff fines and jail sentences for teachers and teachers' union leaders who participate in illegal strike actions.

Teacher unions may be boxed in and unable to gain much more power for teachers within the confines of bureacuratic state schooling, at least in the forseeable future. But during the collective bargaining era in education, teachers have become much more effective in exercising a negative or reactive power to block attempts by school management to increase the efficiency of the basic skills production process. For this reason, conservative critics tend to view teacher unions as an impediment to needed change in the system, as preventing management from achieving its goals. Myron Lieberman, for example, has remarked: "If a teacher union is strongly opposed to any reforms involving terms and conditions of employment, as most reforms do, the teacher union can legally prevent implementation of the reform for a substantial period of time."[48] Reforms Lieberman claims teacher unions routinely block, delay, and/or weaken include: replacing seniority with management discretion in the firing, transfer, and promotion of teachers; merit pay; technological change in instruction; and use of non-teachers to perform "instructional tasks." Lieberman concludes: "As a general rule, teacher unions are opposed to any reform that does not provide more pay, easier working conditions, and/or less work."[49]

Other critics have charged that teacher unions have promoted a form of rigid "role formalization" among teachers, which motivates them to have all their job responsibilities and hours of work explicitly detailed in the wage-labor contract. Kerchner and Mitchell, for example, argue that: "By expanding the requirements for notification, consultation, and review of work assignments..., contracts effectively ensure that every aspect of a teacher's job is planned and rationalized.... [T]he primary motivation for using contract language to rationalize tasks comes from teachers who see rationalization as a mechanism for securing and protecting these interests."[50] Ironically, while collective bargaining has contained the demands of teachers, it has been at a price that many conservatives now find intolerably high; and this leads to calls for union-busting in the schools—generally through support for some sort of voucher plan that would create a private, entrepreneurial, and supposedly non-union system of education, such as that advocated by Lieberman.

A critical response to the thesis that teacher unions stand in the way of needed innovation in the schools may be grounded on several propositions. First, innovations have not been neutral politically or ideologically. The term "innovation" has a whole history of usage by state officials, university-based researchers, and bureaucratic administrators to mean top-down reform of the curriculum and/or instructional process with the objective of increasing the quantity or quality of system outputs—generally defined as achievement test scores. More specifically and concretely, "innovation" has tended to be a code word for further rationalization of the curriculum and the instructional process through new forms of bureaucratic and technical control. In this discursive context, innovations are consistent with a project of fine-tuning existing structures in education without altering the overall design of those structures or the interests they serve; innovations are thus designed to maintain and consolidate centralized steerage of the system.

Teacher union resistance to innovation and negativism thus may be appreciated as adaptive responses to a position of institutional disempowerment. Max Weber observed that if a parliament was limited to token participation in decisions made by the executive branch of government and was unable to initiate change, then it could only carry on "negative politics." Specifically, *negative politics* implies: (1) "stand[ing] over against the government as a hostile power," (2) providing the executive "with the absolute minimum of information," and (3) serving as an obstacle to the government whenever possible.[51] While Weber was referring to relations between two branches of the state, what he had to say is also applicable to an analysis of the relations between management and labor or (more specifically) urban school management and teachers' unions. Teachers' negative politics express the power relations that keep teachers individually and collectively excluded from meaningful participation in school decisions. Rather than blaming teachers for their negativism we need to link this institutional phenomenon to an agenda for the democratic restructuring of the schools, so that teachers need no longer resort to negativistic tactics.

Resistance to innovation may also take on gender connotations within the power dynamics of schooling. The imposition of a technical-rational, hierarchical paradigm in curriculum and instructional design and decision-making is related to patriarchal control in education. Consequently, resistance to innovation by teachers may at least partially involve a tacit or overt assertion of alternative models of curriculum and instruction related to feminist concerns for personalized, non-hierarchical, and discursive or dialectic forms of learning and knowing.[52] It represents both a challenge to the further rationalization of the teaching and learning processes and to the patriarchal interests that lie behind the rationalization project.

In a similar vein, resistance by teachers to working beyond the

Chapter Two

contract needs to be contextualized, that is, understood within the broad institutional and cultural dynamics within which teachers have made a particular work culture. Such resistance reflects a recognition that if teachers do not have their responsibilities, duties, and hours of work clearly stated in the contract, they are more easily taken advantage of by administrators who are continually motivated to get more labor out of teachers. Administrators complain that teachers are acting unprofessional when they refuse to work beyond the contract and take on new responsibilities and duties that consume more of their time and effort, but in doing so teachers are playing the contract game with the only power they have. In the adversarial climate of the school that results from the formalistic and rigid bifurcation of management and labor roles, both administrators and teachers must learn to play the game well; and the contract is the terrain upon which the wage-labor battle is played.

Teachers' support for role formalization may also be related to a desire to gain more control over the process through which they are evaluated. Given teachers' current disempowerment, it is in their interests to have the criteria for their evaluation clearly and formally specified, so that administrators cannot use the evaluation process to punish teachers they do not like and reward teachers they do, and so that some uniformity is maintained in a highly subjective process. As Alice Kessler-Harris has observed of women in industry and their acceptance of scientific management approaches, such mechanized, dehumanizing approaches made women workers "less subject to the whims of individual [male] foremen and to their likes and dislikes. . . ."[53] This may account for support by some teachers for highly formalistic lesson planning formats as well, such as those associated with Madeleine Hunter's work. Teachers may gain a sense of security in adhering to prescribed lesson planning formats mandated by the administration, since they know that if they use the formats they have a better chance of producing the kind of learning outcomes administrators expect, and of receiving positive evaluations.

Ironically, some teachers may also feel more professional when their roles are highly-formalized and the language they use in their work is highly technical. In the basic skills era, role formalization has been associated with the notion that teachers should be given more power to make technical decisions, such as which workbook series to use to teach particular performance objectives, when to administer skill mastery tests, when to group and regroup students according to skill deficits and achievement levels, etc. As Michael Apple observes: "They [teachers] feel that since they constantly make decisions based on the outcomes of these multiple pre- and post-tests, the longer hours are evidence of their enlarged professional status."[54] While such a reductionistic conception of professional decision-making obviously serves managerial interests, teachers' concern with professional status needs to be taken seriously. The effort by teachers to carve out some sphere of autonomy, even if it is a very limited and narrow sphere of technical decision-making, represents an attempt to gain more professional control over their work. The irony is that this sphere of control is carved out within the context of a project of school reform that has served to further de-professionalize teaching.

Finally, it is important to recognize that, while teachers have supported role formalization for a number of reasons, most of this support has come from the top of the bureaucratic hierarchy rather than the bottom. For example, the effective schools discourse, which has been used to legitimate the state-sponsored basic skills restructuring of urban schools, has argued that a high degree of teacher role formalization is related to effectiveness in raising students' test scores. In the effective urban school, according to one researcher, "rules and procedures are specified to handle most behavioral contingencies," while in the ineffective school, teachers suffer from "the absence of clear guidelines about what teachers are to emphasize, and the absence of clear criteria by which teachers are to be monitored and evaluated."[55] To suggest, therefore, that the real culprits in promoting teacher role formalization are teachers is to miss much more powerful influences. Teachers have developed a defensive role formalization designed to play the game as much to their advantage as possible given the existing rules of the game.

For all of the limitations of teacher unionism in its current form, it is clearly more progressive than reactionary, and potentially quite radical in its critique of the current system of schooling. The growing identification of teachers' unions with organized labor, and their active involvement in political lobbying in recent years, have resulted in a broadening of teachers' interests and a contextualizing of these interests. Teacher unions became heavily involved in partisan politics in the early 1970s, when Congress passed legislation allowing for the organization of so-called political action committees (PACs) by interest groups to engage in political lobbying and make campaign contributions. While the objectives of this political agenda do not generally extend beyond "special interest" legislation, teacher union PACs have pushed teachers in the direction of politicizing their concerns. Teacher unions have also become quite influential in the progressive wing of the Democratic party.[56] Teacher unions did not choose to become part

Chapter Two

of Jesse Jackson's Rainbow Coalition in the 1988 election, yet they worked together in support of progressive planks in the platform and built links to anti-racist, feminist, and gay and lesbian agendas in particular. As urban school crisis tendencies deepen and as teachers' discontent grows in the decade ahead, teacher union affiliation with a resurgent democratic-progressive political movement must be considered a distinct possibility.

Teachers' Work Culture and Crisis Tendencies in Urban Schooling

In this chapter I have viewed teachers' work culture in terms of the historical movements and struggles of teachers to articulate an occupational identity and a set of job rights and interests within the context of changes in the structuring of school sites. I have argued that it is important to understand the material and organizational conditions under which teachers construct an occupational identity, along with the role of the teacher within the overall process of schooling. Teachers represent the institution of schooling and are invested with institutional authority in carrying out the plan of instruction in the classroom, and at the same time they are workers within the schools who have been de-skilled and de-professionalized in ways similar to other semi-professional workers. They are, to use the language of structuralist theory, both members of the professional-managerial class and the broad working class. Because of teachers' unique position within class dynamics and power relations, their occupational work culture has been defined in terms of three somewhat different historical movements: a movement to protect and extend craft and professional rights, a movement that identifies teachers' interests with a united professional educational family, and an industrial union movement that organizes struggle around the wage-labor exchange. Teachers have articulated all of these movements to some degree within contemporary teacher unionism.

Professionalism has been a recurrent theme in teachers' work culture throughout the 20th century and, in an empowering form, has strong connections to a craft orientation to work. This empowering model of teacher professionalism has defined education in terms of a personal mediation between teachers and students, the unique orchestration of the learning process, and a redistribution of institutional authority to the school and classroom levels. As such, the movement for the professionalization of teaching has been consistent with the democratization of the schools, and it serves as a continuing threat to dominant structures and discourses in education. Teachers' professional aspirations and values also create motivation problems in urban schools. Professional aspirations for job control clash with the reality of teaching, and this is one reason why urban schools have such a problem retaining qualified teachers in the system. If teachers' professional aspirations cannot be adequately addressed within the framework of collective bargaining, administrators are left with few options in containing rising teacher discontent. Teachers' century-long struggle over professional status has also been related to their struggle against being treated like children, wives, daughters, or personal property by male administrators. The continued treatment of teachers (along with nurses) as semi-professionals and their continued subordination to a masculinized discourse of bureaucratic and technical rationality, suggests that teachers will need to take up gender issues in their professionalization project.

While teacher professionalism has been articulated consistent with a project of occupational empowerment and in opposition to bureaucratic and patriarchal domination within the schools, it also has been articulated consistent with a discourse that aligns teachers' interests with those of bureaucratic elites. First, teachers' claim to expertise and their desire to be included in the professional educational family have sometimes encouraged them to side with administrators and institutions against the intrusion of parents and community groups. Professional discourse and practice in this case has stood in the way of efforts to link teachers and community groups in articulating an oppositional voice in the schools. Second, the conservative discourse on basic skills reform has appealed to teachers' professional aspirations by increasing teacher involvement in a whole range of technical decisions in the school and classroom, while at the same time it has restricted teachers' substantive decision-making power and undermined craft control of work. Such a re-articulation of professionalism appeals to teachers' desires to feel that they are experts, with a highly specialized vocabulary and knowledge base, even though that vocabulary and that knowledge base are increasingly technical in nature. In fact, their professionalism has been limited, particularly at the elementary grades, by the constraints of a purposive-rational, technical language.

The emergence of an industrial model of teacher unionism during the collective bargaining era has resulted in the rearticulation of teachers' interests in instrumental and utilitarian more than professional ways. Teacher unionism during the collective bargaining era has been progressive to the extent that it has recognized that teachers and adminis-

Chapter Two

trators have been placed on opposing sides in the social relations of urban schooling, and that teachers and administrators cannot have common interests in most matters, given the current rules of the game. While teachers' resistance to bureaucratic state reform models has been largely instrumental and self-interested, it has had some effect in slowing down or watering down top-down reforms. Since more than an instrumental, do-the-minimum orientation is needed to achieve excellence or even effectiveness in education, a contract mentality also generates crisis tendencies related to goal attainment that cannot be resolved within the parameters of collective bargaining as it is currently defined. Nevertheless, in the short run, these crisis tendencies may continue to be managed in ways that do not lead to a breakdown of the existing labor-management accord in education. So long as teacher unionism views the fight over the wage-labor contract as the most important fight, and so long as teachers see no clear options that are better, given current realities in the schools, the labor accord in the schools may hold together. However, any effort to move beyond basic skills models of school reform and promote a democratic restructuring of education and the schools would need to challenge the current model of teacher unionism and collective bargaining.

3

Teachers and Basic Skills Restructuring in Midstate

In this chapter I begin to particularize discussion of the urban school crisis and teachers' interests in school reform by examining basis skills restructuring in one Northeastern state, which I call Midstate. My intent is to say something about the specific social and political forces behind basic skills reform initiatives in Midstate, the role and response of the state teacher union to these initiatives, and the contradictions and dilemmas of both reform and resistance to reform. In describing these state developments, I also set the stage for the case study of one urban school district (which I call Urbanville) which follows in subsequent chapters; for events in Urbanville are only understandable when they are first placed within the context of the rise of the educational state over the past several decades. Basic skills reforms have been largely state-sponsored and promoted, and the basic skills restructuring of the urban school curriculum has been coextensive with a dramatic rise in the power of the state over urban school decision-making. This rise in state power, in turn, has been coextensive with a significant shift in school financing from the local to the state level, a shift that in Midstate as elsewhere in the nation was court-mandated and even partially resisted by elements within the state. One of the ironies of educational reform in the late 20th century is that while progressive groups, including teachers, have supported an ever-expanding funding role for state and federal tiers of government, both as a means of increasing educational funding generally and also as a means of over-

Chapter Three

coming local inequities and thus promoting equality of opportunity, the result has been state educational policy which more often serves the interests of bureaucratic managerial, corporate, and political elites than the democratic majority.[1]

In exercising their new-found power over urban schools, state officials in Midstate invoked a new public philosophy of education.[2] According to this philosophy, the state was only responding to widespread public dissatisfaction with declining achievement in urban schools and lack of school accountability. The public philosophy of education articulated in state discourse also presented educational reform in terms of a democratic response by the state to protect the educational rights of all citizens and meet its constitutional obligation to ensure that everyone in the state, including students in urban schools, got a "thorough and efficient" education that prepared them with the real life skills they needed to get ahead and be successful. In effect, the state was able to establish the parameters for discourse on school reform, and teachers and other progressive groups in Midstate seemed unable to articulate a unified and persuasive counter-discourse on school reform. In fact, most progressive groups in the state initially supported the rise of the educational state; although they began to resist state policies that followed from an increase in state power over urban schools.

Data for this longitudinal study of basic skills restructuring in Midstate comes from several sources. These include: state Department of Education bulletins, research reports and other documents; state teacher union newspapers, and articles on urban education in the state's largest newspaper. These sources of discursive data were reviewed and analyzed for the period beginning with the 1968–69 school year (the first year of collective bargaining in Midstate schools) and concluding with the 1988–89 school year. To use Michel Foucault's terminology, this literature constituted an "archeology of discourse" on urban school reform and teachers' responses to state reform initiatives that could be deconstructed and reconstructed to reveal its discursive logic, contradictions, and conflicts.[3] Discourse on school reform in Midstate was also analysed as it organized a discursive field of action—that is, according to the situational interests it revealed and its pragmatic applications within the battle over urban school reform in the state.

The Urban School Crisis in Midstate

Midstate is one of America's most urban states, and throughout the study period it became more urban each year. In 1970, one in every

Restructuring in Midstate

four students in the state was enrolled in an urban district, and by the mid-1980s that proportion had grown to one in three. During the 1960s, the gap between the state's urban schools and suburban schools began to widen rather dramatically as "white flight" to the suburbs accelerated and as poor black and Hispanic families became the demographic majority in urban centers. The result was a rapid segregation of education in the state along racial and class lines. By the early 1980s, Midstate was ranked fourth nationally in the segregation of black students and third nationally in the segregation of Hispanic students. Approximately three-quarters of all black and Hispanic students were enrolled in schools in which minority students made up at least half of the student body; and half of all minority students attended schools that had less than a ten percent white student population.

Industry in the state had always looked to urban schools to provide a steady supply of high school graduates to enter the semi-skilled, entry-level work force. But while the demand for entry-level workers continued to grow during the study period, urban schools were turning out fewer and fewer adequately prepared workers—that is, workers with the functional literacy skills and work norms and attitudes employers sought. The problem of finding enough qualified employees was particularly extreme in the decade between 1970 and 1980, when the number of jobs in the state nearly doubled; of these new jobs, eighty percent required only a high school diploma. Furthermore, the kinds of technical skills needed for entry-level workers were changing, and urban schools had not modified their curricular offerings to reflect these changes. The new jobs in industry required highly transferable and general job skills rather than the specific vocational skills students had traditionally learned in vocational-technical tracks in urban schools; and the general academic track offered only a watered down version of the college preparatory curriculum.

Between 1969 and 1987, the number of traditional manufacturing jobs in the state dropped precipitously from 680,000 to 500,000, and was continuing to drop at a fast rate. In the meantime, the number of jobs in wholesale and retail trades climbed from 360,000 to 560,000; and the number of jobs in the service and maintenance industries rose from 280,000 to 530,000. Most of the jobs in the latter two categories were classified as semi-skilled, with a high school diploma preferred or required for employment. These were the workers industry could not get enough of. According to a 1988 article in the state's leading newspaper, "Employers who have done their hiring at their work site up until now are sending recruiters to flea markets, to inner-city streets fairs and to job banks at shopping malls. Banks that are hungry for tellers

Chapter Three

advertise open houses for job seekers, with refreshments and music." The article warned that the crisis in finding qualified service industry workers in the state "will pinch all of us—as we wait for service in restaurants, at the supermarket check-out line, in stores, at gas stations and every place else." By the end of the 1980s, Midstate was ranked eighth in the nation in the total number of functionally illiterate adults, who constituted 13 percent of the population—a proportion that continued to rise as approximately 30,000 new immigrants arrived in the state each year. One third of Midstate adults over the age of 25 had not earned a high school diploma.

These problems first began to surface during the 1960s, as business leaders complained more and more about the quality of the average urban high school graduate and as state education officials began to articulate a strategy or policy response. The first and most immediate problem to confront state officials in responding to the urban school crisis was a financial one. Midstate had a long tradition of local control and this implied local financial support of the schools through reliance upon the property tax. There was no state-imposed cap on how much a district could spend per pupil; and many wealthy suburban communities had invested heavily in their children's education, and their public schools were among the best in the country, even as urban districts were experiencing fiscal crisis, declining standards, and rising drop-out rates. In 1968, the state legislature began an almost decade-long battle over school financing by adopting a special committee report which urged the state to move quickly to increase its share of the local school budget from then-current 25 percent to approximately 40 percent, consistent with the national average, in order to meet the immediate threat of fiscal insolvency in Midstate's urban school districts. In adopting this full-funding goal, however, the legislature did not specify where the state was to find the money to meet this goal; and the response of the Governor was to propose that full funding be phased in over a five-year period. This meant that for the first several years of the phase-in, state funding goals were set quite low. In fact, the immediate consequence of the state's commitment to full funding was a reduction in the level of state aid to urban districts.

In 1972, a state District Court declared that the state school finance system violated equal protection clauses in both the state and federal constitutions by failing to provide an equal education for urban and suburban students; and in 1973, the state Supreme Court ruled that the state was in violation of an amendment to the state constitution which charged the state Department of Education with ensuring that every child in the state received a "thorough and efficient" education.

Restructuring in Midstate

The legislature was ordered to find a means of financing a full-funding aid formula to raise state aid to 40 percent of the local school budget, to compensate for inequities in local funding, and to develop a plan for ascertaining whether local districts were in compliance with the "thorough and efficient education" clause in the constitution. The court called for the state to assume responsibilities it had long neglected, noting: "A system of instruction in any district of the state which is not thorough and efficient falls short of the constitutional command. Whatever the reason for the violation, the obligation is the State's to rectify it. If local government fails, the State government must compel it to act, and if the local government cannot carry the burden, the State must itself meet its continuing obligation."

It was not until 1975 that the state legislature was able to put together a school finance equalization plan designed to both increase the overall level of state aid and redistribute that aid in a way which favored urban school districts. To equalize per-pupil costs in urban and suburban districts, the state legislature approved a complex funding formula which weighted school districts according to number of classified students, student achievement test scores, and the socioeconomic and racial composition of the community; and it put a cap on how much a school district could spend per pupil in any given year, so that rich suburban districts would not be able to apply new state funds to their already-high school budgets and thus maintain existing disparities. A legislative plan and funding formula, however, is only activated when funds are allocated, and the state legislature proved unable to make the hard choices associated with raising taxes in the state. Consequently, urban school districts in Midstate once more teetered on the edge of fiscal insolvency as the economy headed into recession. The state Supreme Court had to intervene again in 1976, to order the virtual shutdown of the schools until the legislature and the Governor came up with a plan to fund the school financing formula. In this crisis situation, the legislature, in a lengthy all-night session, finally enacted a two percent state income tax to pay for increased state support of the schools—the first income tax ever levied in Midstate. Within one year, state aid to public education doubled in Midstate; and in most urban districts, two-thirds or more of the school budget consisted of state aid, much of this in the form of categorical aid for bilingual, special education, and remedial education students.

Although the "victory of 76", as educators in the state sometimes referred to it, was successful in resolving the immediate fiscal crisis in urban districts and overcoming gross disparities in spending between urban and suburban schools, fiscal problems and inequalities remained.

Chapter Three

For example, in many urban school districts, new state monies did not seem to trickle down very far beyond the central office. The bureaucratic central office staff grew, but in the schools things went on very much as before. Furthermore, some urban school districts had responded to an increase in state aid by lowering local property taxes, so that net increases in funding were minimal. Perhaps more importantly, the state education budget was fought over each year in the legislature, and the Governor sometimes froze funds once they were allocated. Finally, tax money raised for the public schools—much of it targeted for urban schools—was spent elsewhere in the budget, to compensate for declining state revenues and increased state spending during the decade. In this case, the general fiscal crisis of the state affected public education in a particularly adverse fashion.

For these various reasons, the progress made in the late 1970s in overcoming funding disparities between urban and suburban districts was steadily eroded in the 1980s. At the end of the decade, the state Supreme Court once more sided with a group of urban school districts, and ruled that the current state funding formula was insufficient to meet the constitutional mandate to provide a thorough and efficient education to urban school students. Certainly, there was good evidence to support the contention that considerable disparities between urban and suburban schools had continued or even increased in spite of all the state claimed it had done to overcome them. For example, a *New York Times* article on the school financing lawsuit compared two school districts in Midstate, one suburban (Millbank), the other urban (East Bedford).[4] The article noted: "Millbank is rich in property values. Its spacious homes on quaint country lanes fetched an average sales price of $370,000 in 1988, compared with East Bedford's median sales price of $84,000. The gulf in real estate wealth allowed Millbank to spend $6,247 on each school child last year, while East Bedford spent $4,867." The article also noted that, "Continuity of classroom instruction . . . is continually disrupted by a turnover in teaching staff, which . . . is directly related to under-financing. . . . Between 70 and 80 of East Bedford's 900 teachers leave annually, most to seek higher-paying jobs in other school districts. . . ." In opposing the suit brought by urban school districts, the state Commissioner of Education presented evidence before the court from effective schools research which demonstrated that the "determinants" of the quality of education are found elsewhere than in the budget. The primary determinants, according to the Education Commissioner, were ". . . in management, in community relations, in parental interests, in staff attention, and in numerous other characteristics not clearly related to funding." In rejecting this

Restructuring in Midstate

evidence and argument, the Court noted: "The 'effective schools' concept and studies testing it are asserted as proving the validity of this view of the educational process—a radical view in that it explicitly denies the conventional wisdom that the more spent the better the education; the more teachers the better the education; the more experienced the teachers the better the education." While acknowledging that these other determinants did make a difference, the Court held that funding was one important determinant that had to be made equitable.

Throughout the 1970s, the the state's largest teacher union—the Midstate Education Association (MEA)—was a tireless supporter of full funding by the state, and much of its legislative lobbying effort was focused on achieving that goal. It had supported the various suits brought by urban school districts to equalize funding, and it had lobbied tirelessly in the state legislature and with the Governor and his staff for more state aid to deal with the crisis situation in urban school districts. Pragmatically, the MEA supported a dramatic increase in state funding because it believed that state funding would serve to stabilize school budgets, equalize teachers' salaries throughout the state, and increase the overall public expenditure for education in the state (and thereby indirectly increase teachers' salaries.) Furthermore, MEA leadership had developed a good working relationship with state legislators and members of the governor's staff, and it hoped to be able to cash in on its growing political influence at the state level. If key state officials could be influenced, teachers would not need to spend so much time working to influence local school boards.

Publicly, MEA support of increased state funding was always presented in terms of meeting student needs; and teachers' more immediate and tangible interests were downplayed. For example, an MEA editorial in 1972, observed, "We had 'pie in the sky' promises [about increased state funding]. The public was impressed. But our schools have been left in the lurch. Significantly, it was those who were promised the most—the cities and the poor rural areas—that proportionately end up with the least." The prospect of civic bankruptcy in nearby New York City in the mid-1970s, and the laying off of thousands of City employees and freezing of pension funds, prompted the MEA to warn in an editorial: "Let's learn from what we see before it is too late for us. Midstate must keep its strong traditions of raising taxes and revenues sufficient to fund all public expenditures, including promised public pension benefits. . . . There is one horrible prospect of financial dislocation if the State Senate 'defaults' on financing Midstate's new system of school finance." The dominant press image of the state

Chapter Three

teacher union as a powerful and persuasive lobbying force in the state capital was at least partially accurate, if a bit exaggerated with regard to the struggle over full funding. While the battle over school financing had no clear winners, the state teacher union, along with other progressive forces in the state, could claim a number of victories in its effort to make the state assume its fair share of responsibility for the urban school crisis. Teachers had used their lobbying power effectively and they were respected as a major power player in the battle shaping up over school reform.

Teachers and the Battle over the High School Diploma Exam

The irony was that teachers' success in pushing the state to assume a larger funding burden in urban schools resulted in new state-mandated models of curricular and instructional accountability that disempowered teachers, and the state teacher union often found itself in the awkward position of endorsing more state assistance for urban schools in one editorial and opposing state reform models in another. Most of the programs in the state-sponsored urban school reform package that began to emerge in incipient form by the early 1970s were conditioned upon some form of standardized testing in the schools under state auspices. The MEA opposed state testing proposals from the start and continued to oppose them throughout the 1980s, even as the state moved to implement a high school diploma exam to guarantee that high school graduates were functionally literate. An early indication of things to come was the decision by the state Board of Education to conduct, in the spring of 1973, a round of state-sponsored standardized diagnostic testing in reading and math for all fourth and twelfth graders in the state. State officials argued that such testing constituted a means of ensuring that local districts provided a thorough and efficient education, and claimed the new test data would be used to compare only those districts with similar per-pupil costs, class sizes, socioeconomic mix of students, and other factors, so that districts could see how they were doing relative to other districts like them.

An MEA editorial during this period suggests that teachers were already well aware of the possible implications of state testing on their work: "Naturally, teachers are concerned about pressure 'to teach to the test'. . . . [S]chool districts are told that the State program is simply a way for a school system to determine its educational goals and how it is meeting these goals. But, the specter of standardization looms large.... Whatever we call it, the process by which the test items were selected has 'standardized' the anticipated outcomes for 4th and 12th grade reading and math for Midstate.... Once the test is set, teachers who deviate do so at their own risk.... [Standardized testing] is a straight-jacket procedure that can only curb imagination and innovation among children and teachers in our classroom." The MEA was also concerned that the state had chosen to totally ignore teacher input in designing the test. Several years later, an MEA editorial was critical of new state guidelines which suggested that districts should use standardized test data to determine student skill deficiencies and prescribe an individualized curricular program to overcome these deficiencies. The editorial noted: "Reduced to a mechanical paper-shuffling process ... individualized diagnostic instruction can be as stifling as any traditonal whole-class approach.... To the extent that individualized instruction systems use pre-packaged programs—prearranged objectives, programmed materials, pre-tests, post-tests, re-tests, etc.—we are still laying out before students a series of linear learning hurdles.... There are many valuable learning activities that can only be impressively and efficiently organized by teachers on a group basis." In this and other editorials the MEA affirmed its allegiance to the progressive ideals of John Dewey and others who saw the project method and group activity—under the watchful eye and direction of highly qualified teachers—as the best approach to motivating students and relating the subject matter to their everyday lives and interests. While these progressive themes were no longer acknowledged within state discourse, they obviously continued to influence teachers.

In the mid-1970s, much of the discourse on school reform in Midstate began to center on the possibility that the state Board of Education would approve a high school diploma examination to certify that graduating students had achieved certain basic life skills. One group of business, civic, and state leaders argued for a relatively tough test, which would restore the "credential value" of the high school diploma in the face of widespread grade inflation and a tendency to award diplomas to students who merely "put in their four years."[5] Only those students who could demonstrate proficiencies expected of high school graduates by employers and institutions of higher education, so this group argued, deserved "diploma recognition." Pragmatically, supporters of this perspective sought to give employers a better basis for making decisions about who among high school graduates would probably make the best workers or were most literate. But generally this rationale was not highlighted in public statements. In-

Chapter Three

stead, the appeal was more often ideological, and it invoked a romantic image of how things were back in the good old days when a high school diploma meant something. Supporters of this approach were not very concerned by predictions that a tough diploma exam would encourage many urban students—perhaps up to 50 percent—to drop out, since they tended to believe that only those students who were serious about learning should be in school anyway. The state Education Commissioner often appeared to share, or at least appeal to, this group's perspective on school reform, particularly in his public speeches. For example, in supporting a diploma exam, he was fond of paraphrasing a line from a popular television commercial for an investment company: high school graduates in Midstate, he claimed, would be able to say proudly, ". . . they got their diplomas the old-fashioned way—they earned them."

A second group of supporters of a diploma exam, who ultimately prevailed at the state Department of Education, emphasized that the test should serve a diagnostic and referral function. That is, if the test were first administered to ninth graders, it could provide school officials with valuable information on the skill level of each entering high school student, so that students with skill deficiencies could be identified early and given remedial assistance; by the time they were seniors they would be able to pass the test. Interestingly, while the state Board of Education emphasized the diagnostic and referral role of a high school diploma exam in most of its publications aimed at local educators, the state Education Commission continued to lead a state-wide media campaign for the exam based on the proposition that it would restore the credential value to the high school diploma, that it would be a tough exam, and that it would restore old-fashioned work ethic virtues to public education.

Opposition to a diploma exam, in any form, was strong within the state, at least among organized interest groups, including civil rights groups, urban coalitions, the MEA, the state superintendents' association, and some members of the state Board of Education. In 1978, a special committee on high school graduation organized by the state board issued a widely publicized report, the major recommendations of which reflected the general sentiments of the anti-testing forces in Midstate. The report called for assessment of pupil proficiencies in a wide range of subject areas and recognized many alternative, locally controlled forms of assessment, including teacher observations, parent conferences, cumulative student records, and district-designed tests that employed a variety of different quantitative and qualitative indices of student achievement. The MEA praised the report, noting in an

Restructuring in Midstate

editorial that "such a report has made it possible for all students to succeed in school—to get a diploma that means real achievement. Too many voices have been proposing a punitive, simplistic diploma exam." Throughout the late 1970s, the MEA continued to hammer away at two themes suggested in the above comment: (1) a diploma exam would punish urban students who should not be blamed for the inferior education they were receiving in chronically underfunded schools; and (2) a diploma exam would not measure "real achievement," which could only be assessed by qualified teachers who had worked closely with students, and who used a mix of quantitative and qualitative indicators of achievement.

Nevertheless, opponents of standardized testing were clearly in retreat by the early 1980s. This was partly because those who opposed a diploma exam were often depicted by state officials and in newspaper editorials as opposed to holding local educators accountable to taxpayers. Opponents of the exam also had a difficult time countering the charge that they were standing in the way of raising standards in the schools. When a new Governor, elected with active MEA backing and committed to raising teacher salaries, made adoption of a high school diploma exam a top priority in his administration, the MEA began to downplay its opposition. Instead of opposing any exam, the MEA began to talk about the importance of ensuring teacher involvement in designing any possible test. The writing was on the wall; it made little sense to alienate a new political ally by fighting him tooth and nail over a diploma exam when it seemed unlikely teachers could win.

The diploma exam finally approved by the Board of Educuation in 1983, and administered to all ninth graders in the state for the first time in the spring of 1985, was designed by the Educational Testing Service and consisted of three major sections. The reading portion of the test was a series of multiple choice items that asked students to draw conclusions, make judgements, distinguish between fact and opinion, infer a main idea, identify cause and effect relationships, and identify a writer's purpose. The math section consisted of multiple choice items designed to demonstrate mastery of computing percentages, fractions, and decimals, mastery of basic geometric relations, the ability to evaluate whole numbers raised to a given power, the ability to interpret graphs and maps, and competence in solving mathematic problems that involved monetary exchanges. A final, writing portion of the exam, also primarily devoted to multiple choice items, asked students to reconstruct sentences, organize ideas, and edit for errors in grammar and word usage. In a short essay, students were asked to organize thoughts on a given topic, and express these thoughts in fluent,

Chapter Three

grammatically correct English. These, then, constituted the transferable life skills that all students were to be certified as possessing before the state would grant them a high school diploma. The test was pegged to a ninth-grade reading and math level; and students were to have four chances to pass all three sections of the exam between the ninth and twelfth grades. The state required all districts to establish special communication skills and remedial math classes, and students who failed one or more sections of the exam were to be enrolled in the appropriate remedial course or courses until they passed all sections. In addition to the diploma exam, the state also identified "benchmark skills" for the primary and intermediate grades which were related to those tested for on the diploma exam.

In response to criticism from urban school district officials, civil rights groups, and the MEA that the new diploma exam could lead to a soaring drop-out rate among urban students, the state Board of Education president asserted, "No one will fail this test, . . . rather, the test will identify the academic deficiencies that need to be overcome." To ensure that this was indeed the case, the state Department of Education launched a vigorous program of providing technical assistance to local school districts to help them align their curricular and instructional programs with the skills tested on the diploma exam. While local administrators had to ask the state Board for such assistance, those which did not risked losing favor with state officials, and all urban districts in the state asked for help to realign their instructional programs. In workshops in urban schools and in publications aimed at urban educators, state officials adopted an explicitly teach to the test philosophy of instruction. According to one state official: "If the test shows that your curriculum is not providing students with the skills necessary to pass the test, then you should revise your curriculum. There's nothing wrong with teaching to the test." Similarly, in a guide for local educators entitled, "Getting the Most From the Midstate High School Diploma Exam", the state Commissioner of Education posed several questions as the basis for "resolving curriculum design and delivery problems," including: "Do we teach what we test? Do we teach the way we test? Do we teach before we test? and Do we teach enough to ensure a good response on the test?" Summer institutes sponsored by the state allowed local teachers and administrators to spend five days focusing on topics such as: "improving students' test-taking skills; aligning curricula to emphasize the new test skills; motivating students; and finding more instructional time."

Aside from holding workshops and seminars for local teachers and administrators, the state Department of Education developed a series

Restructuring in Midstate

of workbooks and sample test booklets designed to help teachers teach to the test, and these were widely distributed and used in urban school districts. The state also encouraged publishers of curricular materials to develop "skill arrays" that indicated exactly where in various textbook series and skill kits specific testable skills were covered. In effect, the state decided to adopt a Stanley Kaplan and Princeton Review approach to test preparation—one which emphasized drills on items similar to those found on state exams, along with an explicit attempt to teach students test-taking skills and strategies.[6] It was, after all, in the interest of state officials as much as local officials to show progress in the battle against illiteracy and declining academic standards in Midstate; and to do so they were quite willing to endorse the overt coaching of students to help them pass the diploma exam. The presumption seemed to be that in learning to pass the exam, students would of necessity learn basis skills.

The state teacher union found it difficult to oppose the various forms of financial, technical, and consulting assistance provided by the state to local districts since it did not want to appear opposed to efforts designed to help students pass the test, particularly when the state picked up the expenses. Consequently, the response of the MEA was often ambivalent when it came to endorsing or sponsoring special programs to help gear up for the exam. For example, the state sponsored an "Effective Schools" program that provided funds to local urban school districts which agreed to promote the principles associated with effective schools research in one or more of their schools. These principles included, as I indicated in Chapter One, an emphasis on strong instructional leadership by the principal, a clear school mission to teach the basics, agreement among the staff as to this mission, and a strong time-on-task orientation to achieving instructional goals and objectives. The MEA initially opposed the state's effective schools legislative proposal based on the premise that it "is tied, as are so many other state initiatives, to High School Diploma Exam score increases and standardized tests at the third and sixth grade levels rather than comprehensive teacher assessment. . . . Although the Department of Education's goal—ensuring every school in Midstate is effective—is laudatory, its process encourages the top-down management style which researchers indicate inhibits effective change in schools."

In response to the effective schools proposal, the MEA proposed its own legislative alternative, a "School Effectiveness Training" plan which would fund retreats by local school teachers and administrators to help them define the schools' mission and instructional goals, the

Chapter Three

means of achieving these goals, and the appropriate methods of evaluating goal attainmnent. Nothing, of course, guaranteed that local teachers and administrators under the MEA plan would come up with the goals and ways of achieving them that were consistent with teaching to the test, and the proposal was widely seen in the press and the legislature as an attempt by the MEA to get around current collective bargaining laws and gain more power in the schools.

Consequently, when this measure failed to win support in the legislature, the MEA decided to provisionally endorse the states' effective schools proposal, on condition that the legislation be changed to allow for a so-called "local sign-off". This would allow teachers in each district to vote, through their local teacher union, on whether or not they wanted to participate in any effective schools programs. Until teachers voted to participate, a local effective schools program could not be implemented. When the Governor threatened to veto the legislation if it included a local sign-off clause, the MEA dropped its demand and supported the final legislation. In an editorial explaining that a program that would provide some state money to urban schools was better than no program and no money at all, the MEA warned: "Unless all staff members agree to support a project of such importance and magnitude, a truly effective school will not result." Thus, a state program designed to make local schools more effective in teaching to the test came to be supported with reservations by teachers, with the implied threat that teachers might withhold their active participation at the local level and thus undermine the effectiveness of the program if their voices were not heard.

In the late 1980s, with institutionalization of the high school diploma exam completed and with ongoing technical assistance from the state, urban schools in Midstate had largely been restructured to teach basic skills (including test-taking skills), and all of the effort began to pay off. In urban schools, while more than one half of ninth graders had failed to pass all three sections of the exam when it was first administered, by the time these students were seniors in 1989, fewer than 400 students statewide were denied state-certified diplomas. To the state Commissioner of Education, the lesson was clear: "The fact that the great majority of seniors passed the High School Diploma Exam and graduated in 1989 ... is gratifying. The results send a clear message: students who stay in school can learn the basic skills they need and earn diplomas." One might question, of course, whether they earned them the "old-fashioned way." Furthermore, it was not at all clear whether passing a test certified graduates as possessing the basic literacy skills employers in industry had been complaining their workers lacked.

No one seemed to seriously believe that illiteracy had suddenly declined in the state, or that the new certified high school graduates were better prepared for the job market than their predecessors. State officials and business leaders still warned of a growing literacy crisis and urged local educators to do more to respond to the challenge. Yet as scores on the diploma exam rose year after year, state officials talked of designing a new test, which would be more difficult than the current one and would test more curricular subject areas.

The most obvious reason for rising test scores did not appear to be a general rise in student intellectual and literacy skills, at least of the kind that are transferable to real-life work and social settings, but rather a vigorous program of state-sponsored and monitored curriculum alignment at the local level which was grounded in a teach-to-the-test instructional philosophy. Because students were prepared for a particular exam, there was even reason to question whether the skills that students learned to pass that test were transferable to other standardized achievement tests. For example, while diploma test scores rose, a higher proportion of students could not pass the minimum competency tests administered by the state's colleges and universities to entering freshmen. Another reason a high proportion of students passed the test as seniors was that many students who probably would have failed the exam dropped out of school before their senior year; and these students were not included in computing the final proportion of students who did not graduate with their class. Those who were still enrolled as seniors, and thus eligible to graduate, were a relatively select group in many urban school districts, and almost all had passed the diploma exam. Drop-out rates in most urban districts were between 30 and 50 percent; and although these rates did not jump dramatically after the diploma exam was instituted, it seems likely that the exam encouraged students who were already drop-out prone to leave school a bit earlier than they might otherwise have done. Why stay in high school for four years, after all, if you do not expect to receive a diploma after putting in all of that time?

Yet another factor contributing to a high pass rate on the diploma exam was the exclusion of all "classified" students in computing final district scores. Many urban districts in the state had up to 20 percent of their students labeled as bilingual (primarily Spanish-speaking), and up to 20 percent more of their students labeled as "emotionally disturbed," "socially maladjusted", and "neurologically impaired." The use of labeling to help meet the particular learning needs of "exceptional students" is, of course, generally viewed as a progressive development, and in many ways it has been. But the misuse of labeling to

Chapter Three

remove students from test rosters, combined with evidence regarding the likely adverse effects of stigmatizing students with labels, raises serious questions about this practice in urban schools.

Finally, in explaining higher-than-expected test scores on the diploma exam, one must consider the possibility that cheating played a significant if indeterminable role in artificially elevating test scores. Teachers administered and proctored the exams in their own classrooms, and reports of teachers "assisting" students—including providing students with extra time to finish exams, and even changing students' test scores—were common. State officials boasted that their secret monitors in the schools caught three teachers cheating during one administration of the diploma exam; yet there were few state monitors, and cheating by teachers (to say nothing of students) may have been more widespread than state officials cared to admit.

Basic Skills and the Rise of the Educational State

I have suggested that the urban school crisis in Midstate was managed more in terms of image than substance during the 1970s and 1980s. State officials presented a carefully managed impression of acting decisively, of developing a logical plan for action, and they pointed to evidence that their plan was working. Like many other political leaders in America during this period, they learned to manipulate cultural symbols, use the mass media, and rely upon advertising slogans to build a political constituency and sell a reform agenda to the public. Erving Goffman has written of this type of impression management: "When an individual plays a part he [SIC] implicitly requests his observers to take seriously the impression that is fostered before them. They are asked to believe that . . . matters are what they appear to be."[7] In the face of diminishing confidence in public schools, state officials in Midstate presented a carefully managed "face" to the public, one which suggested that school failure was the result of temporary and remedial problems and not from any structural contradictions in the sociocultural, economic, and political systems. The state argued that it had a workable plan for resolving the urban school crisis, and rising test scores were to be taken seriously as signs that the state was doing something to respond to the educational crisis and restore the credential value of the high school diploma. In the meantime, the roots of crisis were largely ignored and the system continued to destabilize. The state had not won the war, or even a battle, in the campaign against illiteracy.

Also ignored in state-sponsored discourse on the literacy crisis in Midstate was the issue of the type of literacy promoted through basic skills reforms. The life skills promoted by the state were almost always defined in terms of economic functionalism and the importance of preparing students for the working world. As Stanley Aronowitz and Henry Giroux have argued, functional literacy in this narrow job-skill sense may actually encourage political and cultural subordination of a "conceptually illiterate" population whose skills are only technical. "They are able to follow orders under the direction of managements that are responsive to bureaucracies and capital, but unable to examine critically public and private life, to determine how and what should be produced and by whom, and to make the public choices that become policy."[8] The teachers' union and other progressive groups in Midstate questioned the means by which the state sought to teach students functional literacy skills, but they rarely questioned what should be taken for literacy, or sought to enlarge the public debate on school reform to include notions of critical, democratic literacy. The schools thus became committed to a notion of literacy that profoundly affected how curriculum and instruction were to be organized, but without much public discourse and debate about what literacy should mean and how students should learn it.

The redefinition of literacy in terms of entry-level job skills in a labor market increasingly dominated by rationalized and routinized forms of labor has been consistent with a general shift in power towards bureaucratic state control of public institutions in America in this century, and more particularly over the past two decades.[9] By "the state" I mean here both state and federal tiers of government in America; although bureaucratic control in education has been most developed at the state level in recent decades, since that is where the money currently is. In 1979, for the first time, state governments contributed more money to education nationwide than did local school districts; by 1985, the state share had climbed to 50 percent of the local school budget.[10] Meanwhile, since the 1960s, the federal government's share of the local school budget has declined to a mere six percent.[11] The real shift in power, then, has primarily been from local school districts to state education agencies during the era of the "new federalism". This rise of the educational state over the past several decades has generally been supported by progressive social groups, including teachers, since it has led to greater equity in school funding, and a more stable local school budget. What happened, of course, in Midstate

Chapter Three

was that the state used its new-found powers to restructure the urban school curriculum in elite managerial ways.

These developments in Midstate certainly call into question the wisdom of the traditional liberal approach to solving problems in America—which is to spend more money on them. In Midstate, liberal discourse on school reform tended to be grounded in a belief that funding disparities between rich and poor schools were the major reason for inequalities in educational outcomes; the urban school crisis, it was argued, could be successfully managed or perhaps even resolved through new funding formulas and plans that shifted the fiscal burden to the state. In direct opposition to this liberal perspective on urban school reform, the conservative Commissioner of Education in Midstate during the 1980s argued that funding was not a determinant of educational achievement, and that the effective schools research indicated that in-school managerial and organizational variables have more to do with determining achievement. Interestingly, although the Commissioner of Education had in mind the better management of urban schools to raise test scores and was using effective schools research to legitimate a policy of underfunding of urban schools, a critical perspective on urban school reform would also suggest that what goes on inside a school, how power is organized and distributed, and how teachers, students, and administrators interact are much more important determinants of student achievement than funding levels.

At best, increased funding is a very limited answer to urban school problems; yet it tends to be the one that progressive elements in society rally behind—perhaps partly because money is tangible, and also because it is such an all-powerful symbol and icon in American culture. Political leadership, within such a context, is reduced to calling for more state aid for particular educational programs worthy of support. Teachers seem to have accepted this pecuniary political logic as much as have other special interest groups in education. In a mid-1980s editorial, for example, the president of the MEA wrote: "I'm talking money. The attitude that throwing money at a problem will not solve it is a rationalization used by those who are not ready to demand the immediate infusion of much larger sums of money into our districts from the state and federal level." Progressives may need to seriously rethink their support for "big government" (either at the state or federal level) and big spending if, in fact, more money does not solve problems and big government brings with it tendencies towards elite managerial rather than democratic control of public institutions. Over the decade of the Eighties, per-pupil expenditures in public education across the nation increased dramatically, by 29 percent after inflation is accounted for, yet educational standards did not improve and may have declined still further.[12] This is not to suggest that more state funding is not needed, only that it alone is not the answer to the urban school crisis.[13]

Teachers also adopted a basically benign view of the state's potential role, believing it could serve to ensure that essential public institutions were properly funded, to overcome or drastically reduce disparities generated in the socioeconomic sphere, and to allow for local decision-making and teacher discretion on curricular matters. Of course, once the state began using control of the local school purse-strings to promote elite managerial models of school reform which conflicted with this progressive view of the state's educational role, teachers increasingly began to view the state with distrust; although they generally maintained an optimistic sense that things would be different under a different administration which was more willing to listen to teachers' concerns. Teachers, however, never lost trust in the idea of working with and through the state as the primary means of achieving occupational objectives. They merely argued that a liberal administration was needed in the state capital, one that would be more sympathetic to teachers' views of needed changes and less biased towards a managerial perspective.

As the current decade began, teachers joined as an important power block in a political coalition in Midstate to elect a liberal Democratic Governor, and the new administration showed early signs of supporting curricular reform initiatives more consistent with teacher and student empowerment, more personalized and non-regimented forms of instruction and student evaluation, and greater local decision-making. There was even some indication that state officials were reconsidering a standardized diploma exam based on growing evidence that teach-to-the-test instruction was not leading to rises in meaningful learning on the part of students. The new Democratic Governor called for "one Midstate educationally" and pledged increased state support to local urban districts. In admitting that it might be difficult to sell increased urban school funding proposals to the state's suburban majority, the Governor argued that: "It is in every individual's interest in the state—not in some ideal, abstract sense, but in a real, tangible sense—to make sure every student gets to be as productive as possible." Interestingly, in this case the emphasis on student productivity, with its implicit economic functionality, suggests that the Democrats had not defined the mission of urban schools in any less narrow or instrumental terms than their Republican predecessors.

What was different in the Democratic reform proposal was the

Chapter Three

emphasis upon responding to low achievement levels through a greater role for the state in compensating for the effects of poverty, and intervening in the "culture of poverty" so that students had a better chance to succeed at school. Schools were called upon by the new Governor to "deal with the totality of problems" which interfered with achievement—including health, drugs, and other family problems. Furthermore, schools were to exercise more discretion in meeting their assigned goals, and in translating goals into specific objectives. The Governor spoke of state policy as a "blend of centralization and decentralization" which would "provide discretion at the local level to meet these [state] expectations—not by putting people at the local level in the straightjacket of saying how it is you're going to meet these goals." The administration also proposed reaching out to the business community and major corporations in Midstate to come into the schools to develop special projects and programs, something the Governor said business leaders were "really primed" to do. Finally, state officials acknowledged that rising test scores on the high school diploma exam had been more manufactured than earned. The Governor called "disconcerting" and "troubling" the failure of students who passed the diploma exam to do well in the state's collegiate basic skills exam. "How is it that you test people at one level and then, when you test the skills that the test was supposed to represent, you get unsatisfactory results? . . . That very well might mean that someone is teaching to the test and that is the very opposite of what we want."

Overall, while the new Democratic administration proposed a significantly less regimented, bureaucratized, and standardized approach to urban school reform, the discourse of reform clearly still defined the role of the schools in ways that were consistent with providing urban school students with the functional literacy skills they would need to be productive members of the semi-skilled labor force. Also unquestioned were limitations in the culture-of-poverty approach to understanding the problem of student achievement. Such an approach fails to address the structurally generated economic roots of poverty and it suggests that white racism is not the primary problem that holds disadvantaged groups back.[14] While the emphasis upon decentralizing decision-making and allowing for a less predetermined and standardized curriculum sound good, the liberal response fails to account for the vicious cycle phenomenon in educational reform, with swings between centralization and decentralization of bureaucratic authority which do not significantly alter power relations in urban education.

In a number of important ways, the Democratic reform agenda was consistent with the principles of enlightened business management, as

Restructuring in Midstate

represented in the 1980s in Thomas Peters' and Robert Waterman's influential book, *In Search of Excellence*.[15] Adaptive institutions supposedly provide room for individual leadership and entrepreneurship in achieving top-down reforms and in responding to unique local conditions and client needs. But the goals of the organization established by centralized management remain unquestioned. The conservative and liberal debate on school reform, consequently, was about the most effective management of the public school system in raising student achievement levels and containing crisis tendencies in urban schooling. Conservative models of state school reform (such as basic skills restructuring) generate problems having to do with a decline in student and teacher motivation and a tendency to go through the motions. Liberal models of state reform help overcome some of these problems. However, in doing so they may not be able to guarantee that the schools are organized in ways that prepare students to be productive and disciplined members of the labor force. After all, the basic skills, top-down approach to the organization of curriculum and instruction in urban schools is designed to closely align what goes on in urban schools with the needs of industry. It remains to be seen, consequently, how far the liberal adminstration in Midstate will be prepared to push a progressive, decentralized agenda for school reform.

A democratic, grass-roots discourse on urban school crisis and school reform unfortunately did not develop in Midstate in the basis skills era to challenge the premises of corporate and state discourse. Teachers voiced opposition, but it was always guarded and hesitant. This was partly due to the fact that teachers' occupational movement was not connected to a broader grass-roots and community-based oppositional movement in the state; and partly it reflected a decision by teacher union leadership to work with state leaders to get payoffs for teachers, so that the union could not afford to alienate political leaders of either major party. However, given the fact that state political leadership proceeded to endorse a reform initiative that further subordinated teachers within a network of hierarchical, bureaucratic controls, teachers may need to rethink their strategy of lobbying state political leaders as a primary means of occupational empowerment. While political lobbying at the state level may have its payoffs, given current realities teachers may want to invest more time and effort in building a power base among various constituencies in the public that have a stake in more progressive approaches to school organization and control and to curriculum and instruction.

4

Teachers and Basic Skills Restructuring in Urbanville

It is now time to shift the focus of analysis to the local school district level and indicate how these developments in Midstate, having to do with a state-declared "war" on illiteracy and with the basic skills restructuring of urban schools, impacted upon the working conditions of teachers in one urban school district. In what follows, I analyze data from the Urbanville school district and from the files of the Urbanville Education Association (UEA), the local teacher union, to piece together a history of the institutionalization of a basic skills package of reforms in Urbanville schools from the late 1960s through the mid-1980s, along with the responses of the UEA to state and central office reforms aimed at making teachers teach the basics. A number of issues are raised in this chapter that pertain to the analysis of urban school crisis tendencies and how teachers constitute a set of interests within the dynamic of urban school reform. Research questions have to do with how the local teacher union interpreted teachers' interests and how effective it was in realizing its objectives within the system. More specifically, I am concerned with the representativeness of the teacher union leadership and its responsiveness to rank-and-file concerns, the relationship between the teacher union and the growing African-American and Hispanic communities in Urbanville, and gender relations and dynamics within the union.

I argue that the UEA was limited in its capacity to mobilize a strong oppositional voice in the schools because it was not able to effectively

Chapter Four

involve rank-and-file teachers, link up with community opposition to existing school discourse-practice, or overcome gender inequalities within the ranks of teachers. The local teacher union was able to slow down and weaken these various central office reform initiatives designed to make teachers conform to new basic skills formats and instructional approaches, but was not able to impede the seemingly inexorable progress of basic skills restructuring. However, because central office administrators did not secure the willing cooperation and commitment of teachers to changes, the administration got its way at a substantial cost that undermined the effectiveness of reforms. Finally, I present evidence that teachers affirmed progressive, student-centered approaches to pedagogy in the face of growing pressure to adopt a performance-based curriculum and a teach-to-the-test instructional style. Teachers associated this more progressive approach to teaching with professional ideals, including some they had learned in their college education courses. The final picture to emerge is thus a complex and multifaceted one. On the one hand, the teacher union was severely restricted in its formal power, crippled by rank-and-file apathy, and unable to work effectively with community groups in building an oppositional voice in the schools. On the other hand, teachers used what formal and informal powers they could muster to oppose basic skills reforms. Many teachers continued to affirm progressive and professional ideals, and in doing so they threatened the capacity of managerial elites to maintain effective steerage of the system.

Data presented and analyzed in this chapter comes from several sources. The first section of the study draws upon ethnographic research conducted by the author from 1984 through 1986 in Urbanville. This data consists of notes taken by the author at teacher union meetings; transcripts of taped meetings; notes from interviews with the teacher union president; notes from informal conversations with teacher union representatives and leaders before and after meetings; and notes on informal observations in the teacher union office. The second section of this chapter, which documents the response of teachers to basic skills restructuring, draws upon data from teacher union files for the period 1968–69 through 1985–86. Most of this data consists of grievances filed by the union or by individual teachers contesting changes in the terms and conditions of employment associated with basic skills restructuring. I also draw upon data in the files documenting incidents in which teachers contested their evaluations by administrators to indicate how teachers affirmed a generally progressive and student-centered curriculum and pedaogy while administrators increasingly emphasized a highly technical "one best way" of basic skills instruction.

Urbanville and Its Schools During the Basic Skills Era

Urbanville was one of over fifty urban school districts in Midstate, and it was fairly typical of the majority of small and medium-sized districts which dotted the state's urban corridor. The headquarters of a large corporation was located in downtown Urbanville, and a state university campus sprawled out on one side of town. Despite these bastions of middle-class culture, Urbanville was, throughout the 1970s and 1980s, a city of poor blacks and Hispanics. The once-large white ethnic neighborhoods had shrunk to a small core of elderly residents, who had no children in the schools. Most of those white working-class and middle-class families who did have children of school age enrolled them in Catholic parochial schools. In the 1980s, there were signs of a gradual "gentrification" in Urvanville, as efforts were begun to revive the downtown neighborhood as a shopping, dining, and entertainment center for the suburban middle class. But efforts to lure the middle class back into the city had not yet paid off as civic leaders hoped it would, partly because Urbanville was still a city of the poor, who had no use for the new boutiques and restaurants designed to cater to middle-class customers, and whose presence in the city actively discouraged many suburbanites from shopping or dining there. The public schools of Urbanville served an increasingly poor black and Hispanic student population throughout the study period. In 1970, white students constituted approximately one third of the total student population, black students made up one half of the total, and Hispanic students represented less than one fifth of the total. By 1975, blacks comprised 60 percent of the student population, whites 20 percent, and Hispanics 20 percent. In 1985, less than ten percent of all students were white, blacks comprised approximately two-thirds of the total, and the Hispanic student population had grown to over one fourth of the total. Overall, the size of the student population declined by approximately one third between the late 1960s and the late 1980s, from 6,000 students to less than 4,000. These students were divided among six elementary schools, three middle schools, and one high school.

The UEA was the local bargaining agent for teachers, although it

Chapter Four

still disclaimed the union label. When, in my first conversation with the UEA president I said I was interested in studying a teacher union, he responded with a smile: "Well, we're a professional association, not a teachers union, you know." In fact, the UEA had became more trade union-oriented over the past decade, as it moved from being a teachers-only association to representing all educational workers in the schools, including maintenance staff, secretaries, and teacher aides. The basis for this so-called "inclusive local" had been established in 1968, in the collective bargaining law for public employees, which distinguished between managerial and non-managerial employees but defined teachers and non-professional employees as a single "community of interest". In 1978, the MEA constitution was changed to allow full membership for support staff, and urban locals in particular rapidly moved to organize support staff and thereby increase membership and (supposedly) bargaining power. Ironically, while the notion of an inclusive local once referred (in the pre-collective bargaining days) to the fact that teachers and administrators were in the same professional association, the notion now links teachers' interests with school labor in opposition to school management.

While teachers and support staff were learning to work together in support of their common interests in Urbanville, power inequalities remained and created some dissention among the UEA leadership. Frank Goodman, president of the UEA during the mid-1980s when the study was initiated, was a high school English teacher who was personally very committed to representing support staff. But at a union meeting he once complained: "I went down last year to the delegate assembly [of the MEA] and thanked everyone there for getting the legislature to raise teacher salaries; and I asked what they were going to do for our support staff. You know, we passed some motions in this county asking the MEA to do something more for support staff salaries. So I asked, 'What happened?' The answer I received was, 'We're working on it.' In November, I called down to the MEA and asked again, 'Where is it? Will it come up at the delegate assembly?' And he answered, 'No, it's not coming up, but another proposal to raise teacher salaries is.' Now, I just think that's an injustice. We need to tie support salaries to teacher salaries. But the MEA won't even adopt a policy statement in that regard. Where's the coordination? It burns me up."

Teachers, then, continued to be the central power block in both the MEA and the UEA, and controlled most key leadership positions, although support staff were pushing to make the union represent their interests better, primarily in relation to increased wages and an improved health and pension package. The support staff representatives

Restructuring in Urbanville

were well aware of their second-class status within the UEA, but they remained hopeful. When I attended a special UEA legislative dinner, a secretary who sat next to me remarked, in a voice meant for my ears only: "We've made progress, I guess. A few years ago, some of these teachers wouldn't be caught dead at the same table with a secretary. We were beneath them. At least now we can sit at the same table." The UEA president generally favored more equality between teachers and support staff in the union, although this implied that teachers' specific concerns would receive less attention, and some teachers were not comfortable with this trend.

This is a difficult issue for critical pragmatists. A teachers-only union, based on an exclusionist notion of professional status (exclusionist in that it excludes "less-deserving" groups such as secretaries and janitors) is less likely to encourage teachers' identification with a broad-based working class movement. In these terms, the inclusive local may be considered a progressive phenomenon. The other side of the picture is that teachers' growing identification with organized labor, as represented by the inclusive local approach, is likely to result in less attention to the unique aspects of teaching and may lead to a de-emphasis upon curricular and instructional issues in the union and a re-emphasis upon "bread and butter" issues that concern everyone. Furthermore, while it is important to recognize that teachers share some common interests with the non-professional staff, within the educational equation teachers share more in common with administrators, from whom they are currently divided. That is, teachers and administrators have curricular and instructional interests not shared by secretaries, janitors, and other school workers, yet no union or association currently brings these interests together.

The UEA was governed by two councils: a representative council consisting of representatives from the various school teaching staffs and support staff units, on the basis of one representative for each 25 members in a unit; and an executive council consisting of the president, vice president, and other officers of the representative council, along with three members elected at large. Because teachers outnumbered support staff by approximately three to one, the representative council was mainly oriented towards teachers' special issues and concerns. In contrast, the executive council was fairly evenly divided between teacher and support staff members, and it tended to focus upon union business and procedural concerns more than substantive issues. However, because the executive council was small, its meetings were most informal. They often revealed more about the real workings of the UEA and the perspectives of its leaders than did the more formal

Chapter Four

representative council meetings, although the latter provided a richer source of information on what rank-and-file teachers were thinking.

Aside from regularly scheduled biweekly and monthly union meetings, the union was kept operational on a day-to-day basis and provided with ongoing leadership by the president. Over the two-decade study period, the UEA had three presidents; but the last one, Frank Goodman, had served the longest, had served separate terms in the early 1970s and the 1980s, and was not seriously challenged for leadership. He had a friendly, disarming personality, and was a committed union man who in the late 1970s had been president of the state MEA for a few years. In that capacity he even spent a few days in jail for supporting a group of teachers in one district who refused to return to work and end a strike, and this incident infused him with a sense of injustice that continued to drive him. In the UEA, he had an inordinate amount of power. He not only organized and ran all meetings, he kept the union going on an everyday basis with very little oversight or help. No one accused the president of hoarding power or being autocratic, however. Rather, the prevalent sentiment was that the UEA was lucky it could find someone to take such a thankless job, especially someone with such close, personal connections to powerful MEA leaders in the state capital.

At the time of the ethnographic study, Frank was in his late fifties, his glory days at the helm of the state teachers' union behind him; and he was struggling to keep himself from becoming burned out by focusing on one battle after another with the administration. It was the battle, he said, that kept him going. The president was paid (in the mid-1980s) $2,000 per year by the UEA, and he received a reduced workload from the district so that he could work in the union office in the afternoons. He claimed: "It is so much better now than back in the 1970s when I was president and had five classes, homeroom, cafeteria duty, and had to do all this anyway. I wouldn't do it that way again. No way. You know, as you get older you need some sleep, your eyes go bad on you, things like that." Yet he obviously relished his work as union president, and that, more than teaching, kept him going. He once confided to me: "I don't enjoy teaching any more. It's just a routine for me now. If it wasn't for this [referring to the UEA], I wouldn't be in this district." Although it might have seemed in his interests, he opposed proposals to raise his salary and to make him a full-time president, as some other districts in the state had done. His reasoning was that "after they pay the president's salary and for a secretary or two, those locals haven't got much money left for anything else. Also, the dues have to be twice as high in those districts." One of

Restructuring in Urbanville

Franks's major priorities as union president had been keeping dues low, something which has won him favor with the rank and file.

Most teachers appeared to prefer that Frank run the union without much oversight, since the constant complaint of union representatives was that teachers in their buildings were too overworked and overcommitted to be involved. Rounding up members to serve on various committees and to run for various positions in the union thus became an immediate objective of the union. At one union meeting, the chair of the nominating committee reported how she had arrived at the current slate of candidates for positions on the executive council, in which most candidates, including the president, were running unopposed: "Everyone was contacted personally through their building reps. We asked people if they would be willing to run for anything at all. And when they declined, this is the slate we came up with." The president thanked the chairperson, and at that, the matter was dropped. However, at another meeting shortly before the scheduled elections, Frank presented the executive council with the need to round up three more members to serve on the elections committee to count the votes. "I don't appoint the elections committee. You have to appoint someone to see that the ballots get out and are counted accurately. Council, I don't have this responsibility, you do. So let's come up with a list. Give me some names." Several names were raised, and one by one dismissed. A member of the executive council volunteered, but was ruled ineligible; another possible candidate had a dinner to attend on the night of committee meeting; another had a class trip that day; and yet another was on the committee last year. Finally, a teacher remarked, "This is getting ridiculous," and the president added, "I will have the ballots all made up, but that's all I'll do because this three-member committee has to approve it. Will we have to postpone the election until someone volunteers?" In the end, with enough personal persuasion from Frank, the requisite number of teachers were rounded up for the assignment and the election of an unopposed slate of candidates proceeded uneventfully.

Executive committee members often blamed the rank and file for being apathetic and then complaining when union leadership made decisions they did not like. Frank was particularly frustrated at times by what he called a "negative" or "bitchy" attitude among many teachers. At one representative council meeting, for example, when he was unable to round up teachers to serve on a calendar committee, he looked over the roster of teachers for each school and half-jokingly asked, "OK. Let's see who bitches a lot at the high school." At which point a teacher representative commented, "We all do." In a suddenly

Chapter Four

more serious tone, the president remarked, "What I'm saying is, we really need somebody from each school to serve on the calendar committee so people in that school can't bitch and complain later that nobody asked them." Occasionally the president seemed aware of the sexist connotations of the term "bitchy", or was made aware by others. For example, at one meeting he began to complain about how teachers in a certain school were always "bitching about something," but stopped himself in mid-sentence and said, "Oh, I shouldn't use that term, I mean complaining. But you know what I mean." Loud enough to be heard around the table, one teacher remarked to her neighbor, "I really wish he wouldn't talk like that." Frank said no more, and went on to another matter. Gender power relations in the UEA were most apparent in the composition of meetings. At at typical representative council meeting with 25 to 30 members in attendance, only two to three were men. One of these would be the president, and another would be the young teacher who was executive council treasurer and "heir apparent" to the current president. The two men ran most meetings, with the president clearly in control but occasionally turning the meeting over to the treasurer to make a report. The vice-president role was occupied by a black woman, and although she sometimes spoke at meetings she was more a figurehead than a powerful or influential figure in the UEA.

Since the UEA organization and leadership structure was expressive of accepted class and gender power relations, it should not be surprising to learn that it was also expressive of racial power relations. The teaching staff in Urbanville was almost 90 percent white throughout the study period, even as their students became more black and Hispanic. Within the teaching staff, black and Hispanic teachers were also heavily overrepresented in lower-status, lower-paying, and less secure positions, such as those in bilingual education and remedial basic skills classes. Race was rarely an overt issue in UEA meetings, although disparaging comments about a decline in the "quality" of students in Urbanville often carried an implicit racial subtext. Informal comments at union meetings, such as, "The schools have really gone downhill since I began teaching here," "A lot of these kids haven't got the ability to learn much," and "Their [students'] attention span isn't very long" were not overtly racist; but they had much the same effect of distancing teachers from students and encouraging teachers to view students as the "other." Some comments were more overtly racist. For example, at a union meeting in which the topic was the decline of the vocational-technical program at the high school, a teacher leaned over to inform me of the background of the current situation. She began: "Some of

Restructuring in Urbanville

our black parents think vocational education is a racist tracking system. They made a real commotion at a [school] board meeting a while back, claiming that black kids were being tracked in voc-tech, so voc-tech courses were racist. Can you believe that? So now we might as well enroll them all in a course for pickpockets." She was alluding to the perception among some teachers that minority students were using the schools as a training ground to become pickpockets—a form of vocational training for their chosen line of work.

Activists in the community often lumped teachers and the UEA together with the superintendent and the school board as part of the "white power establishment" which had managed to maintain its grip on control of major public and private institutions in Urbanville long after most whites had moved to the suburbs; and there was some evidence that UEA leadership was concerned about its image in the black and Hispanic communities. At one executive council meeting the president went over a list of possible invitees to a special UEA-sponsored dinner and dialogue with community leaders, and remarked: "We have Reverend ———, and we have Reverend ——— as two black preachers, alright? Black preachers hold a lot of influence if you get the right ones. Both of these, at least ———, is becoming a force in politics in town. But how about a Hispanic preacher? Why don't I ask Maria Gonzalez [a teacher] if she knows people on the Puerto Rican Action Board. I can ask her to get someone for us." These comments suggest that the UEA leadership was attempting to win favor with the city's minority communities, but also that in doing so it viewed minority participation primarily in terms of tokenism and maintaining good relations with various elements of the community, with little effort made to involve the community in a more meaningful way. Similarly, minority teacher involvement in union committees and decision-making bodies was often viewed in terms of tokenism. The union president, for example, in describing the quota system for sending local members to the state representative assembly, noted: "If you have four delegates, you always were asked [by the MEA] to make sure that one was a minority person of some kind. . . . We used to do very well in that respect for years. And if we have, say, six people run for three delegate seats, it would be nice if one of them was a minority. So we want to encourage minorities to run."

In fact, then, while the UEA was formally committed to overcoming racial disparities, and these commitments seemed genuine if somewhat token, the UEA often remained a neutral or ambivalent party when black and Hispanic community groups accused the schools of promoting a racist curriculum or tracking system. For example, In the early

Chapter Four

1970s, a black teacher at the high school joined several community leaders in publicly charging that "institutional racism is being practiced at the high school" because an inordinate number of black students were assigned to vocational-technical tracks and lower ability tracks. When the teacher subsequently appeared on the auditorium stage at the high school to introduce an assembly program for Black History Month, a number of white students walked out. In response to heightened racial tensions in the school caused by the event, the UEA representative council issued a statement in support of teachers' rights as citizens "to express their personal political views openly without fear of reprisal or intimidation." The UEA also went on record as calling for a district study on the use of standardized tests to place students in ability groups, although no such study was ever undertaken. In this case, the union took no stand on whether or not institutional racism existed in Urbanville schools, and instead focused its concern on the rights of teachers to academic freedom and freedom of speech. The UEA, then, did not appear to express in either its organization or its policy a strong commitment to participatory democratic, anti-sexist, and anti-racist values. Of course, like most organizations in late 20th century America, and perhaps more than most, the UEA was formally committed to equal treatment, equal rights, and social and economic justice; but also like most organizations, it was informally expressive of the accepted class, gender, and racial power relations and beliefs of its members.

The Battle Over Basic Skills Restructuring

The power of the UEA was also undermined by the formal legal structure of collective bargaining that severely restricted the range of issues about which teachers could bargain and thus exercise their power. Because curricular and instructional decisions had been interpreted by state courts as managerial issues about which teachers had no rights to bargain, teachers had to learn how to frame curricular and instructional interests and concerns within the language of the wage-labor contract, and the contract language could only be stretched so far. Throughout the 1970s and 1980s, Urbanville teachers struggled to respond to the basic skills restructuring of their work by framing their interests within the langauge of the contract, and they could claim victory in a few battles in this regard. But they did not prevail in extending their claims to professional job control during the study

Restructuring in Urbanville

period, and they served to delay and weaken, rather than present a forceful alternative to, top-down reforms.

Behavioral Objectives

The first major confrontation over basic skills restructuring in Urbanville schools was in the fall of 1973. When teachers returned to school in September, they found waiting for them packets of new forms to be submitted in preparing "Behavioral Outcomes Learning Units." These, according to an accompanying administrative memo, were to replace the traditional unit and course plans. Changes in lesson and unit planning formats were identified as "necessary to meet new state auditing requirements," which specified that all instructional goals and objectives had to be "quantifiably measurable." Aside from identifying specific behavioral objectives for their courses, teachers in the elementary reading, math, and language arts programs and the secondary remedial math and language arts programs were required to link performance objectives to the use of specific textbooks, workbooks, and skill kits and to use standardized diagnostic tests to evaluate student skill performance. Finally, all teachers were required to estimate what proportion of students they expected would master various objectives within what time frame, based on an evaluation of entry-level skills for each class and test data from previous years. Obviously, these learning units were designed to make teachers use many of the new skill-based series then becoming available on the educational market and to generate through their teaching the kinds of "hard data" needed to satisfy the increasing data demands of the state education agency. Many teachers, though, had to first be retrained through special in-service workshops and summer programs to complete the complex forms, write behavioral objectives, and use the new curricular skill series and tests. Teachers were also given self-guided workbooks on behavioral objectives to review in their own time.

When the new forms and behavioral objective formats were first introduced, the UEA filed a grievance charging that because the changes were imposed without prior consultation with teachers, they constituted "a unilateral change in the terms and conditions of employment in clear violation of the contract." The grievance went on to argue that such a drastic change in instruction "ought to involve the teaching staff, the doers, right from its conception. . . . [Furthermore,] the Behavioral Outcomes Learning Units may be in conflict with academic freedom. The degree of flexibility in the program is not clear." Until these issues

Chapter Four

could be resolved to teachers' satisfaction, the UEA urged that the superintendent delay implementation of the changes. The superintendent responded: "We are going to have to live with these changes. . . . It is no use complaining about something over which we have little control." The teacher union was on very shaky ground in pressing any grievance involving the organization of instruction, and when the superintendent proved immune to its appeal, the grievance was quietly dropped. But the union did continue to attempt to block or delay implementation of new behavioral lesson and unit planning requirements. For example, in 1974, 16 teachers at a middle school were formally reprimanded because they submitted one section of their unit plans late. The teachers argued that they lacked data to complete some of the forms and that the forms were delivered to teachers late. Ultimately, following a formal hearing before the school board, the teachers won their grievance and letters of reprimand were removed from their files. But one union representative warned ominously in a note to the union president that: "Morale can only sink lower when actions against teachers like this occur. We're being snowed under by forms and teachers are just filling them out with anything, just to get them done. Conditions like this can't continue."

Developments in Urbanville, as I have already indicated, were representative in many ways of larger developments in the state; in the 1973–74 school year, teachers throughout the state, but more particularly in urban districts, were being confronted with the new behavioral objectives system of curriculum and instruction. Consequently, the Midstate Education Association (MEA) distributed materials to local unions warning about the possible consequences of over-reliance upon behavioral objectives and suggesting strategies for arguing against behavioral approaches to instruction in their communities. One MEA press release distributed among teachers in Urbanville at this time traced behavioralism "back to its origins in psychology laboratories, where animals such as rats learn to traverse mazes by receiving rewards for correct turns. . . ," and it quoted an education professor as saying: "If these [behavioral] models are adopted uncritically by rank-and-file teachers, education will decline into an inauthentic and spiritless conditioning." Another MEA release distributed among Urbanville teachers argued that: "The behavioral objective movement is primarily concerned with the specific and the concrete, such as the memorization of facts, rather than the liberal and the broad, such as the ability to solve problems and think creatively." More pragmatically, it appealed to teachers' interests in resisting the de-skilling of their work and teacher opposition to being treated like factory workers in industry,

Restructuring in Urbanville

by noting: "Behavioral objectives originated in industry with training projects designed to teach factory workers specific job skills." The implication was that teachers would become more like factory workers if behavioral approaches to curriculum and instruction became the norm in the schools.

Interestingly, this rather politicized conception of the behavioral objectives movement and its likely impact on teachers' work came from the state teacher union rather than the local union. Teachers in Urbanville rarely thought of their struggle against basic skills restructuring in these terms, or perhaps more accurately, never articulated their interests and discontents in these politicized ways. They were always in the position of resisting one change at a time, and they focused their attention on how each change altered the terms and conditions of employment in ways that increased their workload or work hours. Furthermore, under pressure the administration began to ease up on teachers at the high school and did not insist that they link their teaching to standardized post-tests or precise performance objectives. According to one high school teacher: "They [administrators] didn't really care what you put down so long as you were filling out the form and getting it in on time," so that most high school teachers did not feel too directly threatened by the new lesson and unit planning formats, at least in the 1970s.

Professional Improvement Plans

The next major basic skills reform aimed at teachers to meet with active resistance came in the late 1970s, with the requirement that teachers use their yearly Professional Improvement Plans (or PIPs) to detail ways in which they intended to raise student skill levels. PIPs themselves were not new in Urbanville schools and had long been required of all teachers in the state as a way of making them think about how they could improve their teaching. But prior to the late 1970s, administrators in Urbanville did not seek to use the PIP requirement to make teachers commit themselves to an increased basic skills orientation. In these earlier years, teachers frequently listed on their PIPs plans for activities such as taking summer courses at a university, participating in revising a departmental scope and sequence document, doing library research on a particular topic in the curriculum, etc. But all of this began to change when the state department of education decided PIPs could be used by administrators to require specific changes by teachers, and that administrators had a right to review and approve

Chapter Four

or disapprove PIPs submitted by teachers. At a representative council meeting shortly after the new PIP requirements were imposed by the superintendent, the president was directed by a unanimous vote to look into the legality of the reqirement that teachers submit plans for prior approval and whether or not administrators could dictate what teachers included in their PIPs.

At the next meeting Frank reported back on what he had learned: "I talked to ——— at the MEA, and he told me that other court cases around Midstate have recently sustained the rights of administrators to determine the PIPs." A number of teachers moaned audibly and one said: "How could they? They can't do that." Frank sought to calm the teachers by stating: "I'm afraid they can. So please understand that if the administration wants you to write your PIPs this way, they will find a way to force you to participate. But do this. Write on the bottom of your PIP form, 'this is not my personal PIP, and I submit it under protest.' " Once more, teachers had lost a battle, but they succeeded in making a point. Teachers would go through the motions of completing forms according to administrative dictates, but they would not take the forms seriously. Furthermore, over time the administration began to use the PIP requirements more selectively, requiring detailed, performance-based PIPs only from those teachers who had received poor evaluations. This helped defuse some of teachers' immediate discontent, although teachers continued to complain about having to complete the forms and submit them for approval, and the UEA maintained that teachers should receive additional pay or an additional preparation period for completing the forms.

"Time on Task" and "Scans"

In the early 1980s, the battle over basic skills restructuring shifted to the issue of "time on task" evaluation of teachers. Where previously teachers had been held accountable to teach basic skills through a web of forms and paperwork, now teachers were also expected to show real changes in their instructional techniques, demonstrating that they were actually teaching to performance objectives in an efficient manner. The indicator of instructional efficiency was taken to be "time on task," a term used frequently by supporters of effective schools research. Concern with time-on-task approaches to improving instructional efficiency began in Urbanville when the superintendent applied for and received a grant from the state's Effective Schools Program to investigate how student test scores could be raised in the district

Restructuring in Urbanville

through changes at the school building level. Much of the grant money was used to contract with an educational research and development center at a nearby state university, called Research for Effective Schools (RES), to conduct an efficiency study of the schools.[1] As part of the several-year research phase of the study, a consulting team from RES spent two years conducting observations in Urbanville schools and classrooms. Members of the team were given wide leeway by the superintendent to make unannounced observations of teachers and classes as part of their research.

One of the primary research tools employed by the consulting team was called a "scan"—a short (twenty-minute), unannounced observation of the beginning, middle, or end of a class in session, during which time the consultant used a "Pupil Engagement Rate" form to record numbers and compute scores. For every minute of observed class time, the consultant marked how many students (out of the total on the class roster) were present, and how many of those present were engaged in various categories of behavior: on-task behavior (leading to achievement of targeted lesson objectives), socializing, being disciplined, unoccupied, and in transition from one activity to another. At the end of the form was room for the consultant to calculate and record an overall "pupil engagement rate" for the class, which supposedly provided an indicator of how efficient and effective the teacher was in managing class time and focusing student energy and attention on the task at hand. For example, a pupil engagement rate of 80 meant that 80 percent of the time an average student in the class was "on task." In follow-up conferences with teachers after school or during their preparation periods, the consultants reviewed the data and conclusions with teachers and encouraged them to think about, and commit themselves to, plans for raising the pupil engagement rate in their classes. Teachers who were given relatively poor scores on an initial scan (generally lower than 85) were targeted by consultants for further scanning.

When the consulting team finally finished its study, it presented the superintendent with a set of recommendations. Among these recommendations was that principals and other administrators in each school should continue to conduct scans on a regular, unannounced basis to help focus teachers' attention on the need to increase students' time on task, and that they hold post-scan conferences with teachers who needed improvement. This recommendation was adopted, initially for the elementary schools only, and principals began making several visits a week to some classes where students were not up to expected progress in the curriculum. The response of the UEA, following a number

Chapter Four

of complaints from teachers who said they were being "personally harassed," "made to defend everything I do that isn't specifically related to passing tests," and required to "submit plans for raising my scan scores," was to file a grievance charging that scans were teacher evaluations, and that according to the contract teachers were to receive at least two days' advance notice for each formal evaluation. The superintendent argued in response that scans were not evaluations, but rather "a form of quality control information on the achievement of instructional goals." He insisted that "scans have to be unannounced to be effective." Finally, he reminded the union president that the courts would "no doubt side with the administration in this claim." In this, according to Frank, the superintendent was probably right. "The courts always side with the administration when it comes to evaluation," he once confided to me. "So even if the supertintent admitted that scans are evaluation, the courts are going to say: 'Evaluation is a managerial prerogative.' You see, they [the courts] don't acknowledge that any contract language about evaluation is legit. So if we pressed this one, they might even throw out what contract language we now have on evaluation. It's a no-win situation."

For its part, the administration appeared to be playing a waiting game—waiting to see whether teachers were prepared to push the dispute over scans to a court case, based on a claim of breach of contract language on evaluation. When the union did not threaten such action, both sides slowly began to move towards some informal resolution of the conflict in a series of meetings between the union president and the personnel director on the superintendent's staff—a man who often served as an informal negotiating representative for the administration. The administration was receptive to a compromise, since, as the superintendent wrote in a letter to the UEA president: "This matter [of the scans] is unduly affecting morale and professional working relations between teachers and administrators in the schools. I find this an intolerable situation. Surely we can agree on the importance of a quick resolution of this matter." The compromise finally negotiated informally permitted the administration to conduct scans in the elementary schools; but plans to introduce them at the secondary level were dropped. Furthermore, the administration agreed that elementary teachers would be given informal, word-of-mouth, notification several days before they were scheduled to be scanned, so that no one would ever be scanned unannounced.

Frank, who was union president when this deal was "cut" with the administration, believed that "teachers got a pretty good deal." Of course, he was also a high school teacher, and his feelings might have

Restructuring in Urbanville

been different if he had taught in the elementary grades, where the deal seemed less good. He accounted for the discrepency between secondary and elementary teachers by arguing that high school teachers put up more resistance to scans than elementary teachers: "In the high school teachers didn't have the yoke around their neck so long as they did in the elementary schools. So when the superintendent tried to move 'scans' to the high school, teachers resisted." Elementary school teachers were generally presumed among UEA leadership to be less assertive in defending their interests. Even if this was more perception than reality, it seemed to contribute to a perception among administrators that elementary teachers could be pushed around more easily than their secondary school colleagues. Another factor that helps to account for this discrepancy is that the elementary school curriculum was more skill-based and behavior objective-oriented than the high school curriculum, with more use made of standardized curricular materials and tests. It was thus more amenable to time-on-task and teach-to-the-test approaches to evaluation such as the scan. Finally, elementary teachers were generally more subordinated to their principals—a subordination that I have already suggested was at least partially explainable in gender terms. They felt less empowered and they were treated less as professionals than secondary school teachers. A popular elementary school teacher complaint was: "They [the administrators] treat us like children," suggesting that gender power relations are linked to adult-child power relations in school culture (and indeed in the larger culture). All of these factors, of course, worked together to maintain inequalities in the treatment of elementary and secondary teachers by both the teacher union leadership and the administration.

Teacher Evaluations and the "One Best Way" of Teaching

While teachers were partly successful in resisting evaluative procedures, such as the scan, which represented changes in the terms and conditions of employment, they were less successful during the study period in resisting the gradual intrusion of performance-based, teach-to-the-test and time-on-task criteria in regular evaluation of teachers by administrators. Particularly in the elementary and middle schools during the 1980s, and to a lesser extent in the high school, teachers were evaluated on the degree to which their instructional practices and classroom management techniques were consistent with a one best way of teaching. In invoking the notion of a "one best way" to describe the adminis-

Chapter Four

trative model of effective teaching, I mean to invoke as well the particular discursive history of that notion as it has been applied first in industry and then in education during this century. In industry, the notion of one best way is associated with Frederick Taylor and Scientific Management. It implies that scientific task analysis can reveal the one best way of performing any given task with maximum efficiency.[2] Once the requisite task analysis has been completed, all one need do to increase productivity and profit is to train workers to follow the one best way without deviation. In education, the historian David Tyack has drawn upon this discursive history in industry to argue that central office administrators and state education officials throughout this century have sought to build a "one best system" in which teachers and principals are told exactly what to do and are held rigidly accountable for performing accordingly.[3]

Teachers in Urbanville could not file grievances if they disagreed with a negative evaluation of their teaching, but they did have the contractual right to respond to evaluations in writing and have these responses attached to the evaluation in their personnel files. During the study period (fall of 1968 through spring of 1986), this right was exercised by 47 teachers, and almost two-thirds of these cases were in the 1980s, as pressure to teach to the test intensified. In most cases, no direct punitive actions were taken against teachers when they received less than satisfactory evaluations; but several poor evaluations in a row was grounds for concern, since administrators could use this as evidence to build a case for denial of the annual salary increment that moved teachers one step further up the pay scale (something which occurred in 28 percent of the contested cases), or even for termination of a tenured teacher's contract (which occurred in eight percent of the contested cases). In this regard, the power of administrators was significantly enhanced in 1978, when the state Supreme Court ruled that the withholding of increments was a "managerial prerogative" and not a negotiable item.

A discursive analysis of the 47 contested teacher evaluations revealed the following constitutive elements of a one best way of teaching articulated by administrators (particularly during the 1980s): (1) instruction should be directly related to achievement of lesson objectives identified for that day and week in the teacher's Quarterly Topic Plan; (2) appropriate skill-based curricular materials should be used when available; (3) teachers should keep students on task and not waste time; and (4) teachers should keep efficient, well-organized records of student progress. When administrators put negative comments on teacher evaluations, the criticism most often given was that the teacher did not clearly link all instructional activities to the performance objectives and skills that students were to be studying on any given day. At least at the elementary level, these objectives and skills were listed by teachers in writing up their topic plans for each grading period. By requiring that teachers complete these topic plans, administrators were able to get teachers on record as having an instructional program that was closely aligned to the mastery of particular sets of competencies or skills. Administrators then could refer to teachers' own plans when evaluating them. In effect, administrators claimed to be holding teachers accountable to their own stated objectives, although teachers exercised little if any perceived freedom in completing the topic plans. For example, one second grade teacher was criticized in her evaluation because: "Ms. ——— fails to teach to her own Topic Plan objectives for this class. She appears to have completed the Plan without any intention of seriously using it to guide her teaching. She does not seem to understand that by submitting a Topic Plan she is committing herself as a teacher to follow-through."

Aside from having teachers on record in committing themselves to teach to specific skills and performance objectives, elementary teachers and secondary teachers of basic skills and developmental reading and math were also on record in committing themselves to use specified skill-based curricular materials. In their evaluations, administrators often advised teachers to use specific skill based curricular materials which were available in the schools, and a fifth-grade teacher who failed to use such materials was criticized because ". . . you fail to make use of the Developmental Math and Reading Inventories for this class and the appropriate skill kits in the library, although you list these as resources on your Topic Plan." In effect, teachers who sought to develop their own curricular materials or to personalize the curriculum were punished, and this was particularly true in the language arts, reading, and math subject areas at both the elementary and secondary levels. It is also the case, however, that these subject areas grew in importance, and occupied more room in the curriculum, throughout the study period.

Teachers were frequently criticized for inefficient use of time, with instructional efficiency defined in terms of the smooth, uninterrupted flow of student work activities which leads in the most direct path to attainment of the performance objectives identified on teachers' lesson and unit plans. One elementary teacher was criticized for distributing dittos to students one at a time, as they came up in the lesson, rather than all at once at the beginning of the period—the method judged to be more efficient by the administrator. The teacher responded:

Chapter Four

"Although I do understand the logic behind asking that we distribute all dittos at one time (it shoud reduce management transition time), I have also found that it does not substantially increase time on task to distribute one ditto at a time." In this instance, the teacher chose to defend her method as just as efficient as the administrator's preferred method, in effect claiming that there was no one best way of distributing dittos. Of course, in doing so, the teacher also took for granted the administrator's overall notion that lessons should be organized to maximize instructional efficiency.

Aside from these directly instructional criteria, the one best way of teaching emphasized meticulous record-keeping. Grade books were to be filled with appropriate data on student achievement, lesson plans were to be written in the specified format using behavioral objectives, and lesson objectives were to be consistent with those specified for that week in the unit plans submitted for the class. One elementary teacher, for example, was criticized because she was "a week behind schedule in the developmental math series;" another middle school reading teacher was faulted because her lesson was "not consistent with the stated lesson objective you identified in your Quarterly Topic Plan;" and a high school science teacher was criticized because "you failed to have your planning book on your desk and up to date."

To what extent did teachers, in their written responses to negative evaluations, offer a coherent defense of an alternative to this one best way of teaching the basics? In answering this question it is first important to note that there was less congruence and uniformity among teaching models endorsed by teachers in contested evaluations than there was by administrators in support of the one best way of teaching. Some teachers endorsed a rather traditional view of instruction, with the teacher always controlling and directing activities and calling on students to answer questions. One teacher, for example, wrote: "I prefer to lead children through their seatwork assignments because then I know they've learned what they're supposed to. I see nothing wrong with this practice, although I am criticized for being 'old fashioned' by some." More frequently, however, in their responses to evaluations teachers supported humanistic, progressive, and student-centered models of teaching. Approximately 60 percent of the evaluations contained at least one reference to pegagogic styles or curricular approaches consistent with progressive and humanistic models of teaching.

The defining principles or presuppositions of these alternative models of teaching articulated by teachers in defending themselves included the following: (1) lessons should provide for group-based learning

Restructuring in Urbanville

activities as well as individualized seatwork; (2) teachers should provide ongoing guidance of the learning process, rather than merely monitor student seat work; (3) student comprehension is best evaluated in the context of the lesson through teacher-student discourse or dialogue and "teacher observation" rather than through the use of formal evaluation techniques; (4) the best way to teach literacy skills is through creative writing assignments and the use of popular literature and media; and (5) occasional diversions or side tracks from the lesson objectives may lead to valuable learning experiences and promote a friendlier and warmer classroom environment. A number of teachers who responded to negative comments on their evaluations had obviously been influenced by progressive approaches to teaching which they picked up in university education courses. One teacher lamented that: "I am being criticized for following the approaches to teaching I was taught at ——— University. Everything I did in the lesson was consistent with teaching techniques right out of my methods texts, which I have continued to use as a guide. Am I now being told all of that is wrong?" The one best way of teaching endorsed in Urbanville schools consequently was incompatible with some teachers' deeply held pedagogic convictions and beliefs. When they were criticized for teaching in ways that they believed were effective, they tended to view evaluation with less legitimacy and see it as a means of enforcing conformity upon teachers. A third grade teacher commented in her defense: "This experience [of being criticized for not adhering to the one best way of teaching] has demoralized me and made me begin to wonder what I am supposed to be doing as a teacher." This suggests that the imposition of a one best way of basic skills teaching also generates motivation and legitimation crisis tendencies, and that one of the manifestations of these crisis tendencies is a tendency for many idealistic, creative, and intelligent people to become demoralized as teachers and ultimately leave the system.

Teaching the Basics in Urbanville

All of the various components of a comprehensive system of control over teachers' work were largely in place by the mid-1980s, at which point they became explicitly linked to the new high school diploma exam in Midstate, along with the state-mandated third- and sixth-grade reading and math tests which were now aligned with the diploma exam. Urbanville students scored among the lowest in the state on

Chapter Four

achievement tests, and there was widespread fear among local administrators that a high failure rate on the new diploma exam might lead the state to impose instructional and organizational changes upon the district, as part of broad new powers being proposed legislatively which would allow the state to virtually take over and run local school districts that were not providing a "thorough and efficient" education to students. The superintendent in Urbanville became a leader in a statewide coalition of urban school administrators which urged the state to delay implementing the diploma exam until their districts could better prepare for its impact. In addressing the annual state school boards convention in the fall of 1985, he called the diploma exam "a Mack truck coming around the bend"—the implication being that a powerful force was bearing down on urban school districts, that it had come upon the horizon rapidly, and that there was consequently very little one could do to get out of its path. But the diploma exam was not delayed; and while the pass rate on initial administration in Urbanville was slightly under 50 percent, this was somewhat better than expected. Furthermore scores rose significantly in each subsequent year, so that in 1989, the first year students were to be denied diplomas who did not pass the exam, all enrolled seniors in Urbanville graduated with diplomas. An aggressive program of curricular alignment over the 1980s had begun to pay off. Of course, many students had dropped out along the way. Of the original ninth graders who took the test in the spring of 1985, only about half made it through the next four years to pick up a diploma.

By the mid-1980s, Urbanville schools were cutting back significantly on course offerings and school programs not directly relevant to raising student test scores. Partly this was in response to continuing cutbacks and chronic underfunding of the school budget, and partly it was in response to declining student enrollment in certain courses and programs. Teachers complained about cutbacks in course and program offerings, but there was little sense that they could do anything to stop the inevitable. At one executive council meeting, the UEA president announced: "It's being said that we'll lose the Ag[ricultural] and graphic arts programs at the high school. The reason why they are being cut is low enrollment. But I'm afraid that the more you cut these programs and emphasize basis skills, the more you eliminate practical skill programs that motivate students and allow them to move around a bit, and you consequently have more discipline problems.... And the trouble is, once you lose these types of programs, you don't start them up again easily. It's a major financial investment, and let's face it, the school board just can't afford it any more." At another meeting,

Restructuring in Urbanville

when he announced cuts in the shop program, the president remarked: "I've said to the shop teachers, organize some afternoon courses. We've lost two shop courses this year. We need some innovative programs to keep those shops open, after school maybe, special certificates in shop maybe. Those peripheral subject areas will have to do that or they're going to go." But, of course, the shop teachers were very limited in the degree to which they could innovate or change class schedules, and the high school shop progam looked as though it would not hold out much longer. Furthermore, the phasing out of vocational and technical programs was part of the state's urban school agenda. As I noted in Chapter One, vocational and technical training is now often provided on the job, while employers are more interested in prospective employees' acquisition of functional literacy and work discipline skills. In line with this thinking, Midstate education officials continued to cut back funding for vocational and technical programs in urban school districts. Finally, as young people have begun to recognize that the vocational and technical programs cannot guarantee them a good paying job with security, they have stopped enrolling in these programs.

Among other peripheral subject areas to be hard hit in Urbanville were music and art. For example, the high school band was without a director over the course of several years, and participation had finally dwindled to the point where the band no longer met, even though it was still listed in the high school course directory. Participation in extracurricular music and athletic programs was particularly hard hit after the school board adopted a new policy banning students from participating in extracurricular activities if they had failed one or more classes over the past year. Parents and students complained about the new policy, and although the UEA had supported the policy originally, the UEA president remarked: "Theoretically, students who fail courses aren't supposed to have activities. They're supposed to go home and study. But we know that doesn't happen, so maybe the parents have a point. . . . We're reaching a point where our high school is going down the tubes. Pretty soon we'll all be losing our jobs, if we want to think about it selfishly."

The demise of the comprehensive high school in Urbanville was the result of several related factors. First, it was coextensive with the increasing socioeconomic segregation of Americans into urban and suburban populations over the past several decades, a situation James Conant first warned about in mainstream educational research in the late 1950s in *Slums and Suburbs*.[4] In Urbanville the shift in school mission towards teaching the basics reflected the increasing socioeco-

Chapter Four

nomic homogeneity of the students—in this case homogeneous in that they were commonly disadvantaged by race and class, and were being prepared (wittingly or unwittingly) for a future in the semi-skilled work force. This meant that Urbanville schools became highly specialized in the 1970s and 1980s, specialized at preparing disadvantaged youth with the cognitive and attitudinal skills business and state leaders believed they should have; and in becoming specialized, Urbanville schools no longer needed all the frill classes, the vocational-technical programs, the extracurricular activities accociated with the notion of a comprehensive high school.

When progressive educators within the National Education Association advanced the notion of a comprehensive high school in the influential *Cardinal Principles of Secondary Education* report published in 1918, it was associated with the idea that the school should be an "embryonic community" of socioeconomic diversity, where students of all social backgrounds came together and learned to work together and respect one another.[5] This also implied a a rejection of specialized schools designed to prepare students for distinctively different futures, which was the European solution to the problem of education in a highly differentiated class society. Democratic commitments demanded that America reject the European system as elite, that we keep open all students' academic and social options for as long as possible, and that we mix students of all social backgrounds in a great melting pot of public education. Of course, the progressive ideal of the comprehensive high school as an embryonic community grounded on democratic values was never realized in full. Tracking and ability grouping within comprehensive high schools served to separate students of differing class and race backgrounds. But with all of its faults, the old urban comprehensive high school probably provided more opportunity for disadvantaged youth to get ahead than is currently provided by the non-comprehensive, stripped-down, basic skills high school.

Teachers have their own reasons for opposing the dismantling of the comprehensive high school. In Urbanville, the loss of programs was much-lamented by teachers and officially opposed by the UEA for several reasons. Most directly, a loss of programs was associated with a loss of teaching jobs. When programs and courses were closed, teachers generally were not transferred elsewhere, since they had special certification. They simply lost their jobs and no one was hired to replace them, at least for that job. The new teachers hired at the high school were primarily in the remedial or developmental reading and math areas, and more use was made of instructional aides. The second reason why the UEA opposed program cutbacks and closings was that teacher morale "has gone downhill fast," since teachers no longer felt proud of their school's academic and extracurricular programs. As the UEA president, himself a high school English teacher, put it: "Teacher morale is low at the high school, and it gets lower each time another program goes. How can you be proud of a school that doesn't have anything special?" The shift towards a strong curricular emphasis on teaching the basics and away from a comprehensive curriculum thus led to a lowering of teacher morale, which both administrators and teachers seemed to feel was at an all-time low by the mid 1980s, when the ethnographic research was conducted.

Conclusion

I have suggested that teachers' work is structured and restructured through the dynamic of curriculum and instructional reform, and that curriculum reform thereby constructs teaching in predictable ways. Evidence reviewed in this chapter supports the contention that teachers' work became more regimented during the 1970s and 1980s as basic skills ideologies and policies were translated into concrete changes in the schools that impacted on teachers' everyday working lives. Basic skills restructuring was also compatible with a rigidification of labor-management roles, firstly as these roles were clearly demarcated in Midstate's collective bargaining laws, and secondly as they were further demarcated through a series of court decisions which extended the sphere of managerial prerogative. But if teachers appeared to be under much tighter bureaucratic and technical control by the mid-1980s than they had been in the late 1960s when the study began, they also, with some limited success, resisted managerial reform initiatives and in various ways lessened the impact of reforms once they were instituted. Many of the central contradictions and dilemmas of basic skills restructuring were also evident in this regard. When teachers failed to win grievances, they often complied with changes in their assigned duties, but only minimally and without enthusiasm or conviction. They learned to go through the motions and comply under protest, so that the purpose of reforms was often subverted or ignored—a form of goal displacement that impeded the effectiveness of almost all curricular and instructional reforms, although it also represented a form of grumbling acceptance of change and thus a way of adjusting to it.[6] For this reason, it is not entirely accurate to say that the administration won the battle over basic skills restructuring, if winning implies a successful resolution

Chapter Four

of the crisis tendencies that reform is designed to manage. Instead, there was a pattern of adjustment among teachers that allowed minimal achievement (at least in the short run) of managerial goals and objectives for the institution.

Teachers might have been more successful in pressing their grievances, and ultimately in resisting basic skills restructuring, if the rank and file had more actively participated in formulating a collective response to particular problems that developed in the schools, and if they had more generally been more involved in union decision-making. The union president, with the assistance of a small cadre of five to ten committed executive and representative council members, made most important decisions, and this, of course, encouraged rank-and-file passivity and grumbling discontent. Furthermore, so long as the union lacked the power to influence the central curricular and instructional decisions that define and shape teachers' everyday working lives, it should not be too surprising that the rank and file did not devote much time or energy to actively particating in the union. Finally, this study indicates that oligarchic tendencies and rank-and-file apathy were related to gender power relations. In this regard, one can speculate that the UEA might have represented a more powerful force in the schools if the majority of women teachers had felt more empowered within their own union. To the extent that teachers did "bitch" about conditions in the schools and the failure of the union leadership to do enough to represent their interests, this partly reflected the fact that women were not part of the power structure in the union; yet perhaps partly because most teachers preferred to complain about, rather than actively challenge, union leadership, oligarchic and patriarchal tendencies in the union were encouraged. One of the ironies of alienated or non-participative modes of adaptation among subordinates is thus a tendency to reinforce oligarchic, non-democratic forms of leadership and institutional control. My point here is that commonsense beliefs about rank-and-file apathy and "bitchiness" on the one hand, and oligarchical and patriarchal forms of control on the other, are dialectically interrelated, each reinforcing the other.

Racial and class divisions between teachers and the black and Hispanic communities in Urbanville also prevented them from working together very effectively to present a united oppositional force for educational change in the face of basic skills restructuring. There was little open conflict or hostility between teachers and the community in Urbanville during the study period, but then the 1970s and 1980s were politically non-confrontational decades, and community groups were largely uninvolved and acquiescent in discussions of school policy.

Restructuring in Urbanville

Rather than conflict, relations between teachers and the community tended to be dominated by benign neglect, and this in turn was related to the fact that neither teachers nor community groups had much of a voice in school policy-making and curricular decision-making. Perhaps if more teachers (including those in leadership positions) had been black and Hispanic, and more had lived in the community, the union and community groups might have worked together more effectively and recognized their common interests. But the racial and class cleavages that divided teachers from the community continuously acted to undermine efforts at building common interests. This study, then, affirms the general notion that the maintenance of conservative, centralized managerial models of organization and control is related to the segmentation and fragmentation of interests in American society along a number of axes of struggle so that common interests fail to get constructed. This is not to suggest that these various struggles be conflated into a common meta-struggle, only that they be better articulated in building a democratic coalition for change. As Henry Giroux remarks: "At issue here is the need to create a politics that contributes to the multiplication of sites of democratic struggle, sites that affirm specific struggles while recognizing the necessity to embrace broader issues. . . ."[7]

For a number of reasons, then, teachers in Urbanville lost ground in the struggle to see their interests realized in the schools, and they were not very effective in articulating an alternative model of school renewal by linking class, gender, and race issues. But school management had little reason to feel satisfied, since the system lurched towards crisis on a number of related fronts.

5

Role Formalization and "Playing the Game" in Urbanville Schools

In the preceding chapter, I argued that teachers in Urbanville learned to play the contract game in resisting various changes in their work associated with a package of basic skills reforms instituted over several decades. By resisting changes in the terms and conditions of the contract, they slowed down and in other ways impeded the reform institutionalization process, even if they did not stop it. While the contract game was used in resisting administrative innovations, it was also used much more generally and more regularly, as I document in this chapter, to resist all changes in the terms and conditions of employment that had the effect of lengthening the school day or adding to teachers' assigned workload. Teacher unions are often accused, with some validity, of being instrumental and utilitarian in their approach to teachers' interests. They are said to "hold the line" on contract language rather than hold out for loftier purposes and professional ideals in the schools. In fact, this perspective on teacher unions has been used effectively to legitimate the exclusion of unions from significant involvement in educational decision-making. Teachers seek to be treated like professionals, so this argument goes, yet they will be treated like professionals only when they start acting like professionals and place students' interests above their own "selfish" interests in shorter working hours and a bigger paycheck.

Ironically, while managerial elites call upon teachers to act like professionals and not be so self-interestedly utilitarian, these same elite

Chapter Five

groups have promoted an end-of-ideology approach to institutional management, based on the transformation of worker interests into an instrumental calculus. If teachers seem excessively self-interested in articulating and defending a set of interests in the schools, they are only playing the game the way managerial elites have scripted it. On the one hand, administrators and state officials decry teachers' instrumentalism and utilitarianism; but on the other hand, they much prefer it to a more politicized, ideological approach to defining teachers' interests. For these reasons, all the complaints about teachers' self-interestedness must be considered a bit disingenuous and contradictory. This elite perspective on teachers' interests *deconstructs*, since it contains logical propositions that are contradictory. That is, it criticizes teachers for behaving consistent with rules of the game that have been imposed on them by managerial elites and which benefit elites much more than teachers.

In this chapter, I examine the game that teachers and administrators in Urbanville schools played over the terms and conditions of teachers' employment, and analyze teachers' strategic conduct and instrumental logic in pursuing their interests within the game. I divide the case study data and analysis into two major sections. In the first I examine the formal and informal contract negotiation process in Urbanville and discuss, in a general way, how teachers (through the local teacher union) learned to play the game with administrators. Data presented in this section is primarily from ethnographic field notes by the author, including notes from union meetings and informal conversations with union representatives, although I also draw upon some reports and articles in the state teachers' association journal. The second half of the chapter presents and analyzes the major categories of conflict between teachers and administrators which pertained to the enforcement of the wage-labor contract, as documented in the union files for the years 1968–69 through 1985–86. Most of these disputes were over everyday working conditions and concerns—everything from disputes over preparation periods, to after-school meetings and events, to assignment of new classes and responsibilities.

Taken together, these working condition disputes indicate that teachers supported a defensive form of contractual role formalization. Teachers' contract orientation, I argue, was one of the most visible manifestations of the crisis in Urbanville schools; it was an almost inevitable outgrowth of the laborization of teaching and restrictive state collective bargaining laws that locked teachers out of the decision-making process in schools. Although much of what I will have to say in this chapter is critical of the game teachers and administrators

"Playing the Game"

played, this criticism itself needs to be contextualized. Given that school management is motivated by the currently structured rules of the game to more effectively and efficiently control teachers as instructional labor, teachers may well need to play the contract game as much to their advantage as possible in order to prevent being taken advantage of by the other side. Once one is in a game, after all, it is terribly difficult to play by different rules, and one learns to play well in order not to be beaten too badly.

"Playing the Game": A Conceptual Framework

Common to all game theories of human interaction is the presumption that players or actors are, for all intents and purposes, rational beings whose behavior may be understood as motivated by an assessment of utility costs and benefits within the situation at hand.[1] Game theorists tend to view players' actions as "rational" within these bounds and focus analysis upon how individuals maximize attainment of their "utility function" and what "rules of the game" they employ. As Steven Brams writes: "[B]ehaving rationally in game theory means acting to maximize the achievement of some postulated goals, where the outcome depends not only on chance events... but also on the actions of other players with sometimes cooperative and sometimes conflicting interests."[2] Erving Goffman has suggested that games in everyday life provide participants with a sense of purpose ("to best the opposition in some way"), and that this purpose "thrusts the participants into fully interdependent actions, such that a move on one participant's part can have overriding consequences for him [SIC] and for other players. Certain clearly defined elements become determinative: resources (some visible, some concealed...), tactical intent, matrix of possible moves, [and] gaming ability.... All of these factors taken together provide the player with a meaningful field of action and the bases and reasons for making moves."[3] Within the context of the game, "each party attempts to contain the other, and what occurs, in fact, is a competition of containment."[4] Basic to all game theories of human interaction is this assumption that because the outcome of games is contingent on the choices of both sides or players, the strategic conduct and interests of the other player(s) must be taken into account in deciding upon an "optimal" course of action.

Game theorists also distinquish between different types of games, such as those which are strictly competitive and those which involve

157

Chapter Five

some level of cooperation among players. The former type, often called the *zero-sum* game, is one in which "cooperation between the two players is precluded by the simple fact that it leads to no joint gains; what one player wins has to come from the other player . . . [T]he *payoffs*. . . associated with the outcomes for each pair of strategies of the two players, necessarily sum to some constant."[5] In contrast, cooperative games are based on the assumption that players share at least some common interests, and that these interests can only be maximized through joint effort. The outcomes of such games are negotiated settlements of compromise. For example, in the classic buyer and seller exchange, both parties "agree that their common interest dictates that they reach agreement on exchange, so long as no one is made worse off by the deal; but they eagerly complete for the choice of a particular price within these limits."[6] Finally, game theory has been associated with the analysis of constraints on players in maximizing their objectives, related to a lack of "perfect information" in making strategic choices. Games of perfect information are rare in real life, although games such as chess provide an example of a situation where each player is fully informed at each move about the previous moves in the game and about all possible moves open to both players. Poker, on the other hand, is not a game of perfect information, since the player does not know all the cards on the table, and this means that bluffing is possible.[7]

Given the importance of understanding the game-like structure of everyday life, the limitations of game theory are considerable. Game theory is based on a methodological individualism which presumes that the immediate situation is a relatively autonomous sphere of action; that the current "rules of the game" do not participate in, and are not limited or constrained by, anything beyond the situational; and that the situational is non-dynamic and ahistorical.[8] Game theorists and other neo-rationalists conceive of actors as abstracted from, rather than embedded within, wider discourse and practice in the culture. Yet as I have agued, the imputed choices of individuals cannot be analysed as merely rational in some abstract sense, apart from the ideologies or worldviews which individuals use to generate options and apart from the cultural struggles that they participate in and through which they construct identities.[9] Game theory is also inherently structuralist, even though it focuses our attention upon how that structure is concretely constituted in institutional sites by pragmatic actors.

By structuralist I mean a theory that presumes a relatively stable set of "rules of the game" or "constitutive rules" exists, which provides actors with an *a priori* or pre-given structure for regulating their concrete relations. Individuals are treated as rule-following social actors who have no active role in struggling against the current rules or organizing resistances and counter-movements based on democratic or any other values. They are, in effect, controlled by their utility functions which operate within a given rule structure. Research focuses on determining the rules that operate in each individual institutional site to make everyday social life possible, and upon the strategic rationality that guides individual action. The current negotiated order is presumed to serve the interests of all participants to some level of sufficiency. Otherwise participants, as rational actors, would go elsewhere, or decide they no longer wanted to participate in the game. The fact that participants generally follow the rules is taken as an indication that they are happy with the game as it is currently played. In fact, no such *a priori* set of rules exists. The negotiated order in institutional sites represents the end product of an historically emergent order that has been shaped by struggles over power and privilege, and it participates in power dynamics that result in a daily renegotiation of order.

"Playing the Game" in Urbanville: The Wage Package

The heart of the wage-labor contract is the wage and benefit package, and in Urbanville a good deal of time and effort on the part of both union leadership and central office administrators went into developing a negotiation strategy, and revising it as negotiations were conducted during a several-month period every other fall. Negotiations for the pay scale were complex, involving considerations as to the amount of money the city had to spend, how long teachers could hold out, and what other teachers in other districts were settling for. The subtlety and technicality of the wage negotiation process is well illustrated by a UEA contract negotiations meeting in the mid-1980s. The UEA president began the meeting by saying: "The question we have to address, in part, is where do we go from here? The Board has proposed a 6.9 percent increase for teacher salaries in the budget for next year. I asked the Board if it would reconsider; but the answer was 'no.' The City says they don't have the money because they've had to put in new storm sewers and other expenses. . . . A couple of [negotiating] sessions ago we came close to a meeting of minds. They said 6 percent; we said 9½ percent. Then the city dropped this $300,000 sewer thing on us. So at the last meeting they came back and said there's no way we can give 9½ percent . . . They said they'd give us 6 percent the first year,

Chapter Five

and 6½ percent the second year of the contract. We said even to consider that, they'd have to come up with something pretty good to sell it to our members, like changing some [salary] steps around or something like that. So what options do we have? If we strike next year, and end up going back for 8 percent, what do we gain? And neither side really gains from mediation."

After finishing his overview of "where we stand" on negotiations, the UEA president turned the floor over to a "UniServ" representative from the MEA. UniServ is a branch of state NEA affiliates which provides technical assistance and advice to local unions on contract bargaining strategies, and without such assistance the UEA would not have been able to compete effectively with district negotiators, who had access to their own legal assistance. The UniServ representative began by asking for more "hard" data on the local school budget: "I would try to confirm, first of all, those budget figures from the city. I'd look through the city audit and see if they're [the school board] down to the bone on the budget.... If they're not down to the bone, you go back to them and say, 'we're still way off.' But for the sake of argument let's assume they are down to the bone and not playing a game with us. One option is *backloading*—what we don't take this year we'll take next year. Right now in this county we're getting multiple-year contracts that average 8½ percent, and I don't think we'll go above that. So if 8½ percent is average, and we only get 6 percent the first year, we should get 10 percent the next year. But be careful of backloading, because 6 percent and 10 percent are not the same as 8½ percent and 8½ percent. So maybe you shoot for a three-year contract backloaded 6½ percent, 7½ percent, and 9 percent. Those are the things you have to play with. The advantage with backloading is, they can't use the budget argument on you. What you can't do because of City needs this year won't hold true next year...." The MEA representative also cautioned against a practice increasingly prevalent in the state of offering a slight reduction in percentage salary increases for teachers in exchange for extra pay for perfect attendance: "They'd save money that way, because they'd have to pay more to hire subs to fill in for all those absent teachers."

The MEA representative then turned to the subject of salary steps in the salary guide. In this regard, the state legislature was preparing to pass a teacher salary bill that set a minimum of $18,500 per annum for beginning teachers (up from a statewide average of $14,500) and that provided state funds to local districts over the first few years to help them raise the base pay. The MEA representative supported a plan for combining the first nine steps of the current thirteen-step salary scale to bring them all up to the new base pay figure. This meant that for the first nine years teachers would receive no raises, and that there would be only four steps beyond that—a relatively flat or undifferentiated salary guide. One UEA member asked: "Aren't some teachers going to feel cheated? Like, 'I've been working eight years and she's been teaching one, and we both make the same.' " The MEA representative replied: "Sure, but salaries are the same once you reach the top step anyway. Did you know there are only three steps in a police contract. . . . Someday we need to get over these divisions. Right now they've got you so divided by building, by schedule, by titles, they've got you cut up so many ways, they've got you thinking you're different from the person next to you. Now if you differentiate by skills and responsibility, that's one thing. And if you give some recognition to seniority, that's another. But this business of so many steps isn't a meaningful way to differentiate." Finally, the MEA representative inquired whether or not the UEA had considered calling for outside mediation, and advised: "I agree you should try to avoid mediation, because all you have there is another party arguing over mush, but if you decide to I'd like to help pick the mediator." The discussion of the fine points of negotiation strategy continued long into the evening, showing just how technical, and dependent upon professional expertise, the negotiation process has become in public education.

The use of the phrase "playing a game with us" by the MEA representative to describe school board strategy is also indicative of the explicit level of game-playing within the contract negotiation process. It implies a deliberate effort to get away with something or to trick the other side into making concessions. Yet even when it refers to a deliberate act of deception, it is hardly used in a pejorative sense by the MEA representative, since it is presumed that teachers also played the game to their advantage whenever possible. In fact, it pays the other side a compliment of sorts, in that it credits it with playing the game well. "Backloading," too, represents a form of strategic game playing meant to appeal to the short-term interests of the Board to reach a settlement it can live with this year. In this way, it is really a variation on the popular sales promotion designed to ease the customer into a deal by reducing initial payments and ballooning later payments. While not deceptive, such a selling strategy on the part of the union may persuade a School Board to commit itself to a wage settlement that gets it off the hook in terms of current fiscal problems, only to compound these problems later. My point here is that by viewing the contract negotiation process as a game, game players were encouraged to use every trick that they could get away with short of outright lying (and that was not entirely to be

Chapter Five

ruled out) to press their advantage. Not to do so was to play the game poorly and thus be taken advantage of. The UEA negotiations committee meeting described above also suggests that full-time MEA staff may have been considerably more trade unionist in their sentiments, and more political in their perspectives, than were local union representatives and the rank and file. Teacher solidarity and an increased sense of common interests were presented as the means of achieving victory; and teacher divisiveness and differentiation were depicted as the root of teachers' current problems.

"Playing the Game": The Terms and Conditions of Employment

Aside from the wage and benefit package, the contract in Urbanville contained approximately thirty pages of contract language that pertained to the conditions of employment, and that addressed issues relevant to the everyday working lives of teachers. For example, the contract contained language pertaining to: teacher union rights (the UEA president only had to teach a half load, union meetings could be held in school buildings, etc.); number of after-school meetings and events per month that teachers were required to attend (three, without prior notification to the UEA); class size ("The Board agrees to continue its efforts to keep class size at an acceptable number..."); the daily schedule ("In the secondary school the daily schedule will consist of eight periods on a regular day and nine periods on a pupil activity day..."); teacher evaluation ("A minimum of three formal evaluation observations shall be conducted each year for non-tenured professionals.... A minimum of two days' notice will be given to the professional prior to each of the scheduled formal evaluations..."); academic and personal freedom ("The Board of Education respects the rights of all professionals to exercise these freedoms..."); physical conditions and facilities ("To the extent possible ... the Board will provide storage space for materials and supplies, desk, chair, and filing cabinet..."); classroom control and discipline ("When, in the judgment of the teacher, a student is ... seriously disrupting the instructional program... the teacher shall have the right to send that student to the school office..."); and report cards and grading responsibilities ("Teachers are required to submit report cards for students once each term ... and student grades shall be initially determined by the teacher based upon his/her professional judgement....")

As should be apparent from these brief excerpts from the contract,

"Playing the Game"

while some contract language was quite precise, and consequently open to few interpretations, other contract language was quite vague and imprecise, and thus open to competing interpretations. Vagueness and imprecision in language usage may be understood as resulting from a lack of agreement among the teachers and the School Board on a particular issue, and it allowed each side to sponsor its own reading of the language consistent with its particular interests. The School Board, for example, generally supported the use of qualifying language which allowed it an escape clause. Phrases such as "to the extent possible. . ." and "taking into account. . ." allowed administrators to override much of the specific language in various sections of the contract when they felt the need to; although to do so invited retaliatory action by teachers, something that the administration constantly had to consider, even when it was technically not violating the contract.

Contract language was fought over and modified somewhat during each round of negotiations. To a considerable degree, changes in contract language supported by the union represented an effort to translate specific teacher grievances and discontents into formal changes in the structuring of teachers' work; and one got a sense of what the rank and file was thinking by reviewing the "shopping list" of contract proposals drawn up by the union to bring to the table as bargaining chips. Included in a 1984 shopping list of 47 proposals for changes in contract language, compiled by a special UEA committee, were the following working condition items: negotiate the impact on teachers and support staff of closing a building *before* it is done; allow union reps to made announcements at the beginning of all faculty meetings; no employee should have to work in conditions deleterious to health; every elementary teacher should get five (rather than the current three) preparation periods a week; allow teachers to accumulate lost preparation periods from year to year, and make five (rather than the current 15) lost preparation periods equal one sick day; stop cancelling special area classes (music, ESL, art and physical education) and turning those teachers into substitutes; schedule no more than two (rather than the current three) after-school meetings per month and no more than four evening events per year; provide release time to teachers to prepare their required performance-based unit planning forms; ensure that all teaching assistants have the same workload; establish limits on class size and how many students can be mainstreamed in a class; provide written job descriptions for all open positions and do not change them without the approval of the union; provide teachers with lockable, workable, attractive desks (some left-handed) for teachers, on a three-year replacement schedule, with the teacher selecting color and style;

Chapter Five

provide at least one workable typewriter or word processor in each school and department for teacher use; reimburse teachers to buy "reasonable amounts" of books and curricular supplies; hire permanent substitutes rather than rely on teachers to fill in classes; eliminate all scans (see Chapter Four); and cut down on paperwork for teachers.

The list was supposed to reflect what the rank and file wanted, and some rank-and-file teachers had contributed to it as requested by their union reps. But in many buildings, union reps got few if any suggestions from teachers. In discussing this fact at a UEA bargaining meeting, one building rep commented: "I haven't heard from anyone in my building yet. But you can be sure, once we come up with a something they'll complain, including those teachers who aren't members." The union president's response was: "So don't ask them. Chances are we'll come up with ninety percent of what the members would suggest anyway." As in many cases, rank-and-file apathy led to more decision-making by those relatively few teachers who ran the union.

In spite of the fact that working conditions were specified in the contract and bargained about formally and informally, teachers' legal rights in this area were ambiguous and frequently challenged. The first public employee collective bargaining law was passed in Midstate in 1968, with the strong support of the Midstate Education Association (which referred to the new law as the "Magna Carta of the teaching profession in this state"); and the general categories of bargaining established in the collective bargaining statute were at first interpreted in a relatively flexible manner in many local districts. For example, some teacher unions had been able to get included in the contract specific language pertaining to teacher evaluation criteria, teacher involvement in curriculum decision-making, etc., along with language pertaining to the specific role obligations and duties of teachers. The progress made by teachers in the first few years of collective bargaining was, however, increasingly challenged by School Boards, and in a number of cases brought before them the state courts began to interpret the collective bargaining law in a relatively restrictive fashion. Basically, the courts held that the state legislature had intended the terms and conditions of employment to be interpreted narrowly, as referring to the wage and benefit package, the hours of employment, and the physical conditions of work. All other matters, including curriculum decisions, instructional goals, and teacher evaluation, were, according to the courts, "managerial prerogatives" which could not be bargained about. In 1978, in an important and closely watched ruling, the state Supreme Court determined that a local School Board (under the stewardship of the superintendent) had the sole responsibility to establish the school calendar for the year, even though the local teacher union had negotiated the right to be included in such decision-making. Throughout the 1980s, the MEA sponsored revisions to the state collective bargaining law which would allow teachers far more lattitude in bargaining, but with little success. The president of the MEA in the mid-1980s in a speech before the state teacher union convention claimed: "They [the courts] took collective bargaining away, and we've been losers ever since. Fellow MEA members, I did not like losing those hard-won gains. I'm not a loser, and neither are you. With your support we're prepared to take the offensive on whatever field the game must be played. Whether it's at the [negotiation] table, in the administrative offices, or anywhere else, we must fight to bring fairness back to the collective bargaining process."

Despite such optimistic rhetoric, teachers had made no progress on this field of battle by the end of the 1980s. Furthermore, teachers' power to retaliate and make the administration respond to their interests had become more restricted during the period studied, as the strike became a less effective option. There was no law in Midstate against public employee or teacher strikes; although the courts had generally relied on a common-law tradition that dated back to the Colonial era, placing restrictions on strikes against the King which disrupted the provision of governmental services. Throughout the 1970s, the courts reacted harshly to the growing use of the strike to enforce teachers' wage-labor contract demands by levying stiff fines on teacher unions and jail sentences of four to five days on union leaders and participating teachers. In a notable case in the late 1970s, a judge sentenced 106 teachers in one district to serve time in jail for refusing to return to the classroom. The UEA president at the time this study was undertaken had been president of the statewide MEA in the 1970s and was on the scene at the biggest teacher strike in the state in 1979. He recalled: "The local association [teacher union] president was called before the worst 'hanging judge' in the state and told to show cause why teachers shouldn't be ordered to return to work immediately. But all the time he [the union president] was making his case before the judge, the judge had already made up his mind to jail the [union] leadership. So it was just a formality to have this court hearing. We knew this because some of our people saw the local jail bus pull up behind the courthouse before the proceedings even began. So after the judge held the association leaders in contempt of court, he asked them to leave through a side door, where they were photographed, fingerprinted, and ushered into the bus to take them to jail."

The MEA mobilized statewide support for the jailed teachers and

Chapter Five

managed, before nightfall, to obtain an injunction from another judge in the state to release the union leaders from jail. The MEA strike support center also organized a march of hundreds of teachers in front of the jail on a few hours notice. But teachers did not ultimately win the decisive strike battles of the late 1970s; and in the 1980s there were many threats of strikes but fewer confrontations and actual strikes. The one- or two-day walk out, and the adoption of a work-to-rule strategy of meeting only the minimal formal contractual obligations, became more popular among teacher unions in Midstate. But because such tactics posed less of an immediate threat to the system than did the strike, teachers' threats carried somewhat less weight than they had in the 1970s. According to the UEA president: "The courts are now issuing indefinite jail terms. Teachers can be released from jail as soon as they agree to go back to the classroom. That's harder to fight. They keep telling you, 'No one is keeping you in jail but you.' They guilt-trip you."

Teachers' strategic power also was limited by the general apathy of the rank and file when it came to pressing demands through collective action. For example, at one UEA meeting, a teacher representative raised the recurring problem of inadequate street parking space for teachers in several schools. She began by observing that: "I wrote a letter to the mayor and told him I live in this city, I pay taxes in this city, and I work for this city. You mean to tell me I can't park on the street between eight and ten in the morning?" At this point the president interrupted the teacher and said: "Look. The trouble is, that was just you. You have to make a fuss if you want any action on this. Here's what you do. I want a lot of hysterical ladies yelling all at once. You say, 'we're fed up, and we're not going to stand for this anymore.' So I'm giving you a strategy. Make sure your principal hears about it every day. Second, send the superintendent a letter, and send him follow-up letters. Tell him you've met with your principal already and haven't gotten any action. Third, after you wait a fair amount of time, you say, 'We want a meeting with the mayor.' It's election year, and you say to all the members in the building, all of them, that we're going together to the mayor's office, and everybody is attending. I don't want to hear any excuses, anybody suddenly sick, any of this, 'well, they don't need me' stuff. You be there. And you all say your piece to the mayor individually, and I'll guarantee you he'll listen."

But the teachers did not follow through on the president's three-step plan for "getting what you want," and the parking problem remained. From the perspective of the rank and file, "making a fuss" may have been a less than appealing strategy for several reasons. First, it was hard to make a fuss about every issue; and second, making a fuss might exacerbate the already tense working relations between teachers and administrators to the overall detriment of rank-and-file teachers. It is also worth noting that the UEA president presented this strategy as one which women were particularly good at; and in this regard it is a strategy closely linked to the perception of teachers as "bitching" all the time. In effect, the president suggested channeling and making constructive use of teachers' "bitchiness." The sexist term "hysterical ladies" is also used in this context to suggest that teachers can get their way by acting hysterically. Of course, to the extent that administrators ignore or downplay the significance of teachers' complaints because they are viewed as the complaints of "hysterical" women, this sexism works against teachers' strategic interests.

The strategy which teachers ultimately relied upon more than any other to define, articulate, and assert a set of working condition interests in the schools was the grievance, or the threat of a grievance. While rank-and-file demonstrations or dramatic confrontations were hard to organize and increasingly handled in a repressive manner, grievances were easy to file, and they threatened to embroil the school district in legal action unless the administration responded in some way to teachers' discontent. At any given time, the UEA was typically involved in three to five grievances—some of them clear contract violations, and others based on a liberal reading of contract language that union leaders knew could not be sustained in court. But then, most grievances were not meant to get that far. The objective in some cases was merely to "press a case," or "let the administration know we're serious about this," with the hope that a negotiated settlement might be reached or, in the longer term, that contract language would be revised to reflect teachers' concerns. To this extent, each grievance had to be appreciated as a strategic move in a larger game, meant to "sent a message" to the administration that (according to the UEA president) "we're serious about this, and we're going to keep coming back at them with grievances until they have to take us seriously." While many grievances concerned alleged violations of the wage and benefit section of the contract, most alleged working condition violations. I devote considerable space in the following to an analysis of these working condition grievances in Urbanville, for they reveal how teachers' interests are constituted within a dynamic and situational terrain of battle in the schools.

Over the 18-year study period (1968–69 through 1985–86), 241 separate grievances were filed or threatened, with the number reaching a peak in the mid- to late 1970s and tapering off somewhat in the

Chapter Five

1980s, the era of restrictive court rulings on grievances. Eighty-three percent of the grievances involved working conditions as opposed to wage package disputes. Over half (56 percent) of these grievances and grievance threats were either resolved or dropped without adequate resolution at the first step of the grievance process, in an informal meeting between the involved teachers and building representatives. A smaller number (30 percent) were resolved or dropped at the second step, in a meeting between a union representative and the superintendent or one of his staff members (most frequently the personnel director). In only about eight percent of the cases did a grievance reach the third step, at which disputes were resolved by third parties, such as the School Board, an outside arbitrator, the courts, or the state Commissioner of Education.

Although approximately 70 percent of grievances (or threats of grievances) were initiated by individual rank-and-file teachers or groups of teachers (with the rest initiated directly by the union as class action grievances) most teachers were still not directly involved in initiating or pressing grievances. Somewhat less than ten percent of the total teaching force in Urbanville was ever directly involved in initiating grievances; and within this group, building representatives for the union were heavily overrepresented. However, the significance of these disputes, which directly involved a relatively small group of teachers, was enhanced in several ways. As in court cases, individual grievances set precedents, helped clarify ambiguous contract language, and defined the limits of teachers' role obligations. The union leadership played an important role in regard to the determination of what was and was not worth challenging; and once the leadership decided to press a grievance with administrators it was always on the basis of defending or asserting a universal or categorical teacher right. Individual grievances also took on added significance because they often represented the feelings of more rank-and-file teachers than those whose names were on the official grievance form. One building representative for the union commented to me that: "There are teachers out there afraid to complain. They'll complain about things to each other; but when it comes down to acting, they are afraid of their principals. You know, depending upon who your principal is, it can be a big thing to complain. So somebody has to stand up for them." Most often, this was the building representative. In these ways, individual grievances transcended in their ramifications the situational concerns of those particular teachers who filed them.

One further issue is relevant to the analysis of teacher-administrator conflict in Urbanville schools—the difference between the level of con-

"Playing the Game"

flict in elementary and secondary schools. One might think that, because secondary teachers typically enjoy a higher status within the segmented teaching profession, they would be more assertive than elementary teachers in defending their rights and resisting bureaucratic and technical controls. Furthermore, if we assume, for cultural reasons, that women as a group are likely to be less assertive than men within a given occupation such as teaching, then we would also expect that elementary teachers, approximately 90 percent of whom were women, would be less assertive than teachers at the high school, slightly over fifty percent of whom were men. In fact, this hypothesis was not validated by the Urbanville data on grievances and threats of grievances. Elementary teachers comprised approximately 65 percent of the total teaching staff, yet they initiated approximately 75 percent of all grievances. There appeared to be several related reasons for this. Elementary teachers were considered by the union leadership to be more contract-oriented than secondary teachers. One executive committee member remarked: "Elementary teachers know their contract rights and aren't so concerned about their professional image, like at the high school. They [elementary teachers] know you can't trust administrators." In turn, this more overt contract orientation of elementary teachers was related to the fact that relatively more regimented and standardized forms of curriculum and instruction were emphasized in elementary schools, so that the rationalization of teaching may be said to have been most developed at that level. That is, elementary teachers' contract orientation, which union leaders typically viewed positively and administrators viewed negatively, was an adaptive response to the structuring of their work. They had fewer preparation periods, more paperwork and forms to submit, and generally were treated in a more authoritarian manner by administrators.

For purposes of analysis, I have grouped the 199 working conditions contract disputes into a number of categories. In descending order according to the number of incidents grouped in each, these categories include disputes over: change in building assignment (41); inadequate physical conditions in the schools (28); scheduled preparation periods denied (26); after-school and evening events scheduled beyond the number specified in the contract (24); additional report cards and other student evaluation forms beyond the number specified in the contract (23); non-renewal of contract without cause (19); imprecise specification of job duties for new teaching positions (9); assignment of additional classes and duties not previously performed (8); special education students assigned to classes without informing teacher that students were classified (7); denial of duty-free lunch periods (5);

Chapter Five

changes in the length of the school day and school year (5); the number of times each year tenured faculty may be evaluated (2); and charges of sexual discrimination in hiring and transferring teachers (2). I limit my comments to an analysis of some of the most significant of these working conditions disputes—significant, that is, in terms of the issues they raised relevant to an understanding of teachers' role formalization, a contract orientation, and "playing the game."

Building and/or Grade Transfers

The largest single working conditions category involved disputes over building and/or grade transfers. Transfers of teachers were common, particularly at the elementary level (85 percent of all contested transfers were at the elementary level), where the opportunities for transfer were greatest since most teachers were not subject matter specialists. Teachers were often transferred without a reason being given and informed of the decision after it had been made. Often, transfers appeared to result from a more or less rational administrative assessment of staffing changes and needs in various schools. As the student population of some schools grew and the population of others fell, and as teachers entered and left the system through retirement, nonrenewal of contract, or resignation, the central office personnel director shifted teachers around to compensate for these changes. Such a practice of treating teachers as impersonal "slots" or "lines" in a central office staffing plan was consistent with, and made possible by, the standardization and rationalization of the instructional process. Similarly, frequent use of transfers speaks of a model of school management which emphasizes the substitutability or interchangeability of instructional labor. In contrast, a system of education grounded on the principle that teachers should build and develop curricular programs in practice, both as individual practitioners and as members of planning and program development teams in their schools, would place much more emphasis upon staff continuity, and upon allowing teachers to grow and develop their talents within a given school, and this would probably mean fewer transfers overall.

Transfers also often resulted from latent or overt conflict between teachers and their building principals or supervisors. In 30 percent of all contested transfers, teachers alleged that they were being punished in some way and were on an administrator's "hit list." One teacher claimed: "I am being punished for speaking my mind once too often in faculty meetings;" and another wrote, "I suppose I am perceived as

"Playing the Game"

too outspoken and independent by the principal. I have stepped on a few toes to get things done, and now this is my reward." Unfortunately, there is no way of testing the validity of these claims; but if we presume that even half are true, it indicates that transferring teachers who did not fit in or get along with their principals may have been a quite common practice in Urbanville schools. This, in turn, suggests one reason why rank-and-file teachers were reticent to press grievances. Sooner or later, it was assumed, administrators would find a way to "get back at you," and transferring teachers was one way of doing this. The only way to ensure that administrators did not use their power to get back at teachers, according to the UEA president, was to base all necessary transfers upon seniority in the school system: those teachers with the longest service should be the last transferred. "If you give up on seniority, then you give up the ball game," he argued, "because so long as the superintendent has that power to transfer you at his whim, then he can intimidate you." Teachers never won any of these transfer grievances, since staffing decisions were clearly recognized by the courts as a "managerial prerogative", although administrators often agreed to "consider the wishes and desires of the involved parties as much as possible in the future." To what extent they did so is hard to say. What is clear is that there were more contested transfers per year in the 1980s than there had been in the 1970s, by about 20 percent; and that transfers continued to be demoralizing and disruptive to many teachers.

Physical Conditions of Teaching

Perhaps the most obvious and visible symbol of the urban school crisis is the decline of the physical infrastructure of school buildings and the failure to provide teachers with the equipment and materials they need to perform effectively. In Urbanville, disputes over the physical conditions of teachers' work represented the second largest working conditions category. Teachers complained and filed grievances regarding (in descending order): lack of heat or inadequate heat in school buildings on cold winter days, broken windows not replaced, not enough textbooks in usable condition, roaches in classrooms, improper classroom ventilation, leaking ceilings, broken faculty toilets, and broken teachers' desks and other classroom equipment. Usually, teachers got some action from the administration when they filed these grievances, since they pointed in most cases to rather clear violations of building safety and proper maintenance procedures. The trouble was

Chapter Five

that repairs were often limited to the specific complaint identified in the grievance, and often the effect was merely to patch things over rather than remedy the structural problems in the aging buildings. One teacher wrote: "This is my third complaint about the same problem of a leaking classroom ceiling. This time I hope you will locate the source of the leak rather than attempt once more to patch it over." However, when it came to complaints about missing or inadequate classroom supplies or equipment, teachers rarely got what they asked. For example, a typing teacher wrote that there were not enough typewriters in his classroom to permit him to teach effectively: "I have 22 typewriters assigned me, and some of my classes have 24 students. Furthermore, I have to wait until 10 or 12 typewriters are inoperative before I can call a repairman. In some cases, this means I conduct classes with 12 typewriters for 24 students. . . . I had to begin classes this year without a typing chart, demonstration stand, teacher desk, teacher chair, or enough student chairs. I have had to improvise with file cabinets, milk cartons, and the top of a piano being stored in my room. When the piano is being used by the music department, I balance my typewriter on the sink." Yet his grievance resulted in no discernible improvement. At times, teachers' grievances seemed to be related to frustration and discontent over what they perceived to be the relatively opulent working conditions of administrators. The chair of a high school department, for example, asked for a typewriter to meet his responsibilities as chair, but was denied one. He commented bitterly: "I haven't gotten anything. Meanwhile, they buy fancy new word processors for the administrative secretaries and spend $10,000 to repanel the principal's executive suite."

Preparation Periods

Among the most divisive, and revealing, conflicts in Urbanville schools were those which centered around teachers' rights to preparation periods. Typically teachers protested having to give up an assigned preparation period to fill in a class for an absent teacher. Rather than hire substitutes, and also because it was often difficult to find substitutes, administrators had come to rely upon the practice of using a different teacher each period to cover the classes of an absent teacher. And since the teacher absenteeism rate on a given day was approximately 10 percent of the total teaching force in the district, this meant there were many classes to cover, which meant that some teachers lost an average of two to three preparation periods each week. At the high school, teachers had been guaranteed one preparation period each day since the first contract was signed in 1968; yet they still were asked to cover classes during their preparation periods. Administrators argued that when high school teachers were asked to give up a preparation period to cover a class, they were always reimbursed at an hourly rate, so that they were not made to work more hours for the same pay. Nevertheless, teachers felt that they had little choice but to comply when they were asked to take over a class, and that the little extra money they made could not compensate for the loss of a preparation period. In a 1973 case, ten teachers at the high school filed a grievance over the loss of preparation periods, which was ultimately resolved in their favor in court, with the judge ruling that denying teachers their preparation periods was "tantamount to unilaterally lengthening the school day in violation of the contract, no matter what reimbursement is offered to teachers." After that decision, high school teachers experienced fewer problems over denial of preparation periods, although the problems did not stop entirely.

The focus shifted to the battle over preparation periods at the elementary level in the mid- to late 1970s. No preparation periods had been guaranteed elementary teachers in the original contract; when the contract was finally revised in the mid-1970s to grant elementary teachers such rights, they were not equal to those of secondary teachers. Elementary teachers were granted three preparation periods per week, taking into account the schedules for music, art and physical education. This meant that whenever one of these special area teachers was absent for any reason, and a substitute could not be found, elementary teachers lost their preparation period because students could not be left unsupervised. Furthermore, administrators often scheduled special section meetings (for all teachers in a particular grade or special program) during assigned preparation periods. When teachers contested such a practice, the administration argued that "preparation periods are not free periods. They are for planning, and these meetings are consistent with that use of preparation periods." The union finally dropped this grievance, as it did most preparation period grievances in the elementary schools because the leadership believed it was not winnable if teachers took it to court.

Teachers' fight to defend their preparation period "rights" involved a complex interplay of trade unionist and professional concerns. Some teachers obviously viewed preparation periods as scheduled work breaks in a hectic day—an opportunity to recharge batteries and recuperate, most often in the teachers' lounge in conversation with other teachers. For example, in contesting the scheduling of special meetings

Chapter Five

during their free periods, teachers wrote: "I resent anyone telling me what I have to do during my scheduled break;" "My prep period is necessary for me to recuperate and get a second wind;" and "This is the only break I get in a hectic day, and I think I deserve it." The fact that many, if not most, Urbanville elementary teachers viewed preparation periods in this light says something about the intensification of teachers' labor, and about the need to compensate for debilitating work routines by providing workers with periodic breaks. In the industrial union contract, breaks are at least acknowledged as such and rigidly protected by contract. Ironically, teachers, because they were considered professional workers, had fewer rights to unscheduled breaks; yet as their work became more regimented and routinized, in effect less professionalized, during the basic skills era, the need for breaks increased.

Teachers also defended their rights to preparation periods on professional grounds. According to one: "I need my planning period to hurredly prepare for my afternoon classes. If I lose it, my students lose out as well. . . . I am a professional, not a substitute teacher." Another commented: "How am I supposed to run off dittos, get students' folders in order, and take care of other things that are necessary to me being effective as a teacher when I am denied a prep period?" Thus, while administrators had argued that because they were professionals teachers had no rights to breaks (something guaranteed to the school's non-professional employees), these teachers argued that, as professionals, teachers needed rights to preparation periods which could not be taken away at whim. In effect, the teachers' position was: if we are to be treated like subordinated, semi-skilled employees, then we need guaranteed breaks; and if we are to be treated as professionals, then we need guaranteed preparation periods. In either case, we have a right to unscheduled time in the workday. As I said earlier, while secondary teachers largely won their fight for such unscheduled time, elementary teachers were still embroiled in the battle in the mid-1980s. Finally, the battle over preparation periods in Urbanville was closely linked to the high absenteeism rate among teachers, and the related chronic substitute problem, both of which, in turn, were linked to the conditions of teaching in Urbanville schools. In practice, the various aspects of the urban school crisis were thus intricately interconnected and inseparable.

After-school Meetings and Events

By contract, teachers were required to attend no more than three after-school meetings or evening events per month, although the contract also gave the administration the right to call special meetings, given proper prior notification and justification to the union. The administration also contended, although it generally did not press this contention, that teachers had a professional obligation to participate in yearly events such as Back to School Night each fall, quite apart from what the contract said. This meant that in some months teachers might be required to attend four after-school meetings or events. Finally, administrators argued that if fewer than three after-school events were scheduled in one month, more could be scheduled the next month. That is, they read the contract language to refer to the *average* number of after-school meetings or events per month during the school year. Teachers, on the other hand, supported a more literal reading of the contract which disallowed exceptions to the three-events-per-month rule. In essense, they argued that no *single* month should ever have more than a total of three after-school events scheduled.

Most often grievances in this area were filed when special after-school meetings were hastily scheduled and teachers were given only one or two days' notice. These meetings were typically called by grade level to inform teachers about how to complete new record-keeping or program evaluation forms, how to use new diagnostic reading and math tests, how to set instructional goals for the next terms, etc. Often they had been originally scheduled during teachers' preparation periods and were rescheduled after-school when teachers could not attend during the originally scheduled time (often because they had to cover classes during their prepartion periods). Because teachers' reading of the contract language on after-school meetings was a literal one, they had the contract on their side when pressing grievances, and both sides knew this. The result was that when teachers filed grievances the administration generally apologized for the scheduling problems and said it would "make every effort to ensure that this does not happen again." But the meetings were held and teachers were never remunerated for having to "work overtime." This suggests that even when teachers won individual grievances, they often got little—not even a guarantee that such contract violations would not occur in the future.

If there was one thing most Urbanville teachers disliked more than after-school meetings, it was evening events and parent conferences; and they were most unwavering in sticking to the contract language when it came to these events. A good example of a dispute involving evening events was that which surrounded the scheduling of Back to School Night in the mid-1980s. The district's annual open house for parents had originally been scheduled for September; but because of hurricane conditions in the region on the night the event was scheduled, it was postponed for one month. The UEA filed a grievance claiming

Chapter Five

that four after-school events were now on the October calendar in violation of the contract, and that teachers could not be required to attend the rescheduled Back to School Night. The grievance further asked that those teachers who decided to attend, on their own, be paid time-and-a-half for overtime, that they be exempted from attending one after-school event the next month, and that no reprisals be carried out against those teachers who decided not to attend. A frustrated superintendent, in a letter to the UEA president, argued: "Over the two months, the average number of after-school events is three.... Certainly you will agree that 'Back to School Night' is important and that as professionals we have an obligation to our parents to work with them *in the best interest of their children*.... It appears your teachers are being very unbending, especially when all the facts are known" [emphasis mine].

In this instance, the superintendent invokes the image of the good professional, always ready to subordinate self-interest for the good of the children and always on call when needed. But the administration finally agreed to the union's demands, rather than test its looser interpretation of the contract in the courts, since it was clear teachers intended to push it that far if necessary. In this case, the union won a clear victory, yet the victory seemed both counterproductive and rather trivial. Back to School Night was poorly attended by teachers that year, and those who attended did so without enthusiasm. For those few parents who did attend, this only served to reinforce a belief that teachers did not care about their children. However, if teachers' reaction was unfortunate, it was both understandable and almost inevitable within the context of playing the game. It was designed to assert teacher power and extend teachers' wage-labor contract interests. Furthermore, because teachers' strategic victories were few and far between, they pressed their advantage when they could. A victory was a victory, and each one extended in some small way teachers' advantage within the power game played out with administrators.

Ironically, while union leaders supported teachers' resistance to attending any more than the required minimum of after-school meetings and events, they often complained when teachers did not show up for after-school events sponsored by the union. For example, at one executive committee meeting the president spoke about the possibility of getting a speaker from the MEA to make a presentation to teachers on pensions and retirement funds. "Do you want to pursue this?" he asked. "Remember when we had that other speaker from the MEA?" A teacher responded: "Not that many showed up, as usual." The president continued: "Yeh, we finagled it so the elementary teachers

"Playing the Game"

got last period off to come over to the high school to hear this guy. The secondary people didn't get time off, but we arranged it so those who wanted to come could make last period a prep period and attend. So we were all in the auditorium listening to this guy and when 3:15 arrives, a lot of teachers just up and walked out. It was embarrassing, and I sure would not want to do it again if that's going to happen." A teacher suggested, "Then don't do it," and another suggested sending a sign-up sheet around before inviting the speaker to gauge teacher interest. But as the president pointed out, expressions of interest did not always translate into attendance when the event finally occurred. Of course, one of the reasons why teachers liked to leave promptly at 3:15 each afternoon had nothing to do with a contract mentality. Many, teachers complained that they had to cancel other commitments—to their families or a second job—when special after-school meetings and events were scheduled. This refers, then, to a broader problem within late 20th-century America—a growing intensification of the working day in both the institutional workplace and the home which precludes meaningful involvement by many individuals in both the working and middle classes in community organizations and events.

Report Cards and Student Evaluation

The complex changeover to performance-based, test-oriented, basic skills instruction in Urbanville schools, as I have already indicated in Chapter Four, involved the institutionalization of new record-keeping procedures and paperwork duties for teachers that increased their workload significantly. Teachers resisted these increased paperwork duties on the basis that they represented "unilateral changes in the terms and conditions of employment" and, more specifically, that they violated the contract language which specified that teachers had to submit report cards for students only once each term. In most cases, administrators argued that the new paperwork, record-keeping, and reporting forms were not report cards; and their view generally prevailed. However, in several cases, when the new forms were clearly grade cards, teachers prevailed and the administration backed down. One of the most drawn out and divisive of these disputes began in 1974, when the UEA filed a grievance claiming that the Behavioral Outcomes Learning Units teachers now had to submit for each class each term (see Chapter Four), along with new elementary school Pupil Progress Report forms that identified student progress in various skill areas, constituted report cards and increased teachers' workload in

Chapter Five

violation of the contract. To resolve the dispute, a superior court judge ordered that representatives of the union and the Board of Education negotiate a means of meeting all of the new record-keeping and reporting requirements imposed by state officials upon the school district while not increasing teachers' workload any more than necessary.

The negotiated agreement that was formulated in response to this court order maintained all existing reporting forms and requirements, but as a concession to teachers the following was also agreed: "In order to relieve the pressure of learning units, report cards, and pupil performance reports being due at close intervals" they would be more evenly distributed throughout the term; and sections of the forms were to be pre-completed by clerical staff so that teachers had to spend less total time filling them out. When new computerized report card forms were introduced in 1976, the agreement was revised by specifiying that "teachers will mark all objective numbers, mastery levels, and summary grades...; [but] where courses are taught in a unit approach (all students being exposed to the same objectives) objective numbers will be pre-punched on the cards." This resolution of the conflict could hardly be considered a victory for teachers, yet by playing the role formalization game they were able to make the best of a bad situation. However, the fragile accord was broken when "bugs" in the newly computerized student record-keeping and reporting system threatened to delay report cards for spring term. As a result teachers were informed in a memo that, along with the computer report card forms they had already completed, they would need to complete a one-page, handwritten report card form for each student "in order to have a pupil progress report in the hands of the students before or on their last day of school."

The union executive committee immediately filed a grievance and distributed a special flyer to all teachers announcing in bold letters: "SPECIAL CRISIS ALERT: Report Card Agreement Broken By Board of Education." The flyer concluded: "This is an outrage and a contemptible action.... You [the rank and file] told us, unmistakably, that you feel our contract is sacred. This is a contract and we cannot, should not, and must not allow it to be unilaterally altered.... We are hopeful that quick legal action will put a stop to this outrageous usurpation of authority. Unfortunately, courts are often loath to make the kinds of speedy decisions that are essential in these matters. Remembering that, using the force of our group must seriously be considered."
In fact, the UEA did succeed in getting a superior court judge to impose an injunction against the district prohibiting it from making teachers complete the alternative report card forms and ordering that "the

"Playing the Game"

Board must decide which form it wants teachers to fill out." To ensure that no teachers completed the alternative report card forms, building reps for the union collected the forms from teachers and kept them in the union office. Once more, this incident demonstrated that teachers would press their advantage when they could, to resist clear violations of the letter of the contract. The use of the term "sacred" to describe the contract is particularly revealing, for it suggests that enforcement of the contract is almost a moral imperative, that to let the administration get away with such an "outrageous" violation of the contract would be unethical. Of course, it also suggests that in secular American culture the contract serves some of the functions of traditional religious codes of law and is thus invested, by union leaders, with some of the aura of the religious and the sacred—at least when the contract is clearly on teachers' side.

Assignment of Additional Classes and Special Duties

A final cluster of disputes that revealed much about "playing the game" involved resistance by teachers to unilateral changes in their workload through the assignment of new classes. In resisting new class assignments, teachers asserted an interpretation of the wage-labor contract that had not been supported in court cases, and as a result they seldom won these disputes. Their protests were most directly designed to make the administration aware of teacher discontent and of the union's intent to fight any and all increases in workload that were unilaterally imposed on teachers, without a renegotiation of the wage-labor contract. To sustain their claims in this regard, the UEA leadership adopted an *individualistic* as well as collectivist interpretation of the wage-labor contract. That is, the UEA argued that an informal wage-labor contract was established for every individual teacher upon entering the system, and that these entry-level workloads could not be unilaterally raised. In rejecting this interpretation, the administration pointed out that it would "lock some teachers in" to a reduced workload, since they were currently teaching less than a full load. In fact, most teachers had at least one to two unscheduled periods per week (aside from their preparation periods), and some teachers had as many as one unscheduled period per day. These inequalities in workload among teachers were an almost inevitable result of shifting staffing patterns and student populations in schools, along with the need to maintain a small pool of untapped labor power so that teachers with unscheduled periods could be used to cover classes for absent teachers. Consequently, the

Chapter Five

administration viewed these unscheduled periods as privileges which some teachers currently enjoyed because of scheduling exigencies, but to which they had no contractual rights. Because the administration's interpretation of the contract language was consistent with the dominant legal interpretation of teacher contracts in the state, teachers were not able to push their grievances very far. Nevertheless, they let the administration know that they would continue to make a fuss and resist each and every increase in workload, on an individual and collective basis, that was not negotiated.

Teachers also resisted increases in class workload by "playing dumb" about how to teach their new classes and making administrators tell them exactly what to do, what curricular materials to use, etc. The objective here was to shift some of the burden of the increased work load to the administrator who had imposed it on a teacher, and by "making it difficult" for the administrator, encourage him or her to look for a better solution. A good example of gamesmanship involving this "playing dumb" strategy is provided by an incident that occurred during the ethnographic field component of this study. A young, male music teacher had been hired several years previously at the high school, only to have his position cut because of declining enrollment in the music program. He was offered and accepted a transfer to the elementary music program and taught each day in four separate schools, with two unscheduled periods each day for commuting between schools and grabbing a quick lunch. Although this schedule proved a hectic one, it was intensified still further when the teacher was assigned to direct the high school band during one of his unscheduled periods. The band had been on the decline over the past several years as students took more basic skills courses and thus had less room for electives, as fewer and fewer students were allowed involvement in extra curricular activities because they had failed too many classes or not passed the high school diploma exam, and as the charismatic band director who had sustained the band over the previous decade quit.

Without a regular director for almost a year, the band had ceased to exist, except on paper. Still, the elementary music teacher had to show up each day at the high school and go to the band room as if there were a band. After he complained that this situation made no sense, the music supervisor finally agreed and assigned him to direct a group of high school cheerleaders, the "Pom Pom Girls," instead during his unscheduled period. One afternoon, before a scheduled meeting between the teacher and the UEA president to talk strategy, the president explained the situation to the researcher: "Without a band, the number of Pom Pom Girls has dwindled from about 40 to 16;

"Playing the Game"

and ——— [the music teacher] has no idea how to teach routines to these girls, so he's turned it into a study hall for now, but his supervisor says that's not acceptable." When the music teacher arrived, he was obviously upset and demoralized. He began, "I don't want to sound unreasonable. It's just that in terms of learning routines and doing a half-decent job, it's going to take time, and they have to appreciate that." The president assumed control of the conversation at this point and said: "My recommendation is that you tell him [the music supervisor] you don't have the knowledge, background, etc., and all you can do is keep order. If he wants you to do it, he has to give you some information. . . . He's playing a game with you, and you have to play a game back. *Play dumb* and do it under protest. If he wants you to do it he has to provide all the information. I don't want you looking through books and magazines to come up with routines." The teacher finally asked: "SoABCD I go ahead and tell him I'll do it, but. . . ?" The president responded: "Tell him to tell you what to do day by day."

The conversation ended with the music teacher, in a quite emotional manner, talking about the toll all of this was taking on him. "I'm just exhausted, and it's mainly mental I think. I go home and carry all my unhappiness about teaching to my family. Maybe my wife will ask me for a divorce." The president advised, in a half-joking manner meant to cheer up the teacher, that he "go home and take it out on your wife. I used to tell my wife that's what I married her for, wasn't it? Or better yet, you and your wife go take it out on some brick wall, get it out of your system." Sexism aside, his comment reveals much about the psychic costs of the intensification of teachers' labor on both the teacher and his or her family. One can, in these ways, discern the early signs of teacher burn-out and cynicism in such comments from young, often idealistic and committed teachers.

Conclusion

The Urbanville data would seem to lend weight to the critical end-of-ideology thesis as applied to teachers. Teachers did not struggle over the direction of the school or the shape of the curriculum and instruction, and they did not put forward a coherent vision of an alternative way of doing things, based on explicit values and political commitments. Instead, teachers learned to play the contract game and limit their concerns to the terms and conditions of the wage-labor exchange. However, while teachers did reveal a strong instrumental orientation

Chapter Five

in pursuing their interests and seemed to reject ideological appeals, it is clearly too simplistic to imply that teachers' interests had been fully contained or coopted through acceptance of the current rules of the game. Several factors in particular worked to undermine the stability of the current situation. First, teachers learned to redefine many of their professional values and beliefs in terms of wage-labor contract interests; so that their instrumentality hid broader concerns. Ironically, they found ways of challenging their treatment as rigidly subordinated workers by adhering to role formalization. In most of the contract disputes analyzed in this chapter, teachers were fighting for more than what was stated on the formal grievance. To this extent at least, conflict was not contained; and wage-labor disputes were not separable from the broader overriding power conflict between teachers and the administration.

A second factor which destabilized the current situation in Urbanville schools and undermined the containment of teachers' interests was teachers' discontent over their inability to win many battles in the contract game. Only by playing the game effectively, and out-maneuvering the opposition, could teachers hope to hold on to what little power and few rights they did possess in the face of an overwhelming power advantage by the administration. At the same time, given the current rules of the game teachers knew they could not win the game and were obviously disadvantaged by it. They were assigned more responsibilities in an already overly intensified work schedule that sapped their energies and added to their demoralization. They were shifted from school to school and program to program almost at whim, it seemed, with all the attendent stress and disruption; they were supplied few materials and had virtually no access to copying machines, secretarial assistance, or even workable typewriters. What little preparation time they did have in the hectic school day was too often lost as they were asked or told to cover classes for absent teachers. The power that teachers exercised through the Urbanville Education Association was largely reactive and defensive. The game did not, in fact, contain a possible scenario whereby teachers could win in the sense of subordinating the administration to teacher power. The best teachers could do was ensure that the administration had to give some ground here and there. Consequently, there is reason to believe that teachers might not continue to be happy to play the game indefinitely without drastically rewritten rules.

Finally, playing the game represented a form of *goal displacement* among school staff that prevented them from focusing their energies on the educational goals of the schools or on how to improve curricu-

"Playing the Game"

lum and the process of learning. Sometimes it seemed that the game became more important than anything else in the school system, and playing the game gave interest and meaning to everyday life in the school system. Teachers who found that their teaching was not intrinsically motivating could become involved in the union and find some measure of satisfaction in playing the game to beat the administration. The game certainly kept the union president going, and for all the complaining he did about it, he seemed to thrive on the struggle, the sense of engagement with the cunning enemy. And so his advice to the young music teacher assigned to lead the Pom Pom Girls was to fight back, but to fight back within the framework of the contract game. Otherwise, you had no chance against them. Of course, regardless of who won particular battles in the game, the goal displacement involved in game-playing such as this generates crisis tendencies that are central to understanding the current malaise in urban education.

6

"Classroom Management" in the Basic Skills Era

Up to this point I have focused upon the role of the state and local teachers' unions in Midstate in articulating a set of interests in response to a conservative package of urban school reforms, including collective bargaining laws and statutes, that have further differentiated managerial and labor roles within the schools and made teachers more accountable to top-down bureaucratic control. My primary concern, consequently, has been with the structured conflict between teachers and administrators, particularly those at the central office. In this chapter, I want to shift attention to the other major group of school actors with whom teachers must negotiate an everyday life—students. In negotiating classroom order with students, the union has less power than it does in negotiating with administrators. What, then, has a basic skills orientation to the curriculum meant in regard to the construction and reconstruction of teacher-student relations?

The case study data presented in this chapter suggests that the restructuring of teachers' work, the curriculum, and the instructional process during the basic skills era has been coextensive with a shift from authoritarian and repressive forms of student control (the traditional responses to the problem of order in urban schools) towards cool, businesslike, technical-rational forms of control. The trouble with traditional, repressive control of students was that teachers had to personally dominate students and impose the authority of the institution; and this resulted in a personalization of structurally-generated teacher-

Chapter Six

student conflict. The interruption of instruction to discipline and control students also took an inordinate amount of time away from the formal learning process. In the language of basic skills, the student-teacher conflict generated by repressive control tactics reduced time on task. The objective of the newer forms of classroom management is to minimize and contain disruptions as efficiently as possible so that classroom time on task and hence instructional productivity is maximized.

An efficiency discourse thus has replaced moralistic and punitive discourses on student discipline—a development symbolized by the growing use of the term "classroom management." "Dysfunctional" student behavior is to be managed rather than moralistically condemned; and it is to be managed through the rational, detached, depersonalized use of bureaucratic authority by teachers. The discourse on classroom management in education may thus be linked to a broader end-of-ideology discourse which focuses our concern upon the proper management of institutional conflict. This not only takes the existing system for granted, but also depoliticizes highly political power relations and dynamics.

The bureaucratic rationalization of classroom control, however, cannot be expected to effectively manage deep-rooted crisis tendencies in urban schooling any better than bureaucratic rationalization has solved the problem of institutional order more broadly. The attempt to cool out rage and contain conflict through proper businesslike classroom management is not likely to be very effective if the root causes of that rage and conflict go unaddressed. At the same time, a return to repressive forms of control in urban schools may no longer be politically viable, since such a policy would risk making the latent racism and classism of urban schooling more manifest or visible. Bureaucratic elites, consequently, have not been able to effectively manage the problem of order during the basic skills era.

If basic skills reform has been associated with bureaucratic-rational and businesslike forms of control over students, then basic skills forms of classroom management have been associated with the de-skilling and re-skilling of teachers away from a pegagogic to a managerial role. As the curriculum is rationalized and standardized, and in other ways brought under technical control, teaching is reconceptualized in terms of oversight of a curriculum-guided classroom work process. Michael Apple has written of this process: "While the deskilling involves the loss of craft, the ongoing atrophication of educational skills, the reskilling involves the substitution of the skills and ideological visions of management. The growth of behavior management techniques and classroom

"Classroom Management"

management strategies and their incorporation within both curricular material and teachers' repertoires signifies these kinds of alterations."[1] This re-skilling, consequently, reduces the pedagogic dimension of teachers' work in guiding the learning process, so that it also allows the system to make more use of less qualified and experienced teachers.

While teachers have been re-skilled as classroom managers in urban schools, their new management skills have not helped them effectively contain or defuse student resistance to an impersonal, disempowering, non-motivating curriculum. In fact, teachers could be much more effective in maintaining a viable classroom order if they were allowed to personalize their interaction with students and teach from a position of personal caring rather than impersonal authority, and if they could engage students in a curriculum that was motivating and relevant. This suggests that we must be sceptical of the claim that more classroom management training for teachers is what is needed to effectively manage discipline problems in urban schools. The answer to the problem of order in urban schools and classrooms is a new curriculum and a new critical pedagogy that engages students, along with a community and an economy which offers students something worth striving and excelling for. In the meantime, managing the problem of order through current approaches to classroom management can only be partial and contradictory. Businesslike approaches to classroom management are certainly preferable to a return to physically and emotionally intimidating methods of student control, and they may even be more effective in keeping students on task, but they embody contradictions and limitations that must be examined if we are to effectively address the problem of order in urban schooling.

Unlike preceeding chapters, this chapter is based on data from two different urban school districts in Midstate. I begin by examining data on classroom management from Urbanville. Specifically, I analyze the official Assertive Discipline model of classroom management endorsed by the superintendent in Urbanville, which emphasized a depersonalized, bureaucratic-rational approach to teacher authority. I also analyze approaches to classroom management endorsed by the teacher union and indicate how they differed and were also similar to the administrative model. I then examine data from the files of the Urbanville Education Association (UEA) that described incidents of teacher-student conflict, including cases in which teachers were charged with assault. Finally, I present data in this chapter from a participant observation research project conducted in an urban school district near Urbanville that was designed to provide an insider's perspective on teaching and the problem of order in one urban school. The study was

Chapter Six

conducted in conjunction with a practicing teacher in a middle school, which I call McKinley School, during the 1989–90 school year. The McKinley School study supports many of the general findings of the Urbanville study. It also suggests that teachers were frustrated and demoralized because they felt powerless to effectively manage conflict in their classrooms and did not receive adequate support from the administration in their efforts to cope with discipline problems. Both the Urbanville and McKinley School data point to the contradictions between theory and practice in the field of classroom management and the dilemmas of managing the problem of order in urban schools during the basic skills era.

Urbanville Teachers and "Classroom Management"

Probably the most influential system of classroom management over the past decade, particularly in urban schools with a strong basic skills curricular focus, has been Assertive Discipline, an approach developed and marketed by Lee Canter & Associates through a national network of instructors who conduct workshops (both in-service workshops and multi-day retreats) for teachers and administrators, and through books and other instructional materials.[2] In Urbanville, the same consulting team from a nearby university research and development center that had introduced scans in the schools as a means of increasing student time on task also recommended that the district retrain teachers in Assertive Discipline methods through a series of in-service workshops, which were subsequently held over one school year. The district also paid for some teachers to attend special Assertive Discipline workshop series or retreats, with the expectation that these teachers would become "turnkeys" to spread Assertive Discipline ideas among other teachers. Finally, Assertive Discipline principles of effective teaching were used by administrators in evaluating teachers and were thereby incorporated in the one best way of teaching the basics that I discussed in Chapter Four. The basic premises of "assertive" teaching are quite simple. According to the authors of one recent text on classroom management: "Students who do not obey class rules receive one warning and then are subjected to a series of increasingly more serious sanctions. . . . The teacher refuses to devote time or attention to disruptive behavior."[3] Since rules are preestablished for given types and levels of disruptive behaviors, teachers supposedly do not need to spend time explaining or justifying their actions in particular cases. "The goal of

"Classroom Management"

Assertive Discipline," according to these authors, "is to foster in teachers a feeling that they are 'in charge' in the classroom." In order to do this, "at no time does a teacher permit a student to forget who is in charge of the classroom or that class conduct is governed by certain nonnegotiable rules."

The presumption is that "students appreciate having limits placed on their behavior and that they respond to sanctions as well as rewards."[4] Negative consequences endorsed in Assertive Discipline, for use when students disobey rules and fail to live up to expectations, include: after-school and in-school detention, isolation in "time-out" rooms, visits to principal's office, phone call to parents, denial of field trips, recess, and music or art classes, and short and long-term suspensions. Positive consequences include: tokens that may be saved up and cashed in for prizes, awards, happy-face stickers, recognition from the teacher, and a letter or phone call to parents. By consistently repeating what they expect students to do (called the "broken record" technique), by using positive and negative consequences consistently, and by refusing to get "hooked" into conflicts with students, teachers can supposedly "wear down" student opposition without needing to raise their voices or get angry. According to the rationale of central office administrators, if teachers practiced Assertive Discipline techniques in their classrooms, they would have no discipline problems; and if they had discipline problems, it must be because they were not using good classroom management techniques.

The Urbanville Education Association (UEA) took a rather ambivalent stand on the issue of classroom management. On specific local issues in the schools involving student discipline, the union served as a vehicle for rank-and-file teachers to voice their frustration with the administration's "Assertive Discipline" model, with its tendency to blame individual teachers for discipline problems in the schools. But officially, it followed the policy of the state teacher union, which endorsed Assertive Discipline and several other popular models of classroom management. The MEA pressured the UEA and other locals in the state to promote its series of workshops, retreats, and conferences on classroom management. Rank-and-file teachers were guaranteed a "professional day" in the contract so that they could attend regional workshops sponsored by the MEA, and the UEA generally picked up the registration fees for teachers who attended. Rather than endorse one classroom management system, the MEA presented at these workshops a number of competing, slightly different models of classroom management, although the similarities between the models were far greater than their differences. At the 1986 statewide MEA Discipline

Chapter Six

Conference, for example, which drew 500 teachers from around the state, participating teachers were given the choice of attending one of the following workshops, as described in the conference bulletin: "*Least*: A systematic approach to minimizing students' disruptive behavior and maximizing time on task; *Assertive Discipline*: All students can behave when teachers assertively communicate their expectations to them with assertive skills; *Teacher Effectiveness Training*: How to use listening, asserting, and problem-solving skills to give teachers time and energy for teaching; *The O.K. Classroom*: How to better use communication skills to improve students' self-concept, self-reliance, and self-expression; and *Win/Win Relationships*: The skills of conflict prevention, conflict resolution, and artful negotiation."

If there was any significant difference between the approaches endorsed in these various workshops it was minor. All treated discipline problems in the classroom as resulting from a failure to communicate expectations effectively, and all accepted the need to control students so that they could learn. Questions about what they learned and how they learned it were not raised. Which is to say, none of these models of classroom management politicized or contextualized the analysis of the problem of classroom order. Some of the approaches were a bit more humanistic than others in their conception of teacher-student relations. For example T.E.T. presumes that "mutual respect" and trust are the foundation of a good teacher-student relationship and that teachers and students should negotiate resolutions to their conflicts in which both "win," in the sense that both get something out of the resolution. It advocates "a form of negotiation where teacher and student contribute relatively equally. . . . Generally, punishments are not considered viable solutions, since they imply that someone (the students) must lose."[5] T.E.T thus attempts to wed a therapeutic-counselling model (with the student conceived as the client or patient) to a human relationist model of management (with its emphasis upon effective employer-employee communication) to achieve the same basic ends as Assertive Discipline, although the latter approach may be considered more realistic and practical than T.E.T. within a system of urban schooling organized around power relations of domination and subordination. In either case, control of student resistances to the smooth flow of classroom work processes becomes the primary objective of classroom management, which deflects attention away from the deeper, systemic roots of control problems in urban schools. Official teacher union support for dominant classroom management approaches thus suggests a rather uncritical acceptance of an elite managerial perspective on the problem of order in urban schooling.

"Classroom Management"

The MEA adopted a somewhat more critical stance in its lobbying effort in support of legislation to "curb violence and vandalism in our schools." In effect, the MEA acknowledged that the classroom management models it supported and endorsed in its workshop series were not sufficient to deal with the growing discipline problem in urban schools and that stronger measures were needed, at least in the short run, to reestablish order in the classroom. One of the legislative initiatives the MEA supported in the mid-1980s called for special programs of alternative education outside the regular classroom for severely disruptive students "so that such students could be provided educational services suited to their needs while at the same time benefitting non-disruptive students by removing or ameliorating disruption in the classroom." For a number of reasons this piece of sponsored legislation never got beyond committee and was not widely supported by progressive groups in the state. For one thing, it was in opposition to the trend toward mainstreaming special student groups within regular classrooms. For another, it was unclear what or whose criteria would be used for identifying students who were "disruptive of the learning environment." Might minority and disadvantaged students end up being the ones most often removed from classrooms and placed in separate schools for delinquents? A number of other questions were raised in opposition to the union proposal. In such schools, might students merely learn to be more delinquent? Might staff in these alternative programs come to view themselves (and be viewed by students) more as prison guards than teachers? In the end, the union proposal was portrayed in the media as self-interested and narrow-sighted.

Another MEA legislative proposal relevant to the problem of order and discipline was that teachers receive support from local School Boards in pressing assault charges against students, and in defending themselves against assault charges brought by students and their parents. This legislation would "require local Boards of Education to provide advice on legal alternatives" open to teachers in such cases, and it supported the notion that local Boards of Education should help remunerate teachers for legal expenses incurred in pressing charges or defending themselves against charges. The chances for passage of this bill were also slim; but, it did help reveal just how bad the situation had become in Midstate's urban schools, and how vulnerable teachers felt to assault and to assault charges. Disadvantaged students and their families had learned the one great weakness of the current system of bureaucratic state schooling in Midstate: teachers' vulnerability to legal action for using excessive force to control students. If students

Chapter Six

wanted to get back at a teacher, all they had to do was accuse the teacher of shoving or hitting them. All complaints of teacher assault could, if students and parents wanted to push them far enough, end up in court. This piece of sponsored legislation, consequently, was much needed by teachers. But what it lacked was a critical framework which allowed teachers to look beyond their own immediate concerns to understand discipline problems and teacher-student conflict as related to the organization and operation of urban schools.

At the local level, the Urbanville Education Association concerned itself with student discipline problems primarily when teachers sought assistance because students and their parents or guardians threatened to file assault charges. Verbal and/or physical confrontations between teachers and students led, in 15 separate cases over the 1968–86 study period, to formal charges of assault, typically brought by parents and students against teachers (11 incidents), but occasionally brought by teachers against students and parents (4 incidents). Much more frequently, teachers were accused of assault with the threat of possible legal action; but students and parents did not follow through on the threats. Often a meeting between the involved parties in the principal's office was all that was needed to resolve these incidents. Nevertheless, by state law, each time parents complained to administrators about the physical abuse of their children by teachers, the incident had to be written up and filed with the state department of youth services, so that the teachers' names were on file even if teachers were completely exonerated of charges or accusations. In almost all cases that went to court, teachers won or assault charges were eventually dropped, often the result of an out-of-court settlement. Legal fees for court cases were typically paid for by the school board, although in most cases teachers were also suspended without pay pending court decisions, so that even when they won cases, they always lost financially.

A common theme voiced at teacher union meetings whenever discipline problems were discussed (either as part of the formal agenda or on an informal basis among teachers at the meeting) was: "the kids have all the rights, we have none," or some variation thereof. Teachers argued that the courts were "stacked against us" in assault cases; and it was widely assumed that students intentionally tried to draw teachers into fights so that they could sue them, and that they frequently made up evidence against teachers. Teachers' vulnerability to assault charges meant that students could use threats or actual charges as a means of harassing particular teachers they did not like. One high school teacher wrote in her defense: "I was discussing the fire drill rules when [Student A] told me to shut up. She said that she was going to tell her mother

"Classroom Management"

to come to the school and throw me out of the window. She went home and told her mother that I hit her. I did not hit her.... When I was signing out to go home, [Student B] heard my voice and said that I caught (hit) him with one hand by his elbow, and then picked him up off the floor with one hand. I did not touch him. He is as tall as I am and much heavier. I couldn't believe my ears." Another teacher was accused by a young girl's guardian of "slapping her in the face, pulling her by the hair and grabbing her by the neck" in a classroom scuffle. The teacher maintained the incident began when the student had refused to line up with the other children, made faces at the teacher, and then said, "Mrs. ——— [the teacher] is a pig." According to the teacher she took the student out in the hall briefly to talk with her, but "at no time had I come into physical contact with ——— [the student], and in no way struck her." In at least some of the cases, then, teachers appeared to be the victims of fabricated assault charges; and this is one of the reasons few assault charges were sustained in court. Of course, even in these fabricated assault charges, students' anger towards particular teachers or teachers in general needs to be explained. The anger and rage of students, and their strategic use of threats of legal action against teachers, indicates that students feel victimized themselves by the power relations of urban schooling. If teachers are made the victims of student rage, it is within the context of a system of schooling in which students are the greater victims.

When teacher-student scuffles did end up in court, lawyers who represented teachers were, in about three-fourths of all cases, able to get charges dropped. To provide some indication of how these cases were handled, let me refer to one particular case in which the lawyer had carefully detailed steps and tactics in defending a teacher against charges that she "did cause bodily injury" to a second-grade student by "kicking him in the leg." The lawyer wrote in his brief for the teacher: "I will attempt to establish that he [the student] is not capable of knowing the nature of taking an oath in a judicial proceeding," which would effectively block his testimony from being introduced. If the student testified, the lawyer would, "on cross-examination, attempt to establish through his own testimony that he has lied in the past, to his parents and to his teachers on numerous occasions. I will also attempt to establish that his testimony has been carefully rehearsed on numerous occasions with his father, his mother, and/or with an attorney. I will focus on any contradictions between his version of events and the testimony of Mrs. ——— and Ms. ——— [two teachers who heard the scuffle].... Through questioning of the ——— 's [parents] and ——— [the student], we will attempt to establish that he is under

Chapter Six

the total domination of his parents, especially his father, and that his father has taught his son to be extremely aggressive." In preparing the teacher to testify, the lawyer noted that he would begin by asking questions about her educational background, honors and awards she had received, and her many years of teaching in the district. As for the incident itself, the lawyer wrote: "Questions will be asked with regard to the one time your foot accidentally came in contact with ——— 's [the student's] foot when you broke up a fight between he and another boy. You'll emphasize that there was no injury suffered by ——— [the student], and that you were acting professionally in attempting to prevent serious injuries that could have resulted." In this case the teacher was exonerated of all charges; although this came at a substantial cost, both financial and emotional.

Aside from the issue of teachers' vulnerability to assault charges, the Urbanville incidents reveal how difficult it was for some teachers to maintain an impersonal and businesslike demeanor in the face of student resistance and open hostility and how easy it was to fall back, almost unthinkingly, on authoritarian control tactics. Some teachers had more control problems than others, either because they were less effective than other teachers in managing students in a businesslike manner, or because they taught lower ability groups and remedial basic skills classes (where resistance to the schooling process was strongest), or for both of these reasons. One junior high teacher, for example, was the cause of some concern to her principal, since more than 30 student fights had been reported in her classroom over a five-month period. When she was reprimanded for "unprofessional conduct," she defended herself by maintaining that she had the "worst" class in the school: "I checked the records and found that seven children from my class had been suspended during that [five-month] time; two had been suspended twice, four were cited for fighting in the lunchroom; two were fighting outside the school building after dismissal. I have been assigned the most aggressive and emotionally disturbed students in the school, and instead of receiving help, I am reprimanded for attempting to maintain order."

The reprimand had followed two incidents, about three weeks apart, that had resulted in parental complaints and threats of legal action. According to the teacher, the first of these incidents began when "——— [Student A] got out of his seat and began hitting another student. I told ——— [Student A] to stop hitting her and return to his desk. When he continued to hit her I intervened, taking him by the arm and pulling him away. . . . He told his mother that I had scratched him. . . . This was not true." The second incident, a more serious one,

"Classroom Management"

began, according to the teacher, when "——— [Student B] began fighting with another boy. I sent the other boy to the back of the room and told ——— [Student B] to wait by the classroom door to discuss his problem. I walked with him to the door and opened it...." The child later told his mother that the teacher had pushed him towards the door, and that he had cut his lip on the door. The teacher maintained that the boy must have cut his lip "while fighting with the other boy, bumped his head on the door, or hurt it after leaving the room." Whatever the exact truth, this teacher seemed unable to stay out of trouble for long and hence faced denied of her annual salary increment, more reprimands, and possible dismissal if she could not learn to be a more effective classroom manager.

In some cases, teachers' physical intervention in classroom fights seemed almost the only appropriate response, given the circumstances; yet even in these cases, teachers faced reprimands and possible legal action for "overreacting." A good example is provided by a case involving a teacher aide, assisting a special education teacher in a middle school class for "emotionally disturbed" students. The teacher recalled that "——— [Student A] told me he didn't want to work on his reading workbook anymore, became enraged, kicked his desk and chair across the room, balled up his papers and threw them all into the wastebasket, stomping it down with his feet. I asked ——— [the teacher aide] to remove him from the room until he calmed down. But ——— [Student A] refused to leave and kicked the wastebasket across the room. He then shoved the reading table into the board. Mr. ——— [the teacher aide] took his arm to lead him out of the room. He became more physically violent, tried to kick Mr. ———, throwing himself on the floor in the process. Mr. ——— tried to hold on to him, but he broke away and started punching Mr. ———. " The teacher aide recalls what happened next in the hall: "He hit me right in the middle of my [arm] cast, upon which I let his wrist go. He quickly threw his hands up in a boxing position, hopping around, screaming, 'I'll whip your ass, nigger.' I quickly reached out to grab him, but he kept hopping around. Finally, the security guard arrived. Then Mr. ——— [the principal] came out of his office, walked up to me, and said, 'You are suspended... I don't let anyone batter and abuse children in my school building.' I said 'fine,' and walked back to my room to pick up my things."

This is an incident, arguably, of teacher abuse more than child abuse—at least if the accounts of the teacher and teacher aide are at all accurate. It also provides some indication of just how much anger and rage some students have within them, a rage which gets directed

Chapter Six

at almost all school authority figures and which may contribute to the high proportion of urban students who are labeled "emotionally disturbed." Finally, this incident also reveals something about the strategic use of racial slurs and taunts by students to "get to" teachers. In this case, since both teacher aide and student were black, the student's taunt may be self-deprecating. Another possible (and complementary) interpretation is that the taunt was made to make the teacher aide aware that he too, like the student, was a "nigger," one of the oppressed, yet as a teacher he was serving the white institution as an agent of control. I do not mean to suggest that the student meant all of this on a self-aware level, only that at a commonsense level this student's use of the word "nigger" revealed something about racial power relations in the school and the culture, along with the power of words as strategic weapons in conflict.

There were other indications that teacher-student conflicts in Urbanville schools were linked to racial power relations. For example, in the fall of 1968, race relations in Urbanville were perhaps at a low point, and the city erupted in a series of riots, involving burning and looting of shops, and various Black Power and civil rights groups demanded an end to police brutality and control of the city by a small "white power establishment." In the schools, a series of physical confrontations occurred that fall between a group of white teachers and black students, particularly those older high school teachers who had not adjusted well to the rapid rise in the black and Hispanic student population, and those students self-identified with the Black Power movement. One veteran teacher remembered, "It was a terrible time. Teachers were afraid to come to school in the morning. And some of the teachers were of the old school who didn't adapt very well to minorities." The most serious incident that fall involved a white junior high teacher who suffered cuts and bruises from a scuffle with a student and was placed under doctor's care for two weeks. Although the student did not sustain injuries, the parents threatened to sue the teacher for assault. This angered many rank-and-file teachers, and the UEA representative assembly met in special session to pass a resolution demanding that the administration take action to prevent a "climate of fear and intimidation" from taking hold in the school. The resolution read, in part: "This attack, by its very violent nature, indicates some realization by local students that more is to be gained than lost by such attacks . . . [and it] suggests the weaknesses of the school system in its handling of discipline cases [and] its inability to cope with the pressures exerted by certain outside groups" (a reference to the Black Panthers in particular, and more generally Black Power groups in the community). In the language of confrontation typical of that year in America, the resolution concluded: "These outside pressure groups seeking to destroy the present power structure in order to expand into the ensuing vacuum may have shifted tactics from using children as shock troops in a frontal assault to using them in a series of sorties hoping to probe and exploit areas of greatest weakness, instilling fear and suspicion, and destroying the system from within." The teachers were suggesting that students who adhered to the Black Power philosophy were "enemies within" who hoped to intimidate teachers and thus bring the system to a halt, and that they were controlled from without by militant radicals. The implication was that these black students were brainwashed and being used for evil purposes. Here again, the teacher union hardly seemed to be taking a very progressive stance, one that recognized the legitimate grievances of black students and the black community in Urbanville. However, it is also the case that some teachers *were* being attacked by a group of militant black students; and in the immediate situation, their own sense of victimization took priority.

During the last year of the study period, another series of incidents occurred that appeared to have racial overtones, although these incidents also indicate just how much the terrain of conflict had shifted from the late 1960s, when racial conflict was much more politicized, overt, and confrontational. The latter incidents involved complaints by a number of teachers to both administrators and the union about pickpockets operating in the schools, with teachers specially targeted to be "ripped off." In a UEA representative council meeting one building representative complained: "We have no locks in the building for teachers to lock things up, like purses. And somebody has stolen a master key and broken into the building at night. There is one cabinet that has a key, but it's been broken into seven times this year. This has all been reported to the principal, and nothing gets done." Another teacher interjected: "You can't go anywhere in our school without your pocketbook and personal belongings. The kids are all learning to be pickpockets and thiefs. Someone took something out of my wallet while I was out to lunch, and the door was locked. Nobody feels safe anymore." The UEA president inquired of the teacher, "What did ——— [the principal] say?" The teacher responded: "Nothing. He didn't want to be bothered." Teachers were angry and frustrated, but unable to translate that anger and frustration into positive change.

They also articulated their anger in a way that reinforced racial stereotypes and a "them" (students) versus "us" (teachers) perspective. "Pickpocket" became, for some teachers, almost a code word for black male student, and its usage allowed these teachers to vent their anger

Chapter Six

against black students without being overtly racist. One executive committee member made this racism overt by remarking to me: "Black parents don't want vocational programs for their kids, so I guess what we need now is a pickpocket course." Aside from revealing racist attitudes among teachers, this incident also reveals something about the hidden curriculum of urban schooling for inner-city black males. To the extent that there really was a pickpocket problem in the schools, it suggests just how much the schools were training grounds for a certain form of alienated identity construction among minority youth, who learn how to "rip off" and "work" the system which victimizes them. If delinquent students could not win in the overall power struggle with the school and with individual teachers, they could take their revenge in a number of ways, and "ripping teachers off" was one of them. It was not, then, merely a case of white racist teachers unfairly blaming "innocent" minority students. Racial stereotypes and biases were to some degree a joint production of teachers and students. They also encouraged teachers and students to construct institutional identities in opposition to each other, in a them-versus-us manner, that kept teachers and students from recognizing common interests in the institution.

McKinley Middle School and the "Problem of Order"

The McKinley Middle School case study, to which I now turn, complements many of the themes that emerged from an analysis of the Urbanville data; but it provides a somewhat different perspective, since it is based on participant observation data and focuses upon everyday life in one urban school over the course of one school year. McKinley School was in a city which had, up through the 1950s, been heavily Jewish and Italian. But in the early 1960s a group of Puerto Ricans was brought to the city by a major industry which needed cheap, available labor. Once a Puerto Rican community was established in the city, the immigration of Puerto Ricans rapidly accelerated; and in recent years Dominicans also established a growing community in the city, which was overwhelmingly Hispanic by the mid-1980s. At the time of the study, approximately 85 percent of McKinley Middle School's students were Hispanic, ten percent were black, and five percent were white. Approximately one third of all students in McKinley School were classified as bilingual, and many of these were recent arrivals from the Dominican Republic, Puerto Rico or Central America.

"Classroom Management"

McKinley School had a curriculum that was heavily oriented towards passing basic skills tests, and the principal was committed to the notion that "every teacher is a teacher of basic skills" and should be concerned about preparing students for tests. The participant observer was in his second year as a middle school music teacher in McKinley School during the year the study was conducted (1989–90). Although he would have preferred teaching in the suburbs, such jobs were not easy to come by, especially for someone who had only recently returned to teaching and consequently had few connections with the network of teachers who knew about the good jobs in the suburbs. Consequently, he considered himself lucky to be teaching at McKinley; although he also began to feel that we was not really teaching, just baby-sitting. Music was treated as a free period for students, a chance for them to unwind, a place for them to be entertained, not seriously engaged in learning to appreciate and understand the structure of music. Over the course of the year the participant observer and the author engaged in a series of conversations on the general topic of what had been happening in McKinley School and what teachers had been saying and doing. The author took notes during these conservations, and these notes were later written up in more detail. Finally, early drafts of this chapter were reviewed by the participant observer for accuracy and so that he could add detail where possible.

Before proceeding with the description and analysis of the problem of order in McKinley, it is important to say a bit more about the perspectives on student discipline and order used by the author and the participant observer, and the dialectic or interactive development of a common perspective to account for what was going on in McKinley School. From my vantage point as a university-based scholar, and consistent with my political commitments and my working hypotheses, I tended to presume that student resistance in urban schools resulted from a curriculum lacking in intrinsic motivation and personal relevance, lack of student identification with the white, middle class culture represented by teachers, and the role that urban schooling has come to assume in contemporary America of reproducing power relations of domination and subordination. The participant observer, from his vantage point as a practicing teacher at the "scene of the battle," felt this explanation excused students for their misbehavior. He viewed the control problems in terms of individual students who gave individual teachers (and more particularly, himself) a bad time and who "thrive on chaos." This difference between the author's abstract, analytic framework for analyzing student resistance and the pragmatic, situational framework employed by the participant observer was, at least

Chapter Six

initially, the cause of considerable disagreement during our discussions. Nevertheless, rather than view our perspectives as conflicting, we sought to link the pragmatic with the more general and abstract in ways that overcame their apparent incompatibility. In fact, at the concrete classroom level, individual students (and teachers, for that matter) *are* responsible for their actions, and it does not help to absolve them of responsibility for acting self-destructively. At the same time, the social, economic, and cultural forces which promote irresponsible or self-destructive student behavior must be addressed if we seek solutions which move beyond the merely individual and situational. Holding individual students responsible for their behavior will not work in the long run unless these other realities are addressed; although as a teacher, to continue to let students act self-destructively by venting their anger and rage inappropriately at the wrong targets and to fail to hold them accountable to certain rules of conduct, is to participate in the self-victimization of disadvantaged students. What is called for pragmatically, in the here and now of classroom life, consequently may be different from what is called for from a longer time frame and broader perspective. The important point is that present practice is informed in some way by longer-range goals and purposes.

The Official Model of Classroom Management

Let me begin the analysis of data from McKinley School by examining the official model of classroom management and student discipline in the school, as it was articulated in a memo to teachers from the principal entitled "Tips on Discipline from Administrators to Teachers," which teachers were required to keep in their planning book. In this lengthy memo, the principal listed a number of discipline guidelines, in sequential order of importance. At the top of the list was "plan." More specifically: " Plan ahead. Plan more classroom activities than you'll use." Number two was: "Keep students busy on learning tasks ." Both of these guidelines linked student control with the establishment of a busy classroom routine, which kept students out of trouble. Student conflict and resistance were viewed as the inevitable consequence of idle hands. This indicates that the recent concern with increasing student time on task in the urban school classroom is not only about raising test scores—it is also, and perhaps just as importantly, a response to the problem of order and the belief that keeping students busy is the answer to discipline problems. Next on the principal's list of discipline tips was, "Catch the child being good," a domi-

"Classroom Management"

nant behavioralist theme which implies that positive reinforcements, in the form of teacher attention, can solve most discipline problems. The next two tips were: "Avoid making issues personal between pupil and teacher," and "Don't get upset about mild classroom incidents." Here the emphasis was upon not escalating minor disturbances through confrontational language and by maintaining a businesslike voice. The final discipline tip was: "NEVER humiliate a student, make threats you don't plan to carry out, use ridicule or sarcasm...." Such uses of language, according to the principal, were not effective and could incite students more. Aside from these tips, the principal's memo emphasized that discipline was each teacher's responsibility and should not be pushed onto administrators. "If you are constantly calling for assistance you are leaning on the administrator to do what is *basically* your job." The principal thus implied that the problem of student discipline was owned by teachers, that only they could solve it.

The McKinley School principal also linked these tips on classroom management to effective schools research; and he required teachers to keep several effective schools handouts in their planning books to guide their practice and to serve as a basis upon which the principal would evaluate them. One of the handouts claimed: "Over the past two decades, significant gains have been made in acquiring a research-based understanding of the teaching/learning process. This emerging body of knowledge has recently been translated into descriptions of practical, effective and efficient teaching practices.... Due to their *validated influence*, these research-based factors form a foundation for the effective teacher in making *logical choices* and *sensible instructional decisions*" [emphasis mine]. I call attention to these highlighted phrases because they take so much for granted that needs to be questioned. The assumption is that the best approach to organizing teacher-student relations can be revealed by research, as if the science of behaviorism were somehow neutral and objective. Suddenly, in just the past two decades, teachers are informed, the "science of education" has resolved all disputes over student discipline. The one best way of organizing teacher-student relations has been discovered, and not surprisingly, it is a way that is consistent with a bureaucratic state model of basic skills instruction. Now all teachers have to do is to implement this one best way. The basic skills bias of effective schools research is apparent in the handout's claim that "precise teaching is more effective teaching which includes objective skill-based instruction, directed teaching, preparation of total unit planning rather than day to day, and matching student needs to selected programs and mastery learning." "Precise" and "directed" teaching imply teaching that sticks to the approved

Chapter Six

performance objectives, and "mastery" learning implies post-testing to see if students have achieved instructional objectives.

A U.S. Department of Education research newsletter on effective schools research distributed to all McKinley School teachers began with a military battle analogy: "The classroom is the command center where teachers win or lose the battle for academic achievement and order. If disruptive behavior prevails and discipline is weak or lacking, then the chances for victory are slim." It went on to claim: "Research shows . . . that instructors can reduce disruptive behavior and increase scholastic success by setting and enforcing clear rules at the beginning of the year, consistently rewarding good behavior, and promptly punishing misconduct. Within this framework, rewards and punishments should be incremental and designed for speedy application."[6] What gets endorsed, in all of these handouts, is a technical-rational mode of thinking about discipline problems that legitimates a process of schooling that dominates and alienates students. The professional discourse on "effective schools" and "classroom management" thus perpetuates the depoliticization of the power relations of urban schooling.

Finally, the principal at McKinley was a strong believer in the notion that teacher expectations influenced student classroom behavior in important ways, so he placed a good deal of emphasis on "positive thinking" among the staff and on setting high expectations for student achievement and behavior (also consistent with the effective schools model). One in-service workshop for teachers was devoted to a presentation by a speaker whom the assistant superintendent had first heard at an administrators' conference in Atlanta—a multiply-handicapped person whose message was: "We can rise above our handicaps through optimism and the power of positive thinking." The none-too-subtle implication was that McKinley School students were culturally or emotionally handicapped too, but could rise above their educational handicaps if teachers believed they could. The speaker concluded on an emotional note by telling the assembled teachers: "I'd rather spend one day with one leg and a positive attitude than the rest of my life with two legs and a negative attitude. . . . I struggled 16 years to learn how to tie my shoes with stumps of hands. I've overcome my handicaps, and your students can too. . . . Teachers *can* make a difference in children's lives. You can help instill optimism and a belief that you can be anything you want to be in your students." The presentation was followed by an informal session with teachers, at which time the speaker sold and autographed copies of his book. Most teachers did not stay for this informal session, however, and many left the meeting cynical and even resentful. As they drifted off, one teacher asked, "Do

"Classroom Management"

they [the administrators] think we're the reason why students aren't succeeding?" Another teacher remarked, "Positive thinking is fine, but I could do a lot more if they'd reduce class size." Still another asked, "Are they trying to pump us up, give us a pep talk?" Many rank-and-file teachers in McKinley thus rejected the philosophy of positive thinking as an attempt to shift blame to teachers, and they became cynical about the whole administrative approach to classroom management.

Teacher Responses to the Problem of Order

The negativistic comments by teachers leaving the workshop described above also point to a morale problem among teachers. In fact, there was a consensus among the McKinley School staff—both teachers and administrators—that teacher morale was at an all-time low, and that it was most directly related to problems with discipline in the school. For all teachers, discipline was an ongoing problem that affected the quality of their working lives. And, of course, beyond the narrow range of control some teachers were able to establish in their own classrooms, teachers had to worry about the problem of order and the possibility of confrontations in the halls and on the school grounds. Everyone seemed to know that drugs were being sold and used in the middle school, including crack, on a regular basis, yet administrators refused to confront the issue. In one unused classroom on the second floor, students regularly went to buy and use drugs. Teachers were also frustrated (as in Urbanville) by what they perceived to be an inequality between the rights of students and teachers, and by students' use of threats of legal action to intimidate and harass teachers. A popular expression among students in McKinley School was: "You touch me, I sue your ass." It was directed at teachers (some more than others) as a taunt, and as a way of challenging teachers' authority over students. Challenges to teachers' authority also involved threats of violent reprisal, so that teachers lived in a state of fear that someday a student in one of their classrooms would pull a knife or a gun on them. While toy knives and guns had been confiscated from students, so far no lethal weapons had been confiscated at the middle school; although most teachers felt that it was only a matter of time before such weapons appeared in the school. Furthermore, when students got angry, they could always find usable weapons around them. One teacher reported that when he had asked a boy who was being disruptive to sit down, the boy become very angry, threw himself into a rage, and ran out of

Chapter Six

the room yelling, "I'm going to go get a baseball bat and beat your f____in' head in." Within several minutes the boy was back, wielding a bat and advancing on the teacher. The teacher was able to dodge the bat as the boy swung at him, and the boy was later suspended, but when he returned the teacher had to find a way of working with him again. As the guidance counselor remarked of the case, "There's nothing we can do." In fact, the school staff could do little to help the boy, whose rage was partially related to a physically abusive home environment; nor could the school help teachers who justifiably felt the need to be protected from such students.

The staff at McKinley Middle School was severely restricted by districtwide discipline codes, state laws, and the courts in the exercise of authority over students. The discipline options available were listed on a special form which had to be completed each time a "negative consequence" was invoked against a student. These options included: after-school detention, lunch detention, parental note, suspension, conference with counselor, and administrative warning. Furthermore, the form stipulated specific consequences for each of 23 separate categories of student misconduct, so teachers were not free to select the form of punishment. For example, students who cut class (presuming they were caught) were "punished" with a session with the school counselor (for which they got out of class); and if students were assigned to detention but failed to show up, they merely received an administrative warning. Even relatively severe forms of punishment, such as short-term suspensions, were little more than vacations from school for some students and respites for their teachers. It was virtually impossible to expel students under the age of 16, since few alternative programs for juvenile offenders were available. Teachers could, in theory, write up paperwork to begin the process of getting disruptive students labeled as either "hyperactive," "emotionally disturbed," or "socially maladjusted" and removing them to special education "resource rooms" at least part of the day; but there was only so much space in resource rooms, since teacher-student ratios were kept low. Furthermore, there was a huge backlog of cases waiting to be reviewed by the school district committee that made classification recommendations. All of this meant that teachers had to cope with emotionally volatile, disruptive students on a regular everyday basis.

Each teacher in the school had developed a somewhat unique response to the problem of order. At one extreme was an eighth-grade teacher who was known for never yelling at students. If a student was being disruptive, she would tell him to follow her to the hall, where she would warn him: "If you fail my class, you won't get into high

"Classroom Management"

school." Since her math course was one of those students had to pass to get promoted, she could use this threat effectively. If a student became very disruptive, she immediately sent another student to the principal's office to get help. When help arrived, she merely said: "I want this child out of my room immediately." That seemed to do the trick in most cases. Of course, the fact that this teacher was a physically imposing woman probably contributed to her relative effectiveness as a classroom manager. At the other extreme was a fifth-grade teacher who had been over 20 years in the system and who was known to "scream at kids at the drop of a hat." Although there were many fights and confrontations in her classroom, she maintained order by out-yelling the students; and since she did not get into physical confrontations with students, she managed to stay out of trouble and was thus effective in her own way—even though she violated almost all of the guidelines of student discipline officially endorsed by the school principal.

She was also quite open and "unprofessional" in her dislike of certain students. One day in the teachers' lounge she reported that one of her students who had been suspended was back today. "My day is ruined," she said. "Sandra is back. I hate that bitch. I know, I know, I'm supposed to like all these kids, but some of them I can't." The band director, who was sitting next to the participant observer while this comment was being made, represented perhaps the most idealistic and humanistic perspective on classroom management among the teaching staff, and after the teacher described above left, he turned to the participant observer and commented, "I know there are different teaching styles, but I'm not sure about hers. Teaching is motivation. You have to motivate the kids." The participant observer noted that it was easy for a band director to talk about motivation, since all of his students were there because they wanted to be. "In my classes," the participant observer commented, "I've got these jerks who won't let me teach. And they don't care if they flunk my course because music doesn't count." The band director countered, "It's your job to motivate them. 'Cover' yourself and teach what you have to teach, but try to relate the curriculum more to their interests." The band director was generally respected by other teachers in McKinley School, but because of his somewhat unique position, most teachers viewed him as idealistic rather than realistic when it came to teacher-student relations.

Another group of teachers was in a relatively unique position in this overwhelmingly Hispanic school. Although less than ten percent of McKinley School's teaching staff was Hispanic, Hispanic teachers (most of them bilingual teachers) were generally believed to have a

Chapter Six

significant advantage when it came to maintaining student discipline. One of the teachers most respected by students was a Cuban-born bilingual teacher. As a middle-class Cuban, she came from a higher-status Hispanic background than many of the poor Puerto Rican and Dominican students whom she taught, and she believed that "these children are lucky to have me." She rarely yelled at students, but when she did it was in Spanish, and it generally got their attention. She also frequently got on the telephone and called parents and grandparents who could only speak Spanish and enlisted their aid in punishing or rewarding students. While this teacher used her Hispanic cultural background and language to her advantage, Anglo teachers often complained that language and culture differences worked against them. For example, Hispanic students could choose not to hear Anglo teachers when they did not want to hear, on the pretense that they did not understand, and they could mockingly direct obscenities at teachers or make jokes about them in front of the class and get away with it so long as the teacher spoke only English. Male teachers were often called "Pato," which literally meant "duck" in Spanish, but which also meant "faggot" or "queer" in Puerto Rican slang. In this case, boys asserted their macho identity by defining the "other" (in this case, male teachers) as homosexual and presumably therefore non-masculine. This incident also suggests, more generally, that Hispanic student resistance to the schooling process in McKinley School was related to the establishment of a cultural identity separate from, and in opposition to, to the dominant Anglo culture of the school. Because students did not feel the need to establish a separate cultural identity in their relations with Hispanic teachers, these teachers experienced fewer control problems.

Only a few teachers in McKinley School resorted on a regular basis to physical force and verbal intimidation in controlling students. Although these teachers were relatively isolated on the staff and their classroom control techniques frowned upon, the general perspective among teachers was one of "live and let live," and administrators only intervened or reprimanded these teachers when they got into trouble with parents. One of these authoritarian teachers, whom I will call Jim, was a seventh-grade teacher. Jim was a former Vietnam Vet who appeared to be suffering from post-traumatic stress syndrome. Near the beginning of the year he had confided to a fellow teacher and Vietnam Vet that he was having marital problems and had fantasized about shooting his wife and children. The fellow teacher persuaded him to seek counselling from a psychiatrist, which he subsequently did. The psychiatrist had prescribed heavy doses of valium—a tranquilizer—which Jim used when he was teaching. Still, he seemed emotion-

"Classroom Management"

ally unstable and easily angered. Once Jim walked into the faculty lounge at lunchtime and, after complaining about how bad his students were that day, announced that: "the best way to establish discipline in this school would be to hold an assembly on the first day of each year in the auditorium. You get all the students assembled, and you pick one at random. You put him up on the stage and shoot him, and then tell all the other students, 'There, that's for nothing. Now mess up!' " Near Halloween, he told a group of teachers in the faculty lounge that: "I'm tired of those little brats coming around and soaping my windows. This year I'm going to rig up a trip-wire right in front of my window, connected to the trigger of a gun." In both of these instances, other teachers assembled in the lounge did not criticize Jim when he made these comments. For the most part they remained silent. But after he left they were more open in their criticism. One teacher asked, "How can he be saying those things?" Another commented, "Maybe he wasn't cut out to be a teacher." And yet another warned, "Someday he's going to hurt someone. Then we'll all suffer." In fact, later in the year Jim was suspended for a few days after a black student complained to her parents that he had slapped her. But he was allowed to count these as sick days. Once he came back, teachers began to express more disapproval of his behavior among themselves. But unless or until he got himself involved in a more serious infraction, the chances were that Jim would continue to teach in McKinley School. While his troubles obviously had personal roots, it is also likely that his high-stress, high-conflict job made his condition worse.

The Problem of Teacher Morale

Work-related stress also lowers teacher morale, even among effective classroom managers; and teacher morale at McKinley School was, according to many teachers, at an all-time low during the year of the study. Administrators were as much or more concerned with the teacher morale problem than they were with the student discipline problem (although the two problems were closely related) because demoralized teachers undermined the achievement of instructional goals. Consequently, the principal at McKinley School decided to devote a major part of the December faculty meeting to the topic of teacher morale. He began the meeting by saying, "I wanted to have this talk today so we can start off the New Year fresh when we come back from the holiday break." He reported that he had recently conferred with the superintendent about teacher morale at McKinley

Chapter Six

and that "he [the superintendent] shares my concern that something be done about this problem." Part of the problem, according to the principal, was that "because morale is low, teacher absenteeism has been high, so I've had to call on more teachers to give up their unscheduled periods to 'cover' classes, and that lowers morale even more." While this was insightful on the principal's part, the effect was to shift the discussion to teacher absenteeism and the importance of teachers showing up for work every day.

The principal also maintained that morale had been adversely affected by an "atmosphere of rumors and gossip" in the school. The principal referred, more specifically, to recent rumors to the effect that he was pushing one of the older teachers to resign because he believed she was ineffective in managing student discipline problems. The teacher had been assigned a class composed of some of the most delinquent and hyperactive students in the fifth grade, and many teachers presumed this was an intentional effort on the part of the principal to push her out. The most recent rumor concerning this teacher was that a student was seen running out of her classroom into an adjoining class, where he reported that his teacher was crying with her head down on the desk. The teacher later denied she had been crying, but many teachers believed the rumor and took it as a sign that she was was in emotional distress and needed help. About these rumors, the principal commented: "I want you to know I had nothing to do with Mrs. ——— 's assignment this year. I think we would all benefit if there were fewer rumormongers in the school."

Finally, the principal related the morale problem to some teachers' "negativity." He argued that: "The new year can be a new beginning if we all decide to think positively rather than focus on the negative. . . . Remember, we're here for the children." At that, he changed the topic and announced, "We have a new 17-year old student enrolled today who is from the Dominican Republic. He is being assigned to the sixth grade." Several teachers moaned audibly at the prospect of what they presumed would be yet another slow and probably "difficult" student in the school. Interestingly, in a meeting devoted to the topic of teacher morale, the principal consistently managed to frame discussion in such a way that teachers were blamed for lowering their own morale. Furthermore, very little was heard from teachers at this meeting; they would do their own talking (gossiping, the principal would say) once the meeting was over.

The teacher morale problem, and its relationship to the discipline problem, prompted the principal to schedule yet another meeting in January—this time a special after-school meeting on the topic of stu-

"Classroom Management"

dent discipline, with all concerned teachers encouraged to attend and make their views known to school administrators. More pragmatically and informally, the meeting was presented as an opportunity for teachers to vent their anger and frustrations. As the vice principal put it in a conversation with the participant observer, "We need a meeting where teachers can just 'vent.' " The implicit human relational assumption here is that while no real solutions could be offered to raise teacher morale, at least some of teachers' distress with their condition could be temporarily relieved through a cathartic "bitch session" where they were allowed to "get it off their chests." The meeting, held in the teachers' lounge, was attended by approximately fifty teachers (nearly fifty percent of the teaching staff), the three building administrators, the teacher union president, and several building representatives for the union. Teachers dominated discussion in this meeting—it was after all, billed as a teacher "bitch session"—and administrators responded rather briefly and directly to various proposals and suggestions by teachers.

The meeting began with four teachers speaking in support of an "in-house suspension" system, similar to that implemented in an adjoining school district. In that district, according to the teachers, disruptive students could be removed from class and placed in a special classroom under the watchful eye of a militaristic male teacher where they worked on assigned homework, were not allowed to talk, could go to the bathroom only at specific times, etc. Students in the district referred to in-house suspension as "the box" and, the teachers claimed, took it seriously as a form of punishment. One of the teachers concluded: "I think most teachers believe we should reconsider an in-house suspension room as an option." After the teachers had made their points, the principal responded to this proposal in a rather curt manner. He claimed that, "in-house suspension is not a possibility we can consider. As I've explained before, it would require coming up with a vacant classroom all day every day, and we'd have to hire another teacher to staff it." In-house suspension was a proposal that had been raised time and again by teachers, and this time it was quickly shot down as an option.

The next suggestion offered by a teacher was that intercoms be installed in all classrooms so that teachers could contact the office when they needed help in handling a student fight or disturbance. The principal commented: "I agree with you that we need intercoms. I've asked for an intercom system for three years in a row now. Maybe in a few more years, when I retire, you'll get one." The principal did not have to explain his meaning to the teachers; they all knew that their

Chapter Six

school suffered because the principal was not well liked by the superintendent, while the other middle school principal was the superintendent's chosen "heir apparent." While teachers generally sympathized with the principal in this regard, one teacher commented privately to the participant observer: "Why should we have to suffer because he [the principal] can't get along with the superintendent? It's not fair."

After the intercom suggestion was rejected, several teachers then spoke in support of hiring uniformed security guards for each floor of the three-story school building. According to one teacher, "The two security guards we have now are nice people, and I have nothing against them, but the kids don't respect them. They have no authority. Maybe if they wore uniforms kids would respect them more." Another teacher suggested that security guards should have walkie-talkies so that they could communicate with the office. "Without walkie-talkies they're isolated. I've seen Ricardo [one of the security guards] out supervising the playground, yelling at kids to get away from the principal's parking lot, and they yell back, 'Oh Ricardo, get a life.' He's alone out there, isolated, without a way to call for help if he needed it. It's the *pack mentality* you have to face when you're isolated as an authority figure." The teacher union president finally ended the discussion of security guards without administrators having to say anything. He advised: "We can suggest to the Board that it hire more guards and give them uniforms and walkie-talkies, but it's not a negotiable item. So don't expect much." That ended that.

Next, a teacher suggested Saturday detention as a possibility. But the principal cautioned, "If you open the school on a Saturday, even for a few hours, I'm going to have to be present, and you're going to have to pay me and the maintenance staff to come in just to open up the school so you can have detention for maybe 30 students. It doesn't make sense to me." Several teachers also opposed the idea, since teachers would have to take turns staffing the detention classroom on Saturdays. One asked, "Do we have to punish ourselves to punish the children?" So that killed that idea, and the hour-long meeting ended without any progress being made—although teachers had at least "vented." As teachers drifted away from the meeting, they articulated a variety of responses. One teacher felt that the meeting had been worthwhile because it improved communication between teachers and the principal. She commented: "He's trying to do his best. He's caught in the process just like we are." But other teachers were more cynical. One claimed, "If you really open your mouth at one of these meetings and say what you think, you'll be covering classes from now on." Another said, "You waste your time, and nothing changes."

"Classroom Management"

The problem of teacher morale, among other things, made it more difficult to hold and attract highly qualified teachers in McKinley School. For example, the new seventh-grade science teacher lasted only three months before she submitted her letter of resignation because she "couldn't take it anymore." For over two months after she walked out, no replacement could be found for her, so her classes were covered by other teachers in the school during their unassigned periods. None of these teachers, of course, were science teachers, so the class reverted to a study hall. Finally, when a new science teacher was hired, she spent one day observing in the school and said she had changed her mind. Even though a third science teacher was finally hired, who stayed the year, the administration had to presume he might not return next fall. Teachers sometimes talked about getting a job in another district, but the security that tenure provided generally stopped them from pursuing this idea very far. One teacher complained to the participant observer: "You're still young, you can find yourself a better job in a suburban district. I'm stuck here." Teachers with particular talents were sometimes depicted as fools for continuing to teach in the school. One teacher commented of a fellow teacher: "She's got talents; she could be making money. So why is she wasting her time here?" This self-deprecating talk among teachers reflected their demoralization; and it implied that teaching inner-city, primarily minority students, was not a very "good" job. It was a job teachers tolerated because they perceived themselves to be "stuck," or lacking in the talent or initiative to get a better job; but it was not a job of which many teachers were very proud. Rather, they were teaching in McKinley School only until "something better comes along" or because they were "stuck" there. Such an attitude obviously not only reflects, it contributes to, the malaise of urban schooling; and since many students are no doubt aware of this attitude, it probably contributes to a lowering of students' sense of self-worth, along with their respect for teachers, which increases discipline problems. Once more, this points to the close links between student discipline and teacher morale problems, and the vicious cycle they organize.

"Getting Over" at McKinley Middle School

McKinley Middle School was hardly effective in educating and socializing its students, by any standard and according to any definition of effectiveness. It constituted a precarious social order, one in which everyone was involved in "getting over" on those further up the bureau-

Chapter Six

cratic chain of command. "Getting over" was a term in the students' discourse, although it was occasionally used by teachers as well, since it captured so well the sense of life in the school. One teacher reported to the participant observer an example of student use of the term. "When kids were leaving my class I heard them talking in the hall, and they were saying, 'We're going to get over on Mrs. ——— [their next teacher]. Angel's going to start something to distract her, then we'll see what we can get away with." Students also got over on the school staff by doing such things as standing in line for lunch tickets twice, taunting teachers to distract and frustrate them, cheating on tests and copying homework, lying to teachers, and cutting classes. What all of these various forms of getting over had in common was the aim of working what space was left available within the interstices of power to subvert its claims and objectives. Students' instrumentalism in pursuing their perceived interests is a sad ——— ——— narrowing of young people's struggle for self-ideu... ..gic against the educational institution that could potentially empower at least some of them. It is also a symptom of crisis, and of the inability of the school system to win over students. One teacher said that she lectured to her students: "You think you can get through life getting over on everybody. But it won't work."

The trouble was, getting over *did* work within the immediate context, and everyone in the school was engaged in their own game of getting over. Teachers put things in their plan books they never had any intention of teaching, just to get over on the administration; and they made up figures in filling out forms on student skill levels. The principal was engaged in a desperate game of covering up discipline problems and persistent low achievement in the school. When a group of state legislators visited the school they were given a carefully guided tour that kept them away from students as much as possible, and students were assigned to homerooms for the duration of the visit so none would be seen moving in the halls. The McKinley School administrators also sought to manage an impression of a well run school with the central administration, and sometimes this meant not assigning punishments which had to be reported to the central office. The vice-principal once told the participant observer, "I've already suspended seven kids today and ——— [the superintendent] will be on my back if I suspend any more, so no matter what they do, I'm not going to suspend any more students today." The principal also appealed to teachers to help him get over on central office administrators and state officials by getting copies of old tests and teaching to the test in a very direct manner to raise test scores to the desired level. He once told teachers at a faculty meeting: "I never thought I'd hear myself say this, but teach to the test. We're being monitored by the state and if those test scores don't rise, we may lose our certification, and no one wants that." Furthermore, when tests were administered, absent students did not get included in computing average achievement levels, nor did the large number of bilingual and labeled students. The management of crisis was all form and little substance. Just how long everyone would be able to manage an impression and work the system without acknowledging the reality of the crisis remained unanswered and unanswerable.

Conclusion

In this chapter, one of my concerns has been with the issue of how effective modern, bureaucratic-rational models and discourses of classroom management have been in resolving the problem of order in urban schools. Data from both Urbanville and McKinley School support the conclusion that businesslike models of classroom management may have defused some classroom conflict, but that teacher-student conflicts and classroom disruptions continued to be a major source of job stress and burnout for teachers. Student fights, emotional outbursts, and teacher-student confrontations were everyday school and classroom occurrences, and they were more or less successfully contained rather than prevented. The case studies also suggest that teachers' power as authority figures in the classroom has been increasingly restricted over the past several decades as control has become more bureaucratic and technical. Yet because a complete depersonalization or rationalization of oppressive forms of control is not fully possible, high levels of teacher-student conflict may be endemic to the current system of urban schooling. Teachers are confronted with a problem of order they are unable to effectively manage; and this increases teacher frustration and lowers teacher morale. It also leads many teachers to define their students as the "other," the enemy that one has to subdue or be subdued by; and this in turn is encouraged by and reinforces racist interpretations of the problem of order.

The McKinley School data in particular indicate that many teachers were what Gerald Levy has called "chronic" urban school teachers—those who learn to survive within the system and maintain some semblance of order, in the face of ongoing disruptions and challenges to their authority, by "not taking it personally."[7] Levy contrasts chronic

Chapter Six

teachers with teachers who generally do not last in the system—which he calls "acute" teachers. Of acute teachers, Levy writes: "Confronted with the children's irreverence and disobedience the acute teacher responds with anger and deep feelings of personal inadequacy and unworthiness. He [SIC] takes it personally. In not being able to fulfill his image of an educator and becoming instead an object of ridicule and a source of entertainment for the children, he experiences his humiliation directly and intimately. In the act of failing he reacts as if the failure were happening to him.... Eventually, acute teachers realize the impracticality of their emotional responses. They learn to ignore all attempts of children to elicit a personal response."[8] Ironically, the distancing and detachment of the chronic teacher, which Levy associates with teacher resignation and cynicism, is supported in most of the dominant classroom management models as a sign of effective teaching. This also suggests that the system is less concerned with educating students in empowering ways than in controlling them in a narrow, prescriptive way. The ideal teacher from the perspective of the dominant classroom management model is one who effectively controls or manages students in completing routine classroom work assignments.

This raises concerns about whether the more complete rationalization of authority in education should be considered a progressive development. Within the dominant Weberian discourse in Western social theory, the rationalization of institutional authority has been treated as basically progressive and as consistent with an end of ideology in society—a desirable development from this perspective. In some ways, modern classroom management models of control *are* progressive, especially when the alternative is understood to be some form of despotic control of students. We need to guard against a return to the traditional despotic control of urban school children as documented, for example, in Jonothan Kozol's influential *Death at an Early Age*, which graphically described teaching in an inner-city Boston school in the mid-1960s, where control was established through the brutalization of young black children by white teachers.[9] Kozol wrote: "Children are beaten with thin bamboo whips within the cellars of our public schools and ... they are whipped at times for no greater offense than for failing to show respect to the very same teachers who have been describing them as niggers.... At my school ... students were repeatedly grabbed, shaken and insulted.... At least one child in my school was whipped in such a way as to leave on his hand a physical impairment in the form of a large raised scar which may be with him all his life."[10] While some of the physical and emotional intimidation of students documented in these accounts of urban school teaching still go on, the past two decades have witnessed a drastic decline in the use of such control tactics in both schools and in society more generally, and in important ways this has been a progressive development.

From a more critical perspective, however, the classroom management discourse may be said to divert our attention away from the need to restructure teacher-student relations in far more radical, democratic ways. Furthermore, the rationalization of authority in the classroom has been coextensive with the increased rationalization and predetermination of work tasks for both teachers and students, and the more complete subordination of teachers and students to the state and central office plan for basic skills productivity. Dominant classroom management models not only manage classroom conflict, they participate in the disempowerment of teachers and students. If empowering forms of schooling would necessitate personal, caring relationships between teachers and students, then current disempowering forms of urban schooling necessitate some level of bureaucratic impersonality to contain conflict. Consequently, in responding to the problem of order in urban schools, we must challenge more broadly the Weberian presumption that "rational" or "modern" modes of organizing production and structuring organizations have arisen primarily because they represent advancements over earlier, less rational forms.[11] Behind the supposed impersonality and neutrality of the "scientific management" of institutional conflict lies a legitimating ideology that supports particular social interests. This ideology facilitates the efficient appropriation of labor power from students in the interests of achieving certain predetermined skill "outputs," and it presupposes particular social and technical relations of production in the classroom. Consequently, any endorsement of classroom management approaches must be provisional and circumstantial. In many ways, they are better than a return to the tradition forms of control which they replaced in urban schools; but these approaches do not provide the basis for an adequate resolution of the crisis of control in urban schooling.

7

Beyond the Crisis in Urban Schooling

I pursue several interconnected lines of argument in this concluding chapter, which both summarize and develop themes I have explored throughout this study. In doing so, I divide my comments into four major sections. I begin with a brief review of the case study data from the Urbanville school district and McKinley Middle School; and in doing so I suggest one final reading of the case study text and what it has to say about teachers' work culture in the basic skills era of urban school crisis management. I then examine three major discourses in education that offer solutions or remedies in responding to the urban school crisis, and I indicate how teachers get treated in each of these discourses: (1) a conservative, bureaucratic state discourse that continues to push new forms of rationalization and bureaucratic hierarchical control in the schools; (2) a liberal discourse that affirms the Enlightenment or democratic ideals of excellence and equity in education but that is undermined by contradictions; and (3) an emergent democratic-progressive discourse that shifts attention to struggles organized around class, race, and gender and to workplace democratization. My basic argument is that elements from liberal and democratic-progressive discourses need to be articulated (or interrelated) and also rearticulated (or restated in a new way for a new context) in order to develop a democratic oppositional discourse that can challenge the status quo in urban school reform. I also suggest that teacher unionism and collective bargaining will need to be reconceived in restructuring

Chapter Seven

urban schools consistent with principles of workplace democratization, and that economic interests and dominant instrumental worldviews in the culture will need to be challenged.

The Case Studies: Teachers and Crisis

In Midstate, state education officials gained wide new powers over local school and school district sites, particularly those in urban areas, during the basic skills era; and they deployed a discourse of basic skills reform as part of their project of consolidating control over urban school districts. This rise of the educational state resulted from a fiscal crisis in urban school districts which made them increasingly dependent upon the state budget, and also from a movement to raise standards in urban schools through state-mandated minimum competency testing. While these transformations in the control and governance of urban schools were occurring, teachers in Midstate assumed an ambivalent role. They supported increased state spending in education and the new role of the state in raising educational standards; and in fact they were among the strongest lobbying groups (aside from the business community) which supported an increased educational role for the state to save urban school districts. Nevertheless, they became increasingly disenchanted with the state's role in saving urban schools once its reform agenda began to take shape and it became obvious that classroom teachers were one of the big losers in reform. Still, it was difficult to oppose a reform movement that claimed to be about raising standards and making public schools accountable. While teachers could claim a few victories in their lobbying effort at the state level—most particularly a teacher salary bill that significantly raised the base pay for entry level teachers in the state—lobbying at the state level did not pay off very well for Midstate teachers, at least during the era of the conservative state. This suggests that at the state level teachers might have been more productive and successful in advancing their perceived interests and resisting further bureaucratic subordination if they had spent more time developing links and articulating a common oppositional discourse with other movements outside the state, such as civil rights, trade union, and women's rights movements.

The movement to consolidate educational decision-making at the state level was associated at the local school district level with a central office initiative to reorganize the curriculum and the instructional process around a teach to the test philosophy designed to produce the

Beyond the Crisis

paperwork and quantitative output data required by state officials for funding and monitoring purposes. Along the way, teachers—especially elementary teachers—had new peformance-based lesson and unit planning requirements imposed upon them, were scanned by administrators and effective schools researchers to eliminate time wastage in the classroom, and were evaluated according to a one best way of teaching basic skills that was highly prescriptive, prestructured, and output-based. Teachers resisted these changes in their terms and conditions of employment through their local teacher union, but they were largely unsuccessful because the courts and the state legislature interpreted terms and conditions of employment in a very narrow sense as limited to the wage-labor exchange—the hours of labor, the wages paid, the breaks allowed, the meetings that teachers had to attend, and so forth.

While Urbanville teachers may not have been able to block the erosion of job control that accompanied basic skills reform initiatives, they did learn to play the contract game to their advantage as much as possible to resist a broad spectrum of changes in their existing working conditions. In the contract game teachers sought to maximize their pay and minimize their hours of labor and assigned duties, at the same time that the administration, from its side, sought to get more work out of teachers at a given wage and make teachers take on new assignments and duties. Playing the game represented a very limited challenge by teachers to the institutional power relations and structures that subordinated them, and it did not provide teachers with many victories. Nevertheless, without the constant threat that the teacher union would file a contract grievance if the administration pressed its advantage, things might well have been much worse for teachers. Furthermore, even in its current non-threatening form, teacher unionism appears to threaten bureaucratic elite interests by encouraging a work-to-the-contract sentiment among teachers and by sharply differentiating teachers' interests from those of administrators. So long as teachers' and administrators' relations are organized in terms of a zero-sum game, they are likely to devote an inordinate amount of time to the game and to undermining each other's efforts and countering each other's moves rather than to their common interest in the education of students.

Finally, I have argued that basic skills reform has been associated with new responses to the crisis of student discipline and classroom order that have implications for the structuring of teachers' relations with students. The data on classroom conflict and classroom management from Urbanville, along with that from the participant observational study at McKinley Middle School, suggest that basic skills

Chapter Seven

restructuring has involved the institutionalization of a highly rationalized, depersonalized, businesslike approach to student control problems. Repressive and coercive forms of student control in urban schools have gradually given way to more bureaucratically rational and modern approaches to managing institutional conflict. Not only are such approaches to control more consistent with the overall rationalization of curriculum, the instructional process, and the role of the teacher, but they have also been promoted in the attempt to overcome some of the negative consequences of repressive control—i. e., its tendency to arouse more student resistance.

The rationalization of control may have helped defuse some of the conflict associated with the imposition of power relations of domination and subordination through the curriculum and instructional process, but clearly it has not been able to fully contain the rage, anger, and resistances of urban students. Teachers in Urbanville, and more particularly in McKinley Middle School, pressed for more help from the administration in maintaining order in the school and classroom, but with little effect. In fact, administrators had few good options in managing the discipline problem effectively. They had been increasingly restricted by courts and the state legislature which prevented any use of corporal punishment or verbal intimidation (the traditional means of control in urban schools). In an era when urban schools have been doing the most they can to keep students in school and discourage them from dropping out, repressive control also become a less realistic option if school officials want to lower the drop-out rate. Finally, since the civil rights era the use of overtly repressive force in urban schools to contain student resistance may no longer be a viable option politically since such force, more than anything else, would delegitimate the claim that urban schools are about empowering students disadvantaged by class and race. Given these conditions, the problem of order threatens to deepen in the years ahead, especially if urban schools prepare more and more of their students for a growing American underclass. Teachers obviously have interests in the maintenance of order in urban schools, as do students and parents; but they must also work for a better resolution of the problem of order which goes beyond law-and-order appeals and strategies if they are to link up with a progressive movement for responding to the urban school crisis.

Aside from the legal and administratives constraints placed on teachers in attempting to resist the basic skills restructuring of their work, play the contract game more to their advantage, and cope effectively with the crisis of discipline and classroom order, teachers have been constrained by limitations internal to the teachers' union movement.

Beyond the Crisis

One of these is oligarchic tendencies. Of course, the legal and judicial constraints on teacher union power and influence no doubt contributed to widespread rank-and-file apathy in Urbanville, which in turn contributed to oligarchic tendencies in union leadership, which led to more apathy and less involvement by the rank and file. Nevertheless, little was done throughout the study period to counter these oligarchic tendencies or even to directly acknowledge them. Inextricably intertwined with oligarchic tendencies were patriarchal tendencies within the local teacher union. Hegemonic gender power relations of male domination and female subordination were thus enacted through the operation of a union that primarily served women, and these power relations need to be reconstituted in order to counter rank-and-file apathy and oligarchic tendencies.

Finally, the teacher union movement also was contrained by its failure to articulate teacher interests in opposing basic skills reforms with those of various community groups and thus forge a movement to challenge basic skills restructuring in a more comprehensive and politicized fashion. Racial differences appeared to play a significant role in blocking such a potential alliance between teachers and community groups in Urbanville; although more generally teachers' professional values encouraged them to side with the institution in resisting pressure from "outside" (i.e., community) groups. The involvement of urban schools in constituting racial power relations of domination by whites and subordination of other racial "others" also means that white teachers are encouraged to view their conflicts with students in racial terms and are less likely to side with their students and appreciate their perspectives. This contributes to some teachers' support for conservative, law-and-order approaches to student discipline. As with classist and patriarchal tendencies, these racist tendencies within the teachers' union movement need to be confronted and countered if teachers are to play a significant role in challenging the status quo in public education.

The Conservative State Discourse on Urban School Reform

The basic skills reform initiative that participated in shaping these developments in Midstate, Urbanville and McKinley Middle School, and that has provided a context for the construction of teachers' work culture along particular lines, has been coextensive with a "conservative restoration" in American politics that began in the late 1960s.[1]

Chapter Seven

Ironically, the official conservative platform throughout the 1970s and 1980s has been anti-statist, and has supported the notion that power should be decentralized and that the public school monopoly should be broken up and replaced with a free enterprise voucher system of education. Yet once in positions of state power, conservatives have supported policies that have had the effect of centralizing more power in the hands of state officials, although under the "new federalism" much of this power has shifted from the federal to the state tier of government. Despite all the rhetoric about privatizing the schools and providing parents with more choice in the education of their children, designed to appeal to a broad range of white, "middle Americans" and a New Right constituency, conservatives in the state have not pressed for the dismantling of the public schools—far from it. Instead, the conservative reform initiative has restructured and redirected the schools to bring them under more effective centralized economic and political steerage. It has also done so at a time when poor African-American and Hispanic peoples were reclaiming a space within urban America where they were an electoral majority.[2] While the civil rights movement had held out the hope that through control of the political machinery in major urban areas, disadvantaged groups might be able to redirect public institutions to serve new, non-oppressive ends, in education at least, this hope has not been realized.

The conservative state, in cooperation with corporate America, has sold or marketed this reform agenda in a number of ways. First, it has articulated basic skills reforms in terms of upholding traditional cultural values and returning to a romanticized American past. For example, state officials have sought to link minimum competency testing to public concern about a decline in educational standards, suggesting that such testing represented a return to the good old days when people supposedly earned their diplomas through hard work and discipline. They also related basic skills reforms to America's continued economic competitiveness, particularly competition with Japan and other "aggressive" economic powers that threatened American pre-emminence in the new world order. The appeal is to an *authoritarian populism* that looks backward to a romanticized past and taps patriotic and nationalistic sentiments.[3] Ironically, while conservative discourse appealed to a desire to return to the good old days, basic skills reforms were not traditional at all. They represented an advanced technicization and rationalization of the educative process, and the skills they taught were pegged to the skill needs of a new post-industrial work force.

Second, the conservative state discourse has been fairly successful in articulating this package of basic skills reforms in terms of democratic values and traditions that, on the surface at least, appear progressive. Much of this discourse has presented basic skills and functional literacy as the essential prerequisites, the real-life skills that all people (particularly socioeconomicially disadvantaged students) need to participate fully as citizens and advance themselves socially and economically. Because disadvantaged students presumably do not get these cultural capital basic skills in their deprived home environments, urban schools, it is argued, must focus on the basics in order to give urban students a fighting chance in a competitive job market. All of this may sound convincing on one level, and it has a certain truth to it. Disadvantaged students *do* need a fighting chance and they are ill-equipped to compete unless they get a good, basic education. However, by focusing upon mastery of a rationalized set of literacy skills, presented to students in a regimented and routinized form, basic skills reforms have had the effect of setting up many urban students for jobs in the new American working- and underclasses. They do this by orienting students towards a technical-rational use of language, the coding and decoding of data, and self-disciplined adherence to routine. Furthermore, many students tend to to get tracked in basic skills courses by the middle and high school years through placement in some combination of low ability group classes, the new remedial classes designed for students who are at risk of failing the new state-mandated competency tests, and special education classes for emotionally disturbed students and other students with diagnosed learning disabilities. The possibility of going on to college begins to recede for these students rather quickly because they do not take all the courses four-year colleges require for admission, and a whole set of expectations begins to shape their school careers.

A third way in which basic skills reforms have been sold is through the promotion of the notion that school reform is a managerial rather than political concern, and that the most appropriate models to draw upon in reforming the schools come from the world of business. As Thomas Timar and David Kirp report in their recent study of state-sponsored school reform in the 1980s, the conservative discourse "asserts that schools are organizationally similar to business and industry: they are hierarchically structured organizations with a board of directors—the state board of education—at the top and various management units below." Student achievement on standardized tests—the product of education—"can be changed in the same way that industrial production can be changed, by simply altering the factors of production." Curriculum, instruction, the organization of teachers' work, etc., all become manipulable variables in the centralized managerial plan, and the objective is to find the "right combination of factors" to

Chapter Seven

increase output the most.[4] In these ways, business models of organization and control, and business conceptions of the bottom line, productivity, and efficiency, are taken for granted and treated as politically neutral and disinterested, when in reality they are deeply implicated in the construction of power relations of domination and subordination.

Finally, and related to this last point, basic skills reforms have been legitimated through claims that such reforms represent the outgrowth of scientific research on effective schools. The message of effective schools sponsors is a hopeful one, and this no doubt enhances its political appeal among a broad spectrum of middle-class and white Americans who have grown tired of the despairing picture critics have painted of an oppressive, unresponsive, racist urban school system and who do not want to see their taxes raised to pay for expensive new initiatives to save urban schools.[5] The effective schools research has helped state officials maintain the image that they have things under control, that progress is being made, that substantially more money is not needed, and that all that is needed is a better application of the principles derived from effective schools research. Cleo Cherryholmes refers to this as *vulgar pragmatism*, a form of thinking about educational issues that "results when efficiency is pursued in the absence of criticism, when actions are privileged over thought, when practice is valued and theory disparaged, when practice is divorced from theory (as if that were possible) for the sake of making things work better."[6] This vulgar, unreflective acceptance of the existing structure of institutional power relations prevails throughout conservative state reform models; and the end-of-ideology thesis it celebrates serves to depoliticize (and thus legitimate) state intervention in education to support elite rather than democratic interests.

For teachers the basic skills era has led to further bureaucratic subordination and de-professionalization, particularly at the elementary level; and these developments have occurred during the same period that state officials and prestigious commissions have called for the further professionalization of teaching. Basic skills reforms have made teachers much more accountable to central office administrators and state officials than they were in the pre-basic skills era, although top-down accountability models of control have a long tradition that goes back to the 19th century and the early common school movement and includes the "cult of efficiency" and "scientific management" movements in education during the early progressive era.[7] However, by the late 1960s, technological advances in curriculum design, along with the organization of instruction consistent with new systems theory

Beyond the Crisis

models of production, allowed state officials and local bureaucratic elites to come much closer than ever before to standardizing and predetermining the classroom work routine and thus removing substantial control of work processes from teachers. At the same time, the acceptance by the state of the industrial labor relations model, and with it collective bargaining, facilitated the implementation of basic skills reforms, since collective bargaining laws explicitly excluded teachers from involvement in managerial decisions, such as the form and content of the curriculum, the organization of instruction, and the evaluation of teachers and students. Basic skills restructuring thus has been dependent upon an industrial model of labor-management relations, with a clear bifurcation of roles and chain of command. This also suggests that the current form of teacher unionism and the conservative state reform model, while oppositional in some ways, participate in a broader discursive unification.

While the conservative state reform movement of the 1970s and 1980s was fairly successful in getting its reform package implemented in urban schools, its approach to the management of the multi-faceted urban school crisis has not worked in quite the way its supporters claimed it would. The vulgar pragmatic planning model in urban education—which participates in the constitution of class, gender, and racial power relations—also alienates teachers and students in ways that encourage minimal compliance and active resistance to the structuring of their working lives in the school. The ongoing legitimation of basic skills reforms as serving the interests of socioeconomically disadvantaged groups also presents dominant groups with problems, and this becomes more apparent as we move into the post-industrial era. In terms of a Weberian systems theory, the educational goals of the system are displaced towards compliance with regulations and production of standardized, quantitative output data, and the system literally begins to drown in red tape. As Timar and Kirp remark: "The dilemma for central [state] reformers is to create rules for governing bureaucratic behavior without those rules becoming ends in themselves."[8] In striving for uniformity and standardization, the dominant state planning model actually succeeds in fragmenting the educational planning process. While the limitations of conservative, bureaucratic state discourse are considerable, it may continue to play a central role in the management of urban school crisis in the coming decade. Nevertheless, the rough outlines of a liberal response to the conservative state reform discourse have begun to emerge since the mid-1980s, although so far it has been limited in its influence, especially over state-sponsored reform initiatives.

Chapter Seven
Liberal Discourse and "Saving Urban Schools"

The liberal discourse has been articulated by various coalitions of interests operating, for the most part, outside the state, including corporate-sponsored or endowed foundations (notably the Carnegie Foundation for the Advancement of Teaching), a coalition of universities involved in teacher education (the Holmes Group), and networks and coalitions of schools committed to humanistic reform principles (such as Theodore Sizer's Coalition of Essential Schools).[9] Taken as a whole, these liberal groups have presented an insightful critique of current bureaucratic state reform efforts and demonstrated the need for a radical de-bureaucratization and decentralization of power within the system; and their critique has received serious attention in the academy and in the media. However, as I will argue, the liberal alternative to the conservative state reform package lacks a sufficient theoretical analysis of the relationship between schooling and the constitution of socioeconomic inequality, and hence of the impediments that stand in the way of restructuring schools in isolation from restructuring in other cultural spheres and sites.

The most influential foundation during the 1980s to articulate a liberal discourse on the urban school crisis was the Carnegie Foundation for the Advancement of Teaching, under the leadership of Ernest Boyer, and as represented particularly in two influential reports: *A Nation Prepared: Teachers for the 21st Century* (1986), and *An Imperiled Generation: Saving Urban Schools* (1988). The first of these reports, by the Carnegie Forum's Task Force on Teaching as a Profession, is most sophisticated and detailed in its analysis, although the second applies the reasoning developed in the first report more specifically to the issue of urban school crisis. Let me briefly, then, describe the logic advanced in each of these reports in turn and then point out some of the insights, but also the limitations and contradictions implicit in their analysis of the urban school crisis. *A Nation Prepared* stands as perhaps the most succinct liberal response to *A Nation at Risk*, the Reagan administration's blueprint for educational reform; and like that report, it grounds its argument on an analysis of the relationship between the nation's economic strength and the quality of public education. But while *A Nation at Risk* called for higher academic standards, more teacher accountability, more testing, and more emphasis on basic skills to meet the "Japanese challenge," the Carnegie Forum report calls for both economic and educational restructuring to meet this challenge. More of the same, it argues, would not solve the problem; in fact, it would only make things worse. According to the report: "Three years

Beyond the Crisis

ago [when *A Nation at Risk* was published] ... few perceived that the world economy was in the midst of a profound transformation, one that demands a new understanding of the education standards necessary to create the kind of high wage work force that can compete in a global economy." It notes that South Korean workers who produced VCR equipment sold to American consumers worked seven days a week, twelve hours a day, and earned $3,000 per year. "We cannot, nor wish to, compete with these Korean workers on their own terms," it concludes. The alternative the report proposes is to move beyond an economy oriented around a semi-skilled industrial labor force to one "that is based on the use of a wide scale of very highly skilled workers, backed up by the most advanced technologies available." It warns that unless America, like Japan, is willing to upgrade its work force, "the cost of not doing so will be a steady erosion in the American standard of living."

To compete with Japan in the high-tech, managerial-professional job market, all students, the report says, would need to receive essentially the same education, with an emphasis upon higher-order literacy, analytic reasoning, decision-making, and team work. This applies to poor minority and disadvantaged children in inner-city schools as well, who, the report notes, will effectively be locked into poverty unless they receive more than a minimum basic skills education. The report is critical of regimented, basic skills approaches to drilling and testing and of an over-enrollment of students in non-college preparatory or remedial tracks in urban schools, noting that as a direct result of this approach to instruction, "too many students lack the ability to reason and perform complex, non-routine intellectual tasks." Students need to have a "good intuitive grasp of the ways in which all kinds of physical and social systems work, ... an ability to see patterns of meaning where others see only confusion; a cultivated creativity that leads them to new problems. ..." To produce a work force of high-wage and high-skill workers demands a redefinition of the purposes of schooling, "one that goes beyond the inculcation of routine skills and the acquisition of a stock of facts" to teach young people how to become "very adept at thinking for themselves."[10]

After this analysis of the changing world economy and the kind of labor force we would need to compete in it, the report shifts its attention to its primary focus: the restructuring of teachers' work. The needed changes in education, it argues, cannot be accomplished until teachers' work is restructured consistent with the type of work for which they are training students. "In schools where students are expected to master routine skills and acquire routine knowledge, the necessary skills and

Chapter Seven

knowledge can, to a degree, be packaged in texts and teachers can be trained to deliver the material in the text to the students with reasonable efficiency. But a much higher order of skills is required to prepare students for the unexpected, the non-routine world they will face in the future." Thus, while bureaucratic state reformers have sought to adapt and apply a model of teaching and learning that borrows heavily from industrial labor analogies, *A Nation Prepared* looks further up the labor hierarchy to borrow a model of teaching that draws upon professional-managerial conceptions of work organization and control. As highly trained professionals, teachers are to be given the power to personalize instruction, to become facilitators, guides, coaches, and even counselors to their students. Instruction, as thus conceived, cannot be regimented, standardized, or overly predetermined. "Textbooks cannot do it. Principals cannot do it. Directives from state authorities cannot do it. Only the people with whom the students come in contact every day can do it." The type of teacher, and the type of occupation, the Carnegie Forum had in mind would have to be much more professionalized, and this implies several things. First, it implies a restructuring of schools to "provide a professional environment for teachers, freeing them to decide how best to meet state and local goals for children while holding them accountable for student progress." In restructured schools, teachers would also have access to clerical and other support staff to help them prepare instructional materials. Since the services of this support staff (including teacher aides) could be obtained at a low cost, "it is more efficient to use them to perform such tasks than to have them performed by the professionals." Restructuring of the schools should also entail "giving teachers a greater voice in the decisions that affect the school. . . ."

A second way in which teacher professionalism could be promoted, according to the report, is to provide some room for advancement within teaching; it specifically recommends introduction of the position of Lead Teacher, someone "with the proven ability to provide active leadership in the redesign of the schools and in helping their colleagues to uphold high standards of learning and teaching."[11] Lead teachers in each school might help evaluate beginning teachers, be involved in curriculum development, and so on, and they would be paid more than other teachers. Aside from these measures, the report recommends creating a National Board for Professional Teaching Standards to certify outstanding teachers, requiring a bachelor's degree in liberal arts as a prerequisite for professional teacher training, raising teachers' salaries significantly, and increasing minority enrollment in teacher education programs.[12] Only through such a restructuring of schools

Beyond the Crisis

and a re-professionalization of teaching, the report argues, can public education hope to attract and hold "the best and the brightest" in teaching; and only with such highly professionalized teachers can a new American labor force of high-tech, high-skilled workers be produced.

Several years after the Carnegie Foundation advanced this economically functional discourse on school reform in *A Nation Prepared*, it released a special report on the urban school crisis entitled *An Imperiled Generation*, based on observations and data from a broad cross section of the nation's most urban school systems. The report also includes data from a 1987 Carnegie Foundation national survey of urban and non-urban school teachers. The overall conclusion of the report is that while some progress had been made over the past half-decade in public education to enrich the curriculum, improve teacher salaries and teacher quality, and generally raise academic standards, most of these changes have been limited to suburban schools. The report points to examples of a few urban schools and classrooms where significant learning seems to be taking place but concludes that the nation has to face "the harsh truth . . . that the reform movement has largely bypassed our most deeply troubled schools. . . . The failure to educate adequately urban children is a shortcoming of such magnitude that many people have simply written off city schools as little more than human storehouses to keep young people off the streets."[13] The report then goes on to cite a familiar litany of statistics, and provides concrete examples, which suggest how bad the situation is in urban schools: the soaring drop-out rates, the problem of attracting and holding qualified teachers, the bureaucratic system "crippled by a web of regulations," the deteriorating school facilities, the threats of violence, and the continuing low achievement levels. At one Chicago high school, only ten percent of entering tenth graders had the minimum reading skills needed to read textbooks and take tests. In a Houston elementary school, half the students repeated at least one grade. In Boston, 44 percent of high school students dropped out before the twelfth grade, and of those who did graduate, almost half scored below the 30th percentile on a standardized reading test. At academic high schools in New York City which prepare the best students for college, one out of five students was absent on any given day. There was also evidence of a widespread "culture of cutting." In one urban high school, eleven of 28 enrolled students were in attendance for a basic skills course called High School Mathematics and seven of 18 for a biology course. The report noted that chronic class-cutting also tends to escalate to truancy and finally to dropping out of school altogether. Furthermore, as alienated youth drop out of schools, they "are flooding into communi-

Chapter Seven

ties where they confront unemployment lines, welfare checks, homelessness, and even jails." The report argues that "bold, aggressive action is needed now to avoid leaving a huge and growing segment of the nation's youth civically unprepared and economically unempowered."[14]

Like their students, urban school teachers are also disaffected and alienated, according to the report. This the report relates to several factors. First, the professionalism and authority of teachers in urban schools is undermined by mandating in detail everything they are to do. For example, urban teachers are three times as likely as their counterparts in suburban schools to feel uninvolved in setting school goals or selecting curricular materials. They are twice as likely to feel they have no control over the organization of classroom time or course content. Second, urban teachers have much more paperwork than their suburban counterparts, and this takes time away from planning effective lessons. For example, one teacher complained: "If a student is absent three times you have to list him on a special form that goes to the principal with your lesson plans. And you have to call the student. On the fourth day, you have to send a letter to the student's parents, and send another form into the office when the student is absent the sixth time." Third, the working conditions of urban teachers is not conducive to excellence. Many urban teachers reported that they had no permanent classroom, or even a desk; teaching materials were in short supply (one teacher reported that "last year we were out of mimeographed paper for a month, and once we even ran out of chalk"); libraries were inadequate; lab equipment was missing or out-of-date; etc. Finally, urban teachers report not feeling safe in halls, in the parking lots, or even in the classrooms, and this heightens their general job-related stress.[15]

In calling for a "unified" response to the urban school crisis, one designed to promote excellence among both students and teachers, the report proposes a number of changes. The first major set of recommendations is grouped under the general rubric of "excellence for all," and pertains specifically to student achievement and the curriculum. The report affirms that "equality of opportunity, along with the support to make it real and not merely rhetorical, must be seen as the unfinished agenda for the nation's schools. . . . To push for excellence in ways that ignore the needs of less privileged students is to undermine the future of the nation."[16] At the elementary level the goal should be "to assure that every child . . . could read with understanding, write with clarity, and effectively speak and listen."[17] At the secondary level the curricular focus should be on "language skills, acquisition of general

Beyond the Crisis

knowledge, and on the capacity to think clearly."[18] The report affirms that both urban and suburban schools should be in the same business of developing higher-order thinking skills, although it suggests that in the short run the specific subject matter or teaching methods might vary between inner-city and suburban schools, and urban students might, as a whole, take a bit longer to get through the curriculum. No student, at any rate, should be locked into a curriculum track that prepares him or her only for entry-level, low-skill jobs. "While students tackle core courses in different ways, the basic content and purposes should be the same for all. No student should suddenly wake up to discover that, as an adult, he or she is ill-equipped to participate responsibly in life."[19] To implement such a curriculum would require major changes, the report recognizes. Urban teachers would have to set high expectations for all their students, instructional materials and methods would need to be changed to promote higher-order reasoning and literacy skills, and urban schools would need to make available the same kinds of advanced courses that are found in suburban schools rather than the watered down basic skills courses they currently offer.

A second set of recommendations in the report have to do with school governance and the restructuring of teachers' work. The report endorses the heightened professionalization of urban teaching, consistent with the model of professionalization put forward in *A Nation Prepared*. It also goes beyond this to call for a "radical overhaul" of the organization and control of urban schools so that day-to-day decision-making shifts much more to the local school level through some form of "school-based management." While acknowledging that bureaucratic red tape and state regulations are related to the need for public accountability, the report argues that principals and teachers are not given the control they need to effectively tailor instruction to individual students and situations. School-based management implies, according to the report, that principals and teachers be given more authority to run schools through some form of joint governing board, which would also "have authority to allocate funds within guidelines set by the district office."[20] The decentralization of institutional authority is also to be facilitated by breaking large, anonymous urban schools into small instructional units, and encouraging a close working relationship between each student and a teacher mentor.

Along with a decentralization of day-to-day decision-making, however, the report also endorses more accountability. Obviously, there is at some point a contradiction between decentralization of authority to the school level and more accountability to state officials; and in this regard the report recommends a "middle ground" between decentral-

Chapter Seven

ization and centralization of authority. It notes: "Teachers and principals must be given greater freedom to make decisions. But school empowerment is only a means to a larger end. The public deserves to see results. In calling for greater school authority, we acknowledge a parallel and absolutely essential need for evaluation."[21] It suggests, however, that evaluation would have to be pegged to something more than standardized test scores and encompass an overall assessment of school progress; and it recommends this might take the form of a "school report card" to parents, the community, and outside funding agencies. Such an assessment might include both qualitative and quantitative data on the attainment of school goals, student proficiency in the written and spoken word, the general knowledge of students in various curricular domains, numbers and types of books read by students, distribution between remedial and academic courses, organization of the school into instructional units, teaching innovations introduced over the past year, what happens to students once they graduate, and so forth.[22] Finally, to asssure public accountability, the report endorses "intervention" by the state or other funding agencies if local schools are not able to "provide evidence of quality education" for students. This, it suggests, might take the form of School Evaluation Teams, composed of state and local education officials, college faculty members, teachers, and parents, and established by the state or special commissions to investigate schools that fail to demonstrate expected progress. The teams would be empowered to mandate emergency changes in the schools' instructional program, monitoring of schools, emergency financial aid, removal of principals, or (in extreme cases) the closing of schools.

In describing the crisis in urban schooling and teaching, and in calling for drastic measures to turn the situation around, *A Nation Prepared* and *An Imperiled Generation* provide valuable contributions to the development of an alternative paradigm for educational renewal. The general models of curriculum and instruction, school reorganization, educational evaluation, teacher professionalism, and general decentralization of decision-making endorsed by the reports, if instituted, could help overcome the urban school crisis. Furthermore, the emphasis upon both equity and excellence is critical to any democratic resolution of the urban school crisis. However, there are several major problems or limitations in this liberal discourse on reform that undermine its effectiveness as a viable alternative to the dominant bureaucratic state discourse. One of these problems has to do with a conceptual failure to adequately account for impediments that stand in the way of realizing decentralized, non-regimented, empowering models of urban schooling

Beyond the Crisis

within the context of a highly inequitable socioeconomic order. Liberal discourse tends to presume that public schools are open institutions, in the sense that they can be reorganized based on a rational assessment of problems and needed changes—a belief shared with the conservative state discourse. Liberals merely propose a more humanistic model of school effectiveness. Questions having to do with the resistance of the current system to change remain unraised or under-theorized, as does the question of interrelationship between power relations in schools and those in the broader society.

The result is an analysis of the urban school crisis that is seriously flawed. Take, for example, the claim made in *An Imperiled Generation* that urban schools have been "bypassed" in the school reform movement of the 1980s. As I argued in Chapter One, there have really been two reform movements in education over the past several decades—one aimed primarily at suburban schools, and the other aimed primarily at urban schools. It is hardly accurate to suggest that urban schools have been bypassed, in light of the evidence presented in this study. Quite the contrary. Urban schools have been the primary focus of state-sponsored reform initiatives. Urban schools were not bypassed so much as hit with a different, and more far-reaching package of reforms. That reform package restructured the curriculum around functional literacy and the needs of entry-level workers in the new labor force. The notion that urban schools have been neglected by the state thus does not hold up to scritiny. The reforms sponsored there have merely been of a different type from those sponsored in suburban America.

Another central assumption that underlies the reasoning in both Carnegie Foundation reports is that the schools should turn out more high-skilled workers so that more high-skilled, high-wage jobs will be created in the economy. The problem with this scenario is that it assumes the schools lead the economy—that the tail wags the dog, to use a simple analogy. In fact, the schools respond to changes in the economy much more than vice versa. American industry has promoted the further rationalization and de-skilling of labor throughout this century in an effort to reduce labor costs and increase centralized control over production; and this continues to be its guiding purpose in introducing technological changes. Industry has created far more semi-skilled jobs over the past few decades than it has professional-managerial jobs, and it is semi-skilled workers who are in greatest demand on the labor market. Consequently, it does not make much sense to propose a system of public education which trains everyone for high-skilled, professional-managerial work, when the hard reality is that the economy cannot, or will not, accommodate the aspirations

Chapter Seven

of the vast majority. The differences in curriculum and the organization of instruction between urban and suburban schools are not likely to be significantly overcome so long as gross disparities exist between types of work available to individuals in the economy. While the idea of a common curriculum, oriented around higher-order thinking, decision-making, and literacy skills, along with a commitment to "excellence for everyone," are good ideas and worthy of support, a serious proposal to implement such changes would need to develop a plan for economic restructuring so that there was some correspondence between the skills students learn in school and the skill requirements of jobs available in the economy. It would also need the support of a broad-based democratic movement ready to engage in the political struggle required to make these changes.

The proposal to institute school-based management suffers from a similar under-theorizing of power relations in education. While efforts at administrative decentralization are often initiated by system elites in the effort to overcome the irrationalities and inefficiencies associated with top-down control, so long as elite steerage of the system remains an imperative, too much local school diversity and autonomy will inevitably prove threatening. The experience with decentralization in New York City is a case in point. In 1969, after a lengthy Ford Foundation-sponsored study and demonstration project, New York City embarked on a decentralization plan in which 32 democratically elected local boards were established, with broad powers over hiring and promotion of staff, evaluation of teachers, school construction and maintenance, and (within central office guidelines) curricular decisions. But troubles began almost immediately when the local, democratically elected boards used their powers in ways that threatened elite steerage of the system. For example, in the Oceanhill-Brownsville section of Brooklyn, when an all-black Community Board attempted to fire or transfer teachers and administrators it considered racist or incompetent, the central board (with the cooperation of the teacher union) intervened to restore centralized control over school staffing. Consequently, while the project of decentralization began with promise and was hailed by liberal groups, over the next two decades the central board and the School Chancellor slowly whittled away at the powers of the local boards with regard to substantive decision-making and restricted their powers to selecting staff from approved lists of candidates and awarding construction contracts approved by the central office. As this happened, voter apathy increased and local board members were increasingly elected by organized machines, which meant that they became less responsive to the community and served as power bases for graft and corruption. Ironically, the current reform movement in New York City schools, led by Chancellor Joseph Fernandez, represents an attempt to transfer more power *away* from the unresponsive local boards back to the Chancellor and his staff. That is, rather than attempt to re-democratize the local boards, to give them substantive powers and make them responsive to the communities they serve, system reformers have attempted to bypass local boards by holding building administrators more directly accountable to the Chancellor.[23] Given these realities, it seems doubtful that decentralization schemes *alone* can serve as the basis for a radical transformation of urban schooling. To be effective, decentralization will have to be tied to workplace democratization in both the schools and economy.

The same forces that impede efforts at a real decentralization of power within urban school districts also impede refom efforts aimed at increasing the professional autonomy and power of teachers—both individually and collectively. Bureaucratic elites and state officials may like the idea of teacher professionalism, but they are unwilling to pay the costs of empowering teachers. In most direct terms, increasing teachers' salaries significantly seems infeasible in a state already pressed to the edge of fiscal insolvency. Until the fiscal crisis of the state in America is resolved, urban school teachers' salaries will not rise significantly, and they may even fall further. In less direct terms, the professionalization of urban school teaching seems unlikely so long as urban schools continue to be about skilling and disciplining a semi-skilled labor force. A highly professionalized teaching force is unnecessary so long as the curriculum and instructional process are rationalized and routinized consistent with this role. Furthermore, it seems unlikely that highly professionalized teachers would be compliant employees, content to follow central office directives and exercise little discretionary power in the classroom. In this context, reforms aimed at increasing teacher professionalism generally may be expected, in practice, to involve the increased professionalization of a relatively few teachers, (such as those *A Nation Prepared* calls "lead teachers") and a further de-professionalization of the majority of urban teachers. "Lead teachers" or "master teachers" would receive higher salaries, be involved in curriculum revision, have access to support staff, supervise beginning teachers, etc. To compensate for the heightened professionalization of this teaching elite, more unlicensed, untenured teachers might well be hired at the bottom. Consequently, while the notion of a career ladder for teachers has some merit, it is not likely to increase the professional autonomy and working conditions of most urban teachers so long as other things stay the same. Once more, the liberal discourse on school

Chapter Seven

reform under-theorizes the power relations that work against the empowerment of teachers under current conditions.

Along with this tendency to under-theorize complex problems and thus fail to appreciate why the system remains unresponsive to change, the liberal discourse has a tendency to emphasis system reform through small experiments and demonstration projects. Belief in the efficacy of demonstration projects dates back to the early progressive era, when educational reformers established experimental schools across the country to test out the new child-centered pedagogy of John Dewey and other humanistic progressives. Dewey's "laboratory school" at the University of Chicago was the most famous of these progressive experiments in a radically child-centered curriculum and teacher-centered pedagogy. As pragmatists, Dewey and other progressives sought to apply a scientific model of experimentation to social problems and they tended to presume that nothing fundamentally stood in the way of instituting the lessons learned from these demonstration projects throughout the school system, once we had recognized their superiority to existing forms of curriculum and pedagogy. In *Democracy and Education,* Dewey wrote that: "The development of the experimental method as the method of getting knowledge and making sure it *is* knowledge, and not mere opinion—the method of both discovery and proof—is the remaining great force in bringing about a transformation in the theory of knowledge."[24] The scientific method, he maintained, was as valuable outside the realm of physical science as within it. It was as useful "to the forming and testing of ideas in social and moral matters" as to testing of new ideas in the scientific laboratory. If this insight had not yet been widely recognized, Dewey maintained, it was because "men [SIC] still want the crutch of dogma, of beliefs fixed by authority, to relieve them of the trouble of thinking and the responsiblity of directing their activity by thought."[25]

When applied to education, experimentalism implied a strategy of testing out new ideas in educational laboratories or controlled experiments, then attempting to overcome the "natural" tendency of local teachers and administrators to favor traditional methods. But for all the attention given to the promising experiments in progressive education, and all the dissemination of information on experimental programs, this reform discourse failed to transform the public schools. Humanistic reformers failed to recognize that it was not a lack of better ideas that kept the current bureaucratic state system of schooling from changing. The small class sizes, the highly qualified team of teachers and university consultants, the freeing up of the school day by breaking it into large blocks of time during which students worked on interdisci-

Beyond the Crisis

plinary projects, the qualitative and personalized evaluation of student learning problems, the intrinsic motivation provided by a student-centered curriculum—all of these experimental ideas worked to produce better-educated, more self-directed, less alienated, and less instrumentally competitive individuals. But this was not what dominant interest groups in education wanted from the schools. Consequently, to the extent that progressive ideas were adopted in the public schools, they most often served existing purposes. For example, the progressive emphasis on educating the "whole child" (including the social, emotional, and psychological child) was used to promote the more effective socialization of young people to a very conforming model of adjustment. Progressive experimentalism utterly failed to deliver on its promises as a way of restructuring American public education. It also promoted a variation on the end-of-ideology thesis by suggesting that all that stands in the way of change is a few more experiments and demonstration projects to prove that progressive, teacher- and student-centered approaches to education are superior to traditional methods and will work in the nation's public schools.

Dewey himself came to recognize by the 1930s that the experimental method of system change could only work in an ideal democratic society. In the most politically radical book of the late progressive era, *The Educational Frontier,* Dewey acknowledged that, "A society which includes warring class interests will always fight against its [the experimental method's] application outside of a particular limited field. . . . The objective precondition of the complete and free use of the method of intelligence is a society in which class interests that recoil from social experimentation are abolished. It is incompatible with every social and political philosophy . . . which accepts the class organization and vested class interest of present society."[26] We might add that it is incompatible with the maintenance of race- and gender-based relations of domination and subordination as well. Urban schools, after all, are organized in ways that perpetuate racial inequalities in society; and the bureaucratic subordination of teachers within the professional educational hierarchy is related to the perpetuation of gender inequalities. School structures are not the result of applied intelligence based on controlled, scientific experimentation as much as they are the result of applied power in the interests of dominant groups.

The naive optimism of progressive experimentalism, however, has continued to influence liberal discourse on educational reform in ways that limit that discourse's effectiveness in mounting a serious program for change. In the 1960s and early 1970s, progressive experimentalism was rearticulated by educational reformers who looked to experimen-

Chapter Seven

tal "free schools" and "alternative schools" as models for systemwide change. For example, Charles Silberman's influential study, *Crisis in the Classroom* (1971), sponsored by the Carnegie Foundation, reported glowingly on the many experiments and pilot projects that were then underway in public and private alternative schools. Silberman boldly proclaimed the beginning of a new era in public education, to be brought about by widespread dissemination and application of what had been learned in these educational experiments.[27] Silberman quoted from Robert Merton's famous essay on the self-fulfilling prophecy: "[I]t is the successful experiment which is decisive and not the thousand-and-one failures which preceded it. More is learned from the single success than from the multiple failures. A single success proves it can be done. Therefore it is necessary only to learn what made it work." Silberman concluded that "in the face of widespread doubt about the schools' ability to educate black (or Mexican-American, Puerto Rican, or Indian-American) children, therefore, it is useful to recall the 'law' of human society that Merton laid down: 'Whatever is, is possible.' "[28] If there was anything that stood in the way of changing the system of public education consistent with the lessons learned by recent experiments, according to Silberman, it was "mindlessness"—a tendency in American culture to conform, to resist change, to prefer the traditional. But it was more than mindlessness that kept the "free school" and "alternative school" experiments of the 1960s and 1970s from transforming public schools. In fact, at the time Silberman was writing, basic skills restructuring was beginning to transform urban schools consistent with elite bureaucratic state and economic interests, in direct opposition to everything that Silberman claimed was being learned from progressive experimentation. The schools were not so much resistant to change *per se* as they were resistant to change of the type associated with liberal and humanistic experiments. In spite of much sustained effort and adoption by many teachers of progressive approaches to education that benefitted a substantial number of students, state-sponsored reform was steering urban schools in another direction by the early 1970s, away from progressivism and the empowerment of teachers and students.

Liberalism thus faces a difficult task delivering on all of its promises because it fails to account for power relations that impinge upon the educational site and that serve to maintain dominant forms of school organization and control, pedagogy, and curriculum. This does not mean that the liberal project in its broadest and most humanistic sense, the project of the Enlightenment, should be abandoned; only that the liberal project must interrogate the disjunction between its discourse

Beyond the Crisis

and actual practice. Liberal commitments to equalization, individual self-enhancement, cooperation, and a system of education that counters the individualistic ethic of the private sector with a public philosophy must continue to guide us in restructuring the schools. The committment by liberals to expressive and self-enhancing forms of work also is important in holding out against the further de-skilling of teaching and the rationalization of the curriculum. As Svi Shapiro observes, liberalism appeals to "individuals whose educational preparation and professional socialization have raised expectations of work in which notions of autonomy, flexibility, self-regulation, and personal growth are significant features."[29] Once these expectations have been raised, they may be difficult to contain. Furthermore, liberal pilot projects and coalitions which attempt to institutionalize progressive changes in schools provide important lessons for building a progressive curriculum and approach to school restructuring, and they open up some space within school sites for teaching and learning which constitute power relations along more democratic principles. However, we will need to move beyond the current impasse in liberal discourse if we are to significantly advance the democratic project.

Towards a Democratic-Progressive Discourse on the Urban School Crisis

It is, of course, always easier to critique what is—to show how existing institutional structures and the dominant discourse serve to reproduce or prop up non-democratic sets of power relations, and to point out how conservative and liberal discourses on reform deconstruct under sustained analysis—than it is to offer concrete suggestions for moving towards a form of schooling that resolves current crisis tendencies within the context of a general democratization in the culture. In traditional Marxist analysis, the defense against offering constructive alternatives was always that one had to wait for the revolution, for the post-capitalist society, before real progress could be made on various social problems. In the meantime one could only offer criticisms from the sidelines. This simplistic position was based on a mechanistic understanding of system dynamics which presumed that the contradictions and crisis tendencies inherent to capitalist society would lead automatically to its collapse and replacement by socialism, whatever that vaguely defined term implied. Before that happened, little could be

Chapter Seven

done to work within the system to make it less oppressive; after that happened, there would be no need to change the system since socialism would be a non-oppressive society.

This deterministic view of history was still largely taken for granted in the structural Marxist reproduction theory that framed much critical educational discourse over the past several decades, and it promoted a pessimism about the possibilities for effecting any meaningful change within state or economic sites. One thus had to opt out of the system and create alternative, free spaces as much as possible, because working within existing structures meant playing the game by the existing rules and participating in reproductive processes. This was a leftist discourse that emerged out of the counter-cultural and "New Left" movements in the West during the 1960s and 1970s; and while it contained essential insights into the way power is reproduced and maintained, it proved in the long run to be limited in its transformative capacity. Part of the failure of the neo-Marxist critical theory of school and society to serve as a foundation for building a democratic movement for change may be attributed to the fact that it primarily has been an academic, analytic discourse that has not transferred well to concrete political struggles. As Herbert Gintis observes: "Where have 'alienation,' 'objectification,' 'commodity fetishism,' or 'hegemony' served as the rallying cry of class struggle?"[30] Such a discourse has lacked mediating structures to link theory and practice; and it has not adequately taken up the Enlightenment concepts of democracy, freedom, equity, and justice. While these concepts have no transcendental, *a priori* meaning, they have cultural and historical meaning, and they must be taken up anew and extended in their meaning by each new generation. Related to this, the neo-Marxist discourse has failed to adequately suggest how socialism is to be built, or what, specifically, socialism implies beyond an extension of the democratic project.

In taking up democratic concepts, progressive movements will need to reemphasize the centrality of their meaning within existing struggles in society and the necessity of an extended engagement in working to realize democratic values and commitments. Antonio Gramsci argued that a transformation of power relations in society would only be built on a *philosophy of praxis,* a philosophy or social theory capable of entering into the historical struggles of real people, of articulating and helping to shape a public philosophy capable of countering the hegemony of elite groups, and of constituting a democratic political movement capable of gaining control of the state to make it serve democratic rather than elite interests.[31] Like all values, democratic notions of equity, respect for difference, and social justice have no

Beyond the Crisis

meaning outside of, or apart from, the concrete social and educational practices in which they are discursively constituted. They emerge out of, and help shape, discourse on concrete educational questions and concerns, and they provide a basis for building coalitions of interests around particular agendas for short-term and long-term changes in education and society. Let me now be more specific about what a commitment to democratic-progressive values and concerns might imply in the articulation of a new, more powerful response to the urban school crisis.

Critical Literacy, Critical Pedagogy, and Workplace Democratization

First, and most directly, a democratic-progressive discourse may be associated with support for a critical literacy curriculum that emphasizes more than higher order analytical thinking skills and moves beyond economically functional models of the curriculum. Critical literacy has been used within the progressive, democratic Left discourse in education to imply a capacity for self-reflexivity—the deliberate, discursive reflection on experience and identity construction within a culture in which one is positioned as a classed, raced, and gendered subject. According to Peter McLaren, "the purpose behind acquiring this type of literacy is to create a citizenry critical enough to both analyze and challenge the oppressive characteristics of the larger society so that a more just, equitable, and democratic society can be created."[32] What the democratic left needs to support, then, is not simply or even primarily a more effective means of teaching economically functional literacy skills, but rather a new understanding of literacy as a form of discursive practice by students actively involved in constructing meaning and subjectivity within a context of struggle, in which they must give concrete meaning to notions of justice, liberty, democracy, etc. Questions posed by a critical literacy curriculum include: How can students be made aware of and call into question the construction of their identities around various "others"? How can students resist subordination in ways that are not self-defeating and encapsulating? How can students begin to reshape their own personal and collective identities in progressive, empowering ways?

Discursively, the notion of critical literacy always implies as well a notion of critical pedagogy consistent with a theory of teachers as transformative intellectuals and cultural workers who view schools as sites of struggle over meaning, and who understand their teaching as

Chapter Seven

embedded within the dynamics through which culture is made and history is lived. Henry Giroux writes: "Rather than defining teachers' work through the narrow language of professionalism, a critical pedagogy needs to ascertain more carefully what the role of teachers might be as cultural workers engaged in the production of ideologies and social practices. This is not a call for teachers to become wedded to some abstract ideal that removes them from everyday life or turns them into prophets of perfection and certainty; on the contrary, it is a call for teachers to undertake social criticism not as outsiders but as public intellectuals who address the social and political issues of their neighborhood, their nation, and the wider global world."[33] Critical pedagogy also implies engagement by teachers in the struggles of their students to find their own voices and make their own identities rather than acquiesce to domination and passivity.[34]

Another foundation critical educators can look to in constructing a critical literacy curriculum and a critical pedagogy is Jurgen Habermas's theory of "communicative rationality" or "communicative action." These terms imply a form of public discursive practice, open to all, in which issues of general public concern are raised and various perspectives are critically appraised.[35] Various claims of truth are discursively validated or invalidated according to whether or not they are comprehensible (as linguistic utterances) by all parties, make logic sense (obey the rules of propositional logic), are well intentioned rather than deceptive, and advance agreed upon purposes (the normative context of discourse).[36] Only when such a communicative rationality is achieved in a society, according to Habermas, are individuals able to engage in the critical reconstruction of the life-world in a purposive, active manner consistent with the historical realization of ideals of democratic decision-making, compassion, freedom, solidarity, and so on.[37] As Robert Young argues: "It is not the main function of critical educators to attack the life-world of students—to 'make trouble.' Rather, it should be to assist students to make an effective job of reconstructing the already problematic parts of the life-world through communicative, problem-solving learning."[38] The teachers' role, from this perspective, is to help bring out fundamental differences in beliefs and values among students and within various discourses in the culture. This form of communicative action may be aimed at either understanding or consensus building, or some combination of both. The emphasis upon discourse oriented towards consensus is consistent with Habermas's belief that democracy is dependent upon the adoption of a consensual basis for interaction that alleviates the need for force. A curriculum oriented around communicative rationality thus holds out

Beyond the Crisis

the promise of a social life informed by both reason and values, and committed to the reconstruction of culture. The shortcomings of a Habermasian reconceptualization of curriculum have to do with a tendency to overemphasis reason and de-emphasize mood, affect, and desire in directing discourse, and with a tendency to presume that consensus can ultimately override conflict. While these idealistic tendencies limit the value of the notion of communicative rationality, it still provides insights that are important in guiding critical educational theory and practice. Clearly, the language of "pupil performance objectives," "basic skills," and "effective schools" has emerged out of a technical-rational, bureaucratic, corporate, and patriarchal discourse in the schools. A discourse of communicative rationality would generate a more interactive, consensual, dialectic, non-standardized, and contingent model of curriculum and instruction, one that is always evolving and growing as teacher and student interact with subject matter, within the mileau of the school and the broader culture.

Finally, a critical literacy curriculum and a critical form of pedagogy imply a shift towards multiculturalism and the promotion of difference. Cameron McCarthy suggests that a critical multiculturalism is aimed at "bringing the uninstitutionalized experiences of marginalized minorities and working-class women and men 'to the center' of the organization and arrangement of the school curriculum.... A 'new' critical curriculum should privilege the human interests of the least advantaged."[39] McCarthy argues that a critical curriculum that emphasizes anti-classist anti-racist, and anti-sexist social reconstruction, and that utilizes the viewpoints and experiences of oppressed groups, would constitute a fundamental step in the direction of preparing students for democratic participation in a complex and rapidly changing world. He cautions, however, that this should not mean an unproblematic acceptance of the perspectives of those who are disadvantaged within the dominant culture. A critical curriculum "must avoid the tendency to reify the oppressed.... Changes in the curriculum to address the present and the future of race [and other] relations in the United States must therefore be founded in dialogue and the recognition that the production of knowledge is systematically relational and heterogeneous."[40] If relations of domination and subordination are to some degree at least mutually sustained as an everyday accomplishment, everyone is obligated to examine the role they play in helping maintain and in resisting power relations within various institutional sites, including the school and classroom. Minority and socioeconomically disadvantaged youth, for example, need to examine their own resistances to the schooling process, to understand how some may be self-

Chapter Seven

defeating and confirming of their own subordination and presumed inferiority. The challenge, then, is to channel the anger and the passion that lies behind student resistances in more "positive" directions, to help them commit themselves to personal and cultural struggle and not to take the easy or cynical way out.

Obviously, it is not easy to "do" critical pedagogy, teach communicative rationality, and build a true multicultural curriculum in urban schools as they are currently operated to generate basic skills output data; and powerful forces stand in the way of a reconstruction of urban education consistent with these critical theoretical notions. Nevertheless, through the struggle to teach more critically, teachers reject the passivity, apathy, and acquiescence that now contribute to the hegemony of dominant power relations in education. Let me here provide just one brief example of what "doing" critical pedagogy might imply within a particular cultural site context. In a recent article in *Teachers College Record*, William Bigelow describes and self-reflexively analyzes his own teaching in an inner-city high school, and more particularly a social studies course he taught with Linda Christensen.[41] After studying various historical examples of injustice, students in the class were asked to write about a time when they had their rights violated, "to write from inside these experiences and to recapture how they felt and what, if anything, they did about the injustice."[42] One girl wrote about being enclosed in a solitary confinement cell. A black girl whose mother was white wrote about how humiliating it was when an employee in a movie theater refused to believe that the mother and daughter were related. Another girl wrote of being sexually harassed on the way to school and how her story was dismissed and she was blamed for the problem when she reported it to school administrators. A boy wrote about how the convenience store clerks always watched him closely because he was black; and another wrote about being disciplined by the Dean when he wore an anarchy symbol on his jacket. After discussing these papers in class, Bigelow and Christensen had students discuss how they reacted to these perceived injustices. "From the collective text we saw that most people did not resist at all. What little resistance occurred was individual. . . ."

Interestingly, the teachers ran into some resistance from students to this type of critical literacy assignment. "Part of this resistance," Bigelow suggests, "may come from not wanting to resurface or expose painful experiences. . . ; but I think the biggest factor is that they simply do not feel that their lives have anything *important* to teach them."[43] Self-reflexive, dialectic thinking about social reality and identity construction is not easily taught in a society that actively *discourages*

Beyond the Crisis

individuals from raising these difficult questions about purpose, identity construction, and the making of culture. Ironically, because critical pedagogy and critical literacy expose the power relations that are constituted in everyday discourse and practice, they may also encourage students "to see themselves as victims—powerless cogs in a machine daily reproducing the inequities of the larger society."[44] This is a tendency (given current highly inequitable power relations) that must be countered through the explicit study of historical and situational dynamics and contestation in discourse and practice (and hence in the making of culture). Students may also be encouraged to articulate common interests and build coalitions across class, gender, racial, sexual preference and other "boundaries." This implies valuing and respecting difference, but it also implies valuing community and solidarity among groups currently oppressed to build a democratic majority capable of challenging oppressive power relations.

Beyond a reconceptualization of the curriculum and the role of the teacher, a democratic-progressive discourse in education would place emphasis on the restructuring of the schools consistent with the notion of workplace democratization. It is important to distinguish between workplace democratization and site-based management. The latter notion has come to imply a decentralization of bureaucratic authority to local school building administrators and teachers so they can think up creative new ways of raising student scores on state-mandated exams. It is not surprising, consequently, to learn that site-based management has been a top-down reform initiative in most states and school districts. Workplace democratization implies much more, and something quite different. Marx argued that people make themselves and their culture through work; and as such, productive labor is the essential birthright of all, central to the "species being" of humans. "What they [humans] are, therefore, coincides with their production, both with *what* they produce and with *how* they produce."[45] What we need to support, then, is not simply a more effective means of teaching basic skills, but a new organization of work in schools in the direction of making work experiences (for students, teachers and administrators) more rewarding, more equitable, and hence more productive.

Workplace democratization may be understood typically to encompass four broad projects, with the understanding that its specific meaning and structure may vary considerably in various institutional contexts. First, it implies an enhancement in the participation by workers in the decision-making processes which affect their everyday working lives.[46] Second, it implies worker involvement in a wide scope of substantive rather than merely technical or procedural decisions.[47]

Chapter Seven

Third, it implies changes in the content and complexity of job tasks and the demands work places on the individual, as with job rotation and sharing schemes. Finally, workplace democratization implies making fuller use of a broad range of intellectual, social and physical skills on the job.[48]

When applied to schools as work sites, workplace democratization implies movement in all of these directions for teachers, building administrators, and students (particularly secondary students).[49] However, in urban school sites, because of their special public character and importance in distributing and constituting cultural power, democratization also must involve bridging some of the borders and boundaries between school and community. Local schools need to be made accountable to their community "clients" in a much more direct sense through, for example, local governing boards composed of representatives of a number of affected groups. These boards could be granted substantial power to formulate curriculum guidelines and evaluate learning outcomes, consistent with state guidelines designed to ensure that various voices in the community are heard and their rights respected. Teachers' professional and craft expertise need to be respected as well, within this local democratization of educational decision-making, although questions of how much discretionary power should be reserved for teachers, both individually and collectively, would have to be resolved in concrete practice. Ideally, educational leaders (both teachers and administrators) need to be engaged in a protracted discourse on (1) educational purposes within the context of cultural struggles over meaning, (2) the interpretation and evaluation of existing educational practice, and (3) the change process and what impediments stand in the way of reform efforts.

Workplace democratization also suggests a reconceptualization of teaching and teacher education in line with Dewey's notion of "teacher as investigator," in which teachers investigate pedagogical problems through directed inquiry, linking these problems both to the organizational culture of the school and to the culture of the broader community and society.[50] As Joe Kincheloe remarks of this view of the teacher, which he calls "teacher as researcher": "Democratic educational research performed by teachers renders teacher practice more theoretical in that it is supported by reflection and grounded in socio-historical context. Teachers as researchers gain the skill to interrogate their own practices, question their own assumptions, and to understand contextually their own situations."[51] Kincheloe suggests that research in democratized schools needs to be grounded on five themes: (1) a rejection of the "positivistic notion that all educational issues are

Beyond the Crisis

technical and not political or ethical in character"; (2) an awareness by teachers of "their own value-commitments, the value-commitments of others, and the values promoted by the dominant culture"; (3) an attempt to "distinquish between ideologically distorted interpretations [of educational phenomena] and those which transcend ideological distortion"; (4) an analysis of "those aspects of the dominant social order which block our attempt to pursue rational goals"; and (5) an analysis of possible actions they [teachers] might take if they are to overcome the obstacles social structures place in their way."[52] All of this confirms that workplace democratization in schools cannot be separated from a movement for democratization in the broader culture.

Teacher Unions and Democratic-Progessive Agendas

To institutionalize these changes in the curriculum, teaching, and the organization of the school, simultaneous developments on a number of fronts are needed, and a number of movements must be articulated. One of the possible movements that might lead in the formulation of a democratic discourse and reform agenda in education is the teacher union movement. At the same time, it is clear that if teacher unionism is to serve a pivotal role in support of democratic agendas in the schools, it will need to change in significant ways. Perhaps most importantly, teacher unions will need to become more democratic themselves and find better ways of ensuring that oligarchic and patriarchal tendencies are countered so that the voices of rank-and-file teachers are heard and listened to. It will also need to do a better job of building coalitions of interest in urban communities with poor and working-class white, black and Hispanic groups so that its power base extends beyond the school system and the professional educational establishment. Finally, it will need to think beyond the current rules of the game and conflict over the wage-labor contract, and suggest how the rules of the game can be changed. For example, while it makes sense for teachers to think of administrators (as a group and individually) as the "other" in long, drawn-out battles in the schools, teacher unions will need to begin working to overcome these bipolar oppositions between educational labor and management if they are to re-empower the teaching occupation and restructure schools in democratic ways.

This dual focus for teachers' unions—first, continuing to oppose school management and outmaneuver it in the wage-labor game, and second, working to overcome labor-management divisions—will require some difficult decisions in the years ahead about which course

Chapter Seven

of action to pursue in specific, concrete situations. Recently, on the state and national level, both the NEA and AFT leaderships have endorsed proposals for teacher professionalism and collaborative decision-making like those advanced by the Carnegie Foundation for the Advancement of Teaching in *A Nation Prepared*. As I indicated earlier, this liberal reform agenda represents a significant advancement over the basic skills approach to reform and in a number of ways is consistent with democratic values and commitments. However, in working to implement such an agenda, teacher unions will need to ensure that it leads to significant job restructuring for *all* teachers, not just a professional elite, and that collaborative or shared decision-making plans involve teachers in substantive rather than merely technical decisions about curriculum, instruction, evaluation, and school organization.

Distrust of collaboration with administrators runs deep among urban teachers, and for some good reasons. If teacher unions follow the example of the trade union movement as a whole, union leadership may support collaborative decision-making proposals more than rank-and-file teachers. The current enthusiasm of major American corporations for various forms of shared decision-making and work teams (similar to those that supposedly characterize Japanese industry), is related to the enthusiasm of state officials for various forms of shared decision-making and site-based management. Labor leadership has cautiously endorsed these ideas, although rank-and-file scepticism continues to run deep. For example, the rank-and-file New Directions Movement in the United Auto Workers, which works for the democratization of union decision-making, has opposed the "team concept" of having workers assemble cars as a group and work together on improving production quality and efficiency, on the basis that such ideas represent efforts by management to substitute peer pressure to perform for supervisory pressure. It also has opposed collaborative decision-making schemes in which management and union leaders reach consensus on needed changes. According to a leader of the New Directions Movement, "Unions and corporations do not have common objectives at all times. . . . Everybody seeks consensus in this brave new workplace, just like the Japanese. But what happens if a worker is frustrated. . . . What happens when he goes to his union representative and is told 'We don't grieve that anymore'?"[53] In fact, shared decision-making sounds an awful lot like a return to the pre-collective bargaining era notion of a company family, with management and labor leaders working cooperatively rather than in an adverserial relationship, for the good of the company. The reality then was that labor leaders sold out to management and exercised little if any influence

Beyond the Crisis

over substantive decisions. These are important issues that will have to be faced by teachers. Rank-and-file teacher scepticism about shared decision-making proposals is, consequently, understandable and may serve as a useful check on teacher union leaders who may be more tempted to embrace these new reform proposals which promise to make them part of the school management team.

For all of the limitations of teacher unionism I have pointed to in this study, its emphasis upon understanding teachers' interests as educational workers provides the basis for a potentially radical critique of the existing social and technical relations of work in the school, including students' work. While teacher unionism has not to this point done much to explicitly link teachers' interests as educational workers with students' interests as workers, the possibility for developing such links is inherent in the teacher union perspective. For example, Albert Shanker, president of the American Federation of Teachers (AFT), observed recently in one of his regular *New York Times* columns that while teachers' voices are beginning to be heard in the schools and in public, "another group of workers in our schools are ignored—just like the assembly-line workers in a factory used to be. I'm talking about the students." Shanker argued that just as assembly-line workers must want to come to work and feel that they are listened to by managers, students "must want to come to school, and they must be willing to work, even when no one is hanging over them. If we can't achieve this, no kind of school reform, however ambitious, will improve student learning and public education."[54] The implication here is that curriculum and instruction have been organized consistent with a factory method of production, and that the learning process is an assembly-line of routine labor. What is less clear is where Shanker stands on the implications of this analysis. Should our objective be to organize students into their own trade unions to negotiate with school management over adequate compensation for their labor in the classroom, or to change the way students' work is organized so that it is less alienating and more motivating? Perhaps student unionism is a viable option given current realities, especially at the secondary level. But at some point teacher unions will also need to promote a democratization of decision-making in schools that moves beyond wage-labor, contract approaches to teachers' and students' interests.

Other Axes of Struggle

Racial power relations also play a central role in constituting the urban school crisis and in organizing teachers' work experiences and relations

Chapter Seven

with students, and teachers will need to link up with anti-racist movements in attempting to reclaim urban schools as sites of empowerment, in which teachers and students are on the same side. One strategic objective worthy of support within the immediate situation would be to dramatically increase the proportion of African-American and Hispanic teachers in urban schools. To some extent this will involve challenging the conventional liberal belief that poor, minority students are somehow better off when they receive instruction from white, middle-class teachers, or (conversely) that the racial and ethnic background of students' teachers is irrelevant. If predictions are accurate, by the year 2000 only five percent of all public school teachers in the nation will be members of a racial minority (down from the current ten percent), while one out of every three students in American public schools will be members of racial minorities.[55] Currently, 80 percent of the students in New York City public schools are members of racial minorities, while 70 percent of their teachers are white.[56] Such racial disparities between urban school teachers and students serve as a highly visible symbol of white power over minority groups. Furthermore, because minority students lack racial role models among teachers with whom they can identify, their alienation from the schooling process is heightened. It is imperative, consequently, that some means be found of countering the decline in the pool of minority teachers and dramatically increasing their proportion in the teaching force. This, in turn, cannot be separated from the institutionalization of a curriculum in urban schools that empowers rather than disempowers students so that more of them aspire to become public school teachers—both because they have the requisite academic skills and high self-expectations, and because they view the public schools positively as sites where they would want to work as adults.

It is worth noting in this regard that in 1990 a district court ruled that Boston must begin a vigorous policy of hiring more minority teachers, until they represent at least 30 percent of the teaching force. The Boston teacher union, which represents the current, primarily white teaching staff, has adamantly resisted such a policy, which will entail non-renewal of contracts for a significant number of white teachers, some of whom have up to 20 years' experience in the system, and their replacement by less experienced black teachers.[57] Such court-ordered affirmative action in urban school teaching could increase racial tensions in the short run. Nevertheless, a more racially integrated or balanced teaching staff would not only reduce racial tensions in urban schools, it would probably serve as well to better articulate teachers' interests with those of other democratic struggles in the culture.

Beyond the Crisis

While race and class divide teachers and students in urban schools, gender divides teachers from administrators and has encouraged the subordinatation of teachers within the bureaucratic hierarchy. A number of commentators have pointed out that teaching is defined in the culture as women's work and that as such it is organized similar to other forms of women's work. The sociologist Amitai Etzioni, for example, argued that the high proportion of women in teaching is the single most important factor which has worked against the fuller professionalization of teaching, and he consequently labeled teaching a "semi-profession."[58] The response to this predicament, on one level, is to revalue women's work, and thereby raise the status and power of teachers. This is an important social and economic objective for the coming decade and one over which teachers need to be prepared to struggle. The feminization of teaching has been concurrent with the masculinization of control within the bureaucratic hierarchy in public education, which has been associated with greater use of technical-rational models of organizing the curriculum and the instructional process, which subordinate and dominate teachers. Patriarchal and bureaucratic rationality have gone hand in hand; to challenge one is to challenge the other.[59] Another strategic response to challenge gender power relations in education is to support the active recruitment of women into administrative positions and men into elementary education. Of course, so long as women are discriminated against in most occupational fields, they may benefit from keeping some occupations highly feminized. The current feminization of teaching is also related to a homophobic ideology, which is related to a patriarchal ideology. That is, because teaching (particularly elementary teaching) is not considered men's work within a patriarchal and homophobic culture, this further discourages men from entering the profession. This indicates, once more, the need to articulate struggles within teaching to broader struggles in the culture.

The road to teacher re-empowerment must be through a movement that rearticulates or reintegrates these various dimensions of struggle in democratic ways. Not only must these different *dimensions* of struggle be better articulated, different *levels* of struggle must be as well. Struggles over discourse and practice in school sites need to be related to struggle in other institutional sites and in the culture generally. Whether and how these struggles get articulated remain very open questions. These are difficult times for the democratic opposition in America, and the fragmentation and marginalization of opposition to the dominant cultural discourse and practice may increase in the immediate years ahead. Certainly, the Gulf War indicated the continued strength of a conservative discourse of *authoritarian populism*

Chapter Seven

designed to appeal to nationalism, patriotism, anti-muslim sentiment, and (more instrumentally) consumerism and protection of a high standard of living. The past several decades have witnessed the virtual collapse of the old Democratic party coalition and political machine. This partly reflects the decline of organized labor as a powerful, cohesive political bloc as America has moved into the post-industrial, union-busting era. In contradistinction to the trade unionism of the early decades of this century, late 20th century trade unionism has been remarkably instrumental and apolitical in its articulation of workers' interests and concerns.[60] Nevertheless, trade unionism has a way of turning political in times of economic crisis; and while the traditional industrial power base of the trade union movement has eroded, it has found a new power base in the public sector and among women and minority workers. The collapse of the Democratic party coalition during the era of the "conservative restoration" also reflects the emergence of new political movements that are not organized around class, including feminist, gay and lesbian, and environmental movements. Finally, the decline of the Democratic party coalition is related to its overemphasis upon budgetary solutions to pressing social problems. Urban schools *do* need more funding, and more secure and stable school budgets. However, in order to provide for these fiscal needs some way most be found of resolving the fiscal crisis of the state, and more particularly of urban school districts, and Democrats have offered few solutions to fiscal crisis. Furthermore, more money alone will not resolve the deep-rooted crisis tendencies in urban schooling.

While the fragmentation of democratic-progressive politics in America along racial, class, gender, sexual preference, environmental and other axes of struggle has hindered the articulation of common themes, some significant progress also has been made in recognizing common interests in change. Should these various axes of struggle get rearticulated within a democratic-progressive discourse, the very breadth of concerns addressed would provide a strength hitherto lacking in American democratic-progressive politics. This, of course, is what Jesse Jackson had in mind in organizing his 1988 Presidential campaign around a Rainbow Coalition theme, and the strength of this incipient democratic Left movement was more important than the fact that it failed to wrest power from the neo-liberal faction in the Democratic party. Furthermore, the "landslide" Republican victory in the 1990 presidental campaign should not be overstated. Those who voted for the Republican ticket represented a minority of the potential adult voting population. Widespread voter apathy among the poor and working class, women, and other dissatisfied groups is more responsi-

Beyond the Crisis

ble for the Republican "landslide" than is public support of the Republican agenda.[61] Meanwhile, the limitations of state intervention to save urban schools have become increasingly obvious, and there is growing evidence that the contradictions endemic to urban schooling in advanced capitalist America will lead to deepening crisis in the years ahead. Given the limitations and contraditions of the conservative discourse and practice in urban school reform and deepening economic, political, and cultural crisis tendencies in America, it may be possible to build a new political movement that rearticulates the interests of various groups around a democratic agenda for change.

Notes

Series Editor's Introduction

1. Linda M. McNeil, *Contradictions of Control* (New York: Routledge, 1986).
2. Lois Weis, *Working Class Without Work* (New York: Routledge, 1990).
3. See Sheldon Danziger and Daniel H. Weinberg, eds., *Fighting Poverty* (Cambridge: Harvard University Press, 1986).
4. Marcus G. Raskin, *The Common Good* (New York: Routledge, 1986).
5. Arthur Wise, *Legislated Learning* (Berkeley: University of California Press, 1979).
6. Quoted in James W. Fraser, "Agents of Democracy: Urban Elementary-School Teachers and the Conditions of Teaching," in Donald Warren, ed., *American Teachers* (New York: Macmillan, 1989), p. 128.
7. *Ibid.*
8. *Ibid.*, p. 138.
9. *Ibid.*, p. 144.
10. For an argument that these two approaches must be combined if we are to more completely understand institutions and power relations in this society, see Erik Olin Wright, *Class, Crisis and the State* (London: New Left Books, 1978).
11. Michael W. Apple, *Education and Power* (New York: Routledge, ARK Edition, 1985) and Michael W. Apple, *Teachers and Texts* (New York: Routledge, 1988).

Notes

12. See Michael W. Apple, *Ideology and Curriculum,* second edition (New York: Routledge, 1990).
13. For further elaboration of what this means for teaching and teacher education, see Daniel P. Liston and Kenneth M. Zeichner, *Teacher Education and the Social Conditions of Schooling* (New York: Routledge, 1991).
14. See Apple, *Education and Power* and Apple, *Teacher and Texts.*

Introduction

1. The ethnographic and historical documentation phase of research in Urbanville was completed over two school years, 1984–86 and was funded through a grant from the Rutgers University Research Council. The study of urban school reform and teacher unionism in Midstate was conducted over the 1987–88 academic year using documents in Alexander Library at Rutgers University. The participant observation study in McKinley Middle School was conducted during the 1988–89 school year. Finally, I was able to undertake an historical study of trade unionism in America while at Princeton University during the summer of 1985 on a Woodrow Wilson Foundation fellowship.
2. Ernesto Laclau and Chantal Mouffe, *Hegemony and Socialist Strategy: Towards a Radical Democratic Politics* (London: Verso, 1985).
3. See Louis Althusser, "Ideology and ideological state apparatuses," in *Lenin and Philosophy and other essays,* trans. B. Brewster (London: New Left Books, 1971); and Samuel Bowles and Herbert Gintis, *Schooling in Capitalist America* (NY: Basic Books, 1976).
4. See Paul Willis, *Learning to Labour: How Working Class Kids Get Working Class Jobs* (Westmead, England: Saxon House, 1977); and Michael Apple, *Education and Power* (Boston: Routledge & Kegan Paul, 1982).
5. The 'correspondence' theory or principle is most associated with Bowles and Gintis, *Schooling in Capitalist America* .
6. Herbert Gintis and Samuel Bowles, "Contradiction and reproduction in educational theory," in Mike Cole, ed., *Bowles and Gintis Revisited; Correspondence and Contradiction in Educational Theory* (NY: Falmer Press, 1988), p. 17.
7. Michael Apple, "The politics of common sense: schooling, populism, and the New Right," in Henry Giroux and Peter McLaren, eds., *Critical*

Notes

Pedagogy, the State, and Cultural Struggle (Albany, NY: SUNY Press, 1989), p. 45.
8. The notion of hegemony is most associated with the work of Antonio Gramsci, the Italian, early 20th-century neo-Marxist. See Gramsci, *Selections from Prison Notebooks* (New York: International Publishers, 1971).
9. See, in particular, Jürgen Habermas, *Legitimation Crisis* (Boston: Beacon Press, 1973).
10. James O'Connor, *The Meaning of Crisis; a Theoretical Introduction* (NY: Basil Blackwell, 1987), p. 155.
11. Max Weber, *From Max Weber: Essays in Sociology*, trans., ed., and with an introduction by H. Gerth and C. Wright Mills (New York: Oxford University Press, 1981), pp. 225–226.
12. Daniel Bell, *The End of Ideology*.
13. See Alvin Gouldner, *Patterns of Industrial Bureaucracy* (Glencoe, Ill.: The Free Press, 1954). Other classic studies that address the issue of unanticipated consequences or vicious cycles of control include Robert Merton, "The unanticipated consequences of purposive social action," *American Sociological Review*, 1 (1936), pp. 894–904; and Philip Selznick, *TVA and the Grass Roots* (Berkeley: University of California Press, 1944). For a discussion of the contributions of this research tradition see Michel Crozier, *The Bureaucratic Phenomenon* (Chicago: University of Chicago Press, 1964).
14. Thomas Timar and David Kirp, *Managing Educational Excellence* (NY: Falmer Press, 1988), p. 5.
15. Max Weber, *The Protestant Ethic and the Spirit of Capitalism* (London: Allen & Unwin, 1976), p. 181.
16. I mean in particular the work of Max Horkheimer and Theodor Adorno, writing in the 1940s. See the Frankfurt Institute for Social Research, *Aspects of Sociology* (Boston: Beacon Press, 1972).
17. See Jürgen Habermas, *The Theory of Communicative Action, Volume I: Reason and the Rationalization of Society* (Boston: Beacon Press, 1984).
18. See Harold Garkinkel, *Studies in Ethnomethodology* (Englewood Cliffs, NJ: Prentice-Hall, 1967) as an example of this discursive tradition in social theory.
19. Cleo Cherryholmes, *Power and Criticism: Poststructural Investigations in Education* (New York: Teachers College Press, 1988). In curriculum studies, where poststructuralism has been most influential within education, the "paradigm shift" to poststructuralism may be associated with the publication of a compilation of essays by the leading figures in the curriculum field that is organized around the notion of curriculum "discourses" (and their historic development) rather than curriculum "theo-

Notes

ries." See William Pinar, ed., *Contemporary Curriculum Discourses* (Scottsdale, Arizona: Gorsuch Scarisbrick, 1988).

20. Michel Foucault, *The History of Sexuality, Volume I: An Introduction*, NY: Vintage Books, 1980), pp. 11–12.

21. Michel Foucault, *Power/Knowledge: Selected Interviews and Other Writings, 1972–1977* (NY: Random House, 1980), p. 204.

22. The notion that the dominant discourse constructs reality and thus identities around bipolar oppositions is most associated with Jacques Derrida, *Positions* (Chicago: University of Chicago Press, 1981). See also Terry Eagleton, *Literary Theory: An Introduction* (Minneapolis: University of Minnesota Press, 1983), p. 132–134. In education, a number of studies have begun to address the identity construction process of students in terms of the interrelationship of class, gender, race, and sexual preference. See, for example, Cameron McCarthey and Michael Apple, "Race, class, and gender in American educational research," in Lois Weis, ed., *Class, Race, and Gender in American Education* (Albany, NY: SUNY Press, 1988); James Sears, *Growing Up Gay in the South: Race, Gender and Journeys of the Spirit* (Binghamton, NY: Haworth Press, 1990); and Lois Weis, *Working Class Without Work; High School Students in a Deindustrializing Economy* (NY: Routledge, 1990).

23. For a discussion of the notion of deconstructionism in the theory of Jacques Derrida see Cherryholmes, *Power and Criticism; Poststructural Investigations in Education*, pp. 36–40, and 120–124.

24. Herbert Gintis, "Communication and politics: Marxism and the 'problem' of liberal democracy," *Socialist Review*, 10 (Nos. 2/3, 1980), p. 218. See also Michael Apple, "Redefining equality: Authoritarian populism and the conservative restoration," *Teachers College Record*, 90 (Winter, 1988), pp 167–184.

25. For examples of the liberal discourse in education, see the reports by the Carnegie Foundation for the Advancement of Teaching, *A Nation Prepared: Teachers for the 21st Century* (New York: Carnegie Forum Task Force on Teaching as a Profession, 1986), and *An Imperiled Generation: Saving Urban Schools* (Lawrenceville, NJ: Princeton University Press, 1988); Theodore Sizer, *Horace's Compromise; the Dilemma of the American High School* (Boston: Houghton-Mifflin, 1984); and The Holmes Group, *Tomorrow's Teachers* (East Lansing, Michigan: The Holmes Group, 1986).

26. Gintis, p. 225.

27. See Ira Shor, *Culture Wars; School and Society in the Conservative Restoration, 1969–1984* (Boston: Routledge & Kegan Paul, 1986).

28. See Laclau and Mouffe for a discussion of Gramsci's notion of hegemony consistent with poststructuralism.

Notes

29. Philip Wexler, *Social Analysis of Education; After the New Sociology* (NY: Routledge & Kegan Paul, 1987), p. 16.
30. See Henry Giroux and Roger Simon, "Schooling, popular culture, and a pedagogy of possibility," *Journal of Education*, 170 (No. 1, 1988), pp. 9–26.
31. See Henry Giroux, "Public philosophy and the crisis in education," *Harvard Educational Review*, 54 (May, 1984), pp. 186–194.

1 Crisis Tendencies in Urban Education

1. Carnegie Foundation for the Advancement of Teaching, *An Imperiled Generation; Saving Urban Schools* (Lawrenceville, NJ: Princeton University Press, 1988), pp. xiv–xv.
2. See David Tyack, *The One Best System: A History of American Urban Education* (Cambridge, Mass.: Harvard University Press, 1974).
3. See James O'Connor, *The Meaning of Crisis; a Theoretical Introduction* (Oxford, UK: Basil Blackwell, 1987); Chapter Three, "Social and political crisis theory," pp. 108–157. For a poststructuralist perspective, see Ernesto Laclau and Chantel Mouffe, *Hegemony and Socialist Strategy: Towards a Radical Democratic Politics* (London: Verso, 1985). While Laclau and Mouffe argue that all Marxism is "in the last analysis" deterministic and reductionistic, I see this determinism as existing primarily in a vulgar strain of structural Marxism.
4. See in particular Jürgen Habermas, "Crisis tendencies in advanced capitalism," Part II of *Legitimation Crisis* (Boston: Beacon Press, 1973), pp. 33–94. See also Madan Sarup, *Education, State and Crisis; a Marxist Perspective* (London: Routledge & Kegan Paul, 1982); and Eric Olin Wright, *Class, Crisis and the State* (NY: New Left Books, 1978).
5. Habermas, p. 35.
6. Habermas, p. 71.
7. Habermas, p. 49.
8. Habermas, p. 49.
9. Habermas, p. 78.
10. Habermas, p. 42.
11. Habermas, pp. 92–93.
12. The term "muddling through" is most associated with Charles Lindbloom's analysis of the policy-making process. While Lindbloom writes within a political science tradition, it is one that treats the political very narrowly as entailing the application of an administrative rationality to

Notes

governmental policy-making. See Lindbloom, *The Policy-Making Process* (Englewood Cliffs, NJ: Prentice-Hall, 1980).
13. Herbert Simon, *Administrative Behavior; a Study of Decision-Making Processes in Administrative Organization* (NY: Free Press, 1976 [first edition, 1945]), p. xxix.
14. See Allan Luke, *Literacy, Textbooks and Ideology: Postwar Literacy Instruction and the Mythology of Dick and Jane* (NY: Falmer Press, 1988).
15. For a recent appraisal of both the usefulness and limitations of the "correspondence principle" in leftist analysis see Herbert Gintis and Samuel Bowles, "Contradiction and reproduction in educational theory," in Mike Cole, ed., *Bowles and Gintis Revisited: Correspondence and Contradiction in Educational Theory* (New York: Falmer Press, 1988), pp. 16–32.
16. This economic rationale provided the conceptual grounding for most of the major commission reports on excellence in education in the 1980s, including: The Carnegie Foundation for the Advancement of Teaching, *A Nation Prepared; Teachers for the 21st Century* (New York: Carnegie Forum Task Force on Teaching as a Profession, 1986); The Education Commission of the States Task Force on Education for Growth, *Action for Excellence* (Denver, Colo.: Education Commission of the States, 1983); and The National Commission on Excellence in Education, *A Nation At Risk* (Washington, D.C.: U.S. Government Printing Office, 1983).
17. See Elizabeth Useem, *Low Tech Education in a High Tech World; Corporations and Classrooms in the New Information Age* (NY: Macmillan, 1986).
18. See Linda McNeil, *Contradictions of Control; School Structure and School Knowledge* (NY: Routledge, Chapman & Hall, 1988). The relatively low achievement and low-order thinking skills of suburban students is also a theme in Theodore Sizer, *Horace's Compromise; the Dilemma of the American High School* (Boston: Houghton-Mifflin, 1984).
19. According to the Department of Labor, roughly 25 percent of the nation's work force is composed of college graduates, higher than in any other industrial nation. Furthermore, this figure is increasing at a time when demand for college graduates has begun to decline. See Louis Uchitelle, "Surplus of college graduates dims job outlook for others," *New York Times* (June 18, 1990), p. 1.
20. Uchitelle, "Surplus of college graduates dims job outlook for others," p. 1.
21. See Henry Levin and Russell Ruberger, *Educational Requirements for*

Notes

New Technologies (Palo Alto: Stanford Center for Educational Research, 1986).
22. See Edward Fiske, "Impending U.S. jobs 'disaster': work force unqualified to work," *New York Times* (September 25, 1989), p. 1.
23. See David Livingston, "Class, educational ideologies, and mass opinion in capitalist crisis: A Canadian perspective," *Sociology of Education*, 58 (1985), pp. 1–24.
24. *New York Times*, "Companies teaching workers 3 R's to compete in age of high technology," (May 1, 1988), p. 26.
25. Cited in David Harman, *Illiteracy; a National Dilemma* (NY: Cambridge, 1987), p. 1.
26. Adult Performance Level Study, *Adult Functional Competency* (Austin,Texas: University of Texas Press, 1975). Also see Harman, p. 7.
27. Carman St. John Hunter, *Adult Illiteracy in the United Nations, a Report to the Ford Foundation* (NY: McGraw-Hill, 1979), p. 27.
28. St. John Hunter, p. 28.
29. W. Ross Winterowd, *The Culture and Politics of Literacy* (NY: Oxford University Press, 1989), p. 5.
30. Jonothan Kozol, *Illiterate America* (Garden City, NY: Anchor Press, 1985), p. 4.
31. Harman, p. 1.
32. Fiske, p. 1.
33. This thesis was popularized by William Ryan, *Blaming the Victim* (NY: Random House, 1971).
34. For a critical assessment of the discourse on functional literacy and an analysis of more democratic, critical pedagogic forms of literacy, see Peter McLaren, "Culture or canon: Critical pedagogy and the politics of literacy," *Harvard Educational Review*, 58 (May, 1988), pp. 213–218; and McLaren and Colin Lankshear, eds., *Critical Literacy* (Albany, NY: SUNY Press,1992).
35. See Signithia Fordham, "Racelessness as a factor in black students' school success: Pragmatic strategy or pyrrhic victory?" *Harvard Educational Review*, 58 (February, 1988), pp. 54–84.
36. I provide an ethnographic example of "teaching to the test" in Dennis Carlson, "'Updating' individualism and the work ethic: Corporate logic in the classroom," *Curriculum Inquiry*, 12 (No. 2, 1982), pp. 125–160. For a discussion of "teaching to the test" and rising test scores see Michael Sedlak, C. Pullin, and P. Cusick, *Selling Students Short: Classroom Bargains and Academic Reform in the American High School* (NY: Teachers College Press, 1986), p. 31. See "Study challenges standardized test results," *New York Times* (November 28, 1987) for an account of a

Notes

report by the Friends for Education Inc. which contends that apparently superior performances by today's students on the Iowa Test of Basic Skills, the Metropolitan Achievement Test, and other standardized tests may merely indicate that school districts are tailoring curriculum and instruction to increase test scores.

37. Philip Jackson, *Life in Classrooms* (NY: Holt, Rinehart & Winston, 1968).
38. Michael Apple (with Nancy King), "Economics and control in everyday school life," in Apple, *Ideology and Curriculum* (London: Routledge & Kegan Paul, 1979), p. 55.
39. Samuel Bowles and Herbert Gintis, *Schooling in Capitalist America* (London: Routledge & Kegan Paul, 1976).
40. Samuel Bowles and Herbert Gintis, "The correspondence principle," in Mike Cole, ed., *Bowles and Gintis Revisited; Correspondence and Contradiction in Educational Theory* (London: Falmer Press, 1988), p. 2.
41. Bowles and Gintis, "The correspondence principle," p. 3.
42. Patrick McGuire and Leonard Lund, "The role of business in precollege education," (The Conference Board, 1984), as quoted in Paul Boyer, "Work habits, not skills, cited," *Education Week*, August 22, 1984, p. 13. See also Robert Crain, "The quality of American high school graduates: What personnel officers say and do about it," a report of The Center for Social Organization of Schools, John Hopkins University, 1984.
43. Cited in Peter Passell, "Forces in society, and Reaganism, helped dig deeper hole for poor," *New York Times* (July 16, 1989), p. 1. Data is from a March, 1989, House Ways and Means Committee report.
44. Max Weber, "The types of legitimate domination," in *Economy and Society, Vol. 3*, ed. G. Roth and C. Wittich (NY: 1968), p. 953.
45. In its most conservative form, this interpretation of Weber is associated with the systems theory of Talcott Parsons. See Parsons, "The school class as a social system: Some of its functions in American society," *Harvard Educational Review*, 29 (Fall, 1959), pp. 297–318.
46. See Habermas, "Max Weber's concept of legitimation," in *Legitimation Crisis*, pp. 97–102. I explore Habermas' notion of a legitimation crisis in Dennis Carlson, "Legitimation and delegitimation: American history textbooks and the Cold War," in Suzanne De Castell, Allan Luke, and Carmen Luke, eds., *Language, Authority and Criticism; Readings on the School Textbook* (NY: Falmer Press, 1988), pp. 46–55.
47. A number of revisionist historians of education have challenged the conventional wisdom that urban schools were the primary mechanism for the advancement of ethnic minorities in the 19th and 20th centuries. See Michael Katz, *Class, Bureaucracy, and Schools* (NY: Praeger, 1975);

Notes

David Tyack, *The One Best System: A History of American Urban Education* (Cambridge, Mass.: Harvard University Press, 1974); and Marvin Lazerson, *American Education in the Twentieth Century* (NY: Teachers College Press, 1987).

48. See W. Norton Grubb and Marvin Lazerson, *Broken Promises: How Americans Fail Their Children* (Chicago: University of Chicago Press, 1982).

49. Michelle Fine, "Schooling and nurturing voice in an improbable context: Urban adolescents in public school," in Henry Giroux and Peter McLaren, eds., *Critical Pedagogy, the State, and Cultural Struggle* (Buffalo, NY: SUNY Press, 1989), p. 157.

50. Cameron McCarthy, *Race and Curriculum; Social Inequality and the Theories and Politics of Difference in Contemporary Research on Schooling* (New York: Falmer, 1990), p. 27.

51. The professionalization of discipline and the associated "normalizing" of deviants is a central theme in the work of Foucault. See Foucault, *Discipline and Punish; the Birth of the Prison*, trans. Alan Sheridan (NY: Vintage Books, 1979).

52. The recent effective schools movement owes much to the conceptual and research framework provided by Wilber Brookover, *et al.*, *School Social Systems and Student Achievement: Schools Can Make A Difference* (NY: Praeger, 1979); and Ronald Edmonds and John Frederiksen, *Search for Effective Schools: The Identification and Analysis of City Schools that are Instructionally Effective for Poor Children* (East Lansing, Michigan: Michigan State University Institute for Research on Teaching, 1979).

53. William Bennett, *What Works* (Washington, D.C.: Department of Education, 1987), p. V.

54. Susan Rosenholtz, "Effective schools: Interpreting the evidence," *American Journal of Education*, 93 (May, 1985), p. 361.

55. Philip Hallinger and Joseph Murphy, "The social context of effective schools," *American Journal of Education*, 94 (May, 1986), p. 338.

56. Hallinger and Murphy, p. 334.

57. Hallinger and Murphy, p. 335.

58. Hallinger and Murphy, p. 333.

59. Bruce Biddle and William Ellena, *Contemporary Research on Teacher Effectiveness* (NY: Holt, Rinehart & Winston, 1964), p. vi.

60. J. M. Stephens, *The Process of Schooling* (NY: Holt, Rinehart & Winston, 1967), p. 84.

61. Christopher Jencks, *et al.*, *Inequality; a Reassessment of the Effect of Family and Schooling in America* (NY: Harper & Row, 1972), p. 91. The so-called Coleman report was the report of the U.S. Commission on Equality of Educational Opportunity that had been created by the Civil

Notes

Rights Act of 1964 and was chaired by James Coleman. See Coleman, *Equality of Educational Opportunity* (Washington, D.C.: U.S. Government Printing Office, 1966).

62. Joan Weitzman, *City Workers and Fiscal Crisis; Cutbacks, Givebacks, and Survival* (New Brunswick, NJ: Rutgers University Press, 1979).

63. National Education Assocation, *Estimates of School Statistics: 1969–1970* (Washington, D.C.: NEA, 1970).

64. I lay out some of the history of performance-based state budgeting and evaluation systems and their impact on instructional reorganization in Dennis Carlson, "Curriculum planning and the state: The dynamics of control in education," in Michael Apple and Landon Beyer, eds., *The Curriculum: Problems, Politics, and Possibilities* (Albany: SUNY Press, 1988), pp. 98–115.

65. National Center for Educational Statistics. *The Condition of Education* (Washington, D.C.: U.S. Department of Education, 1985).

66. See Albert Shanker, "Nationwide threat to school funding; disincentives for change," *New York Times*, weekly AFT column (May 27, 1990), p. E7.

67. James O'Connor, *The Fiscal Crisis of the State* (NY: St. Martin's Press, 1973), p. 6.

68. O'Connor, p. 9

69. O'Connor, p. 9.

70. O'Conner, p. 235.

71. See The Council for Basic Education, *Making Do in the Classroom: A Report on the Misassignment of Teachers* (Washington, D.C.: CBE, 1985); and Fred Hechinger, "'Dirty little secret' of unlicensed teachers," *New York Times* (October 8, 1985), p. C8.

72. See Anthony Giddens, *Central Problems in Social Theory; Action, Structure and Contradiction in Social Analysis* (Berkeley: University of California Press, 1979), p. 93.

73. Cleo Cherryholmes, *Power and Criticism; Poststructural Investigations in Education* (NY: Teachers College Press, 1988), p. 5.

74. See Anthony Giddens, *Capitalism and Modern Social Theory; an Analysis of the Writings of Marx, Durkheim, and Max Weber* (London: Cambridge University Press, 1971), pp. 154–163 on "legitimation, domination, and authority."

75. William Heard Kilpatrick, *Foundations of Method; Informal Talks on Teaching* (NY: Macmillan, 1925), p. 12.

76. Giddens, *Capitalism and Modern Social Theory*, pp. 160–164.

77. Max Weber, *From Max Weber: Essays in Sociology*, ed. and trans. H. H. Girth and C. Wright Mills (NY: Oxford University Press, 1946), p. 426.

Notes

78. Weber, *From Max Weber: Essays in Sociology*, p. 243.
79. Harry Braverman, *Labor and Monopoly Capital* (London: Monthy Review Press, 1974).
80. See Richard Edwards, *Contested Terrain: The Transformation of the Workplace in the Twentieth Century* (NY: Basic Books, 1979).
81. Giddens, *Capitalism and Modern Social Theory*, p. 159.
82. Alvin Gouldner, *Patterns of Industrial Bureaucracy* (Glencoe, Illinois: Free Press, 1954).
83. Habermas, p. 77.
84. Charles Silberman, *Crisis in the Classroom; the Remaking of American Education* (NY: Random House, 1970), p. 95.
85. I explore this issue of individualized, basic skills instructional materials and the "cooling out" of classroom conflict in Dennis Carlson, " 'Updating' individualism and the work ethic: Corporate logic in the classroom."
86. Linda McNeil, p. 158.
87. Samuel Weiss, "As class-cutting rises, 'snowball effect' is feared," *New York Times* (June 27, 1988), p. B1.
88. See J. Johnson, "Nation's schools termed 'stagnant' in federal report," *New York Times*, (May 4, 1989), p. 1.

2 Teachers and Crisis: Teachers' Work Culture in Sociohistorical Perspective

1. Kevin Harris, *Teachers and Classes; a Marxist Analysis* (London: Routledge & Kegan Paul, 1982), p. 124.
2. Henry Giroux and Peter McLaren, "Introduction: Schooling, cultural politics, and the struggle for democracy," in Giroux and McLaren, eds., *Critical Pedagogy, the State, and Cultural Struggle* (Albany, NY: SUNY Press, 1989), p. xxiii.
3. Louis Althusser, "Ideology and the ideological state apparatuses," in B. Cosin, ed., *Education: Structure and Society* (Harmondsworth, England: Penguin Books, 1972). For a discussion of Althusser's general structural theory, see Anthony Giddens, *Central Problems in Social Theory; Action, Structure, and Contradiction in Social Analysis* (Berkeley: University of California Press, 1979), pp. 155–160, and 179–181. For a discussion of Althusser's essay on ideological state apparatuses see Henry Giroux, *Theory and Resistance in Education; a Pedagogy for the Opposition* (Mass.: Begin & Garvey, 1983), pp. 79–83; and Robert Moore, "The correspondence principle and the Marxist sociology of education," in

Notes

Mike Cole, ed., *Bowles and Gintis Revisited: Correspondence and Contradictions in Educational Theory* (NY: Falmer Press, 1988), pp. 51–85.
4. Althusser, p. 245.
5. Althusser, p. 261.
6. The term "new middle class" is used by Guglielmo Carchedi, *On the Economic Identification of Social Classes* (NY: Routledge & Kegan Paul, 1977); the term "professional-managerial class" is used by Barbara Ehrenreich, "The Professional-managerial class," in Paul Walker, ed., *Between Labor and Capital* (Montreal: Black Rose, 1978), pp. 5–48; and the term "petite bourgeoisie" is used by Nicos Poulantzas, *Classes in Contemporary Capitalism* (London: New Left Books, 1975).
7. Harris, p. 90.
8. Philip Wexler, "Ideology and education: From critique to class action," *Interchange*, 13 (No. 3, 1982), pp. 53–68.
9. For an analysis of the de-skilling and proletarianization of labor in industry in the early 20th century see Harry Braverman, *Labor and Monopoly Capital* (London: Monthly Review Press, 1974). Poulantzas and Carchedi are also associated with the thesis that the new middle class is proletarianized and de-skilled.
10. Michael Apple, "Curricular form and the logic of technical control," in Michael Apple and Lois Weis, eds., *Ideology and Practice in Schooling* (Philadelphia: Temple University Press, 1983), p. 151.
11. Harris, p. 73.
12. Paul Willis, *Learning to Labour; How Working Class Kids Get Working Class Jobs* (Westmead, UK: Saxon House, 1977).
13. Quoted in Geoff Esland, *et al.*, *People and Work* (Milton Keynes, England: Open University Press, 1980), p. 203.
14. John Goldthorpe and David Lockwood, *The Affluent Worker in the Class Structure* (London: Cambridge University Press, 1969). The notion that work is not a "central life interest" of workers was originally formulated by Robert Dubin, "Industrial workers' worlds: A Study of the central life interests of industrial workers," *Social Problems*, 3 (1956).
15. Cited in Joseph A. Banks, *Marxist Sociology in Action: A Sociological Critique of the Marxist Approach to Industrial Relations* (London: Faber & Faber, 1970), p. 48.
16. Willis, p. 119.
17. See Jacques Derrida, *Positions* (Chicago: University of Chicago Press, 1981).
18. Willis, p. 119.
19. Harry Wolcott, *Teachers Versus Technocrats: An Educational Innovation in Anthropological Perspective* (Eugene, OR: University of Oregon Press, 1977).

Notes

20. Gerald Grace, *Teachers, Ideology and Control; a Study in Urban Education* (London: Routledge & Kegan Paul, 1978).
21. Grace, p. 218.
22. Grace, p. 217.
23. Willis, p. 59.
24. Willis, p. 1.
25. In America, Michael Apple did the most to popularize Willis' study of the "lads" and to develop and explore the implications of Willis' research. He also pointed out many of the limitations of this line of research in seeking to apply it to teachers, female students, and people of color. See Apple, *Education and Power* (Boston: Routledge & Kegan Paul, 1982), Chapter 4: "Resistance and contradictions in class, culture, and the state: Culture as lived," pp. 91–134.
26. I rely for this analysis of craft unionism in America upon a number of sources. See Banks, *Marxist Sociology in Action*, pp. 250–266; Susan Hirsch, *Roots of the American Working Class: The Industrialization of Crafts in Newark, 1800–1860* (Philadelphia: University of Pennsylvania Press, 1978); David Montgomery, *Workers' Control in America: Studies in the History of Work, Technology, and Labor Struggles* (NY: Cambridge University Press, 1979), pp. 8–90; and Selig Perlman, *A Theory of The Labor Movement* (NY: Macmillan, 1928), pp. 155–236.
27. Dan Lortie, *Schoolteacher; a Sociological Study* (Chicago: University of Chicago Press, 1975), p. 12.
28. Cited in Maurice Berube, *Teacher Politics; the Influence of Unions* (NY: Greenwood Press, 1988), pp. 145–146.
29. Lortie, p. 202.
30. See Magali Larson, *The Rise of Professionalism: A Sociological Analysis* (Berkeley: University of California Press, 1977).
31. Quoted in David Tyack, *The One Best System; a History of American Urban Education* (Cambridge, Mass.: Harvard University Press, 1974), p. 257.
32. See Celia Zitron, *The New York City Teachers Union, 1916–1964; a Story of Educational and Social Commitment* (NY: Humanities Press, 1968).
33. The term "company unionism" is used by Perlman, *Theory of the Labor Movement*, p. 21; and by Richard Henry Tawney in *The American Labour Movement and Other Essays* (NY: St. Martin's Press, 1979), p. 59.
34. Perlman, *Theory of the Labor Movement*, p. 211.
35. Lortie, *Schoolteacher; a Sociological Study*, p. 20.
36. Charles Kerchner and Douglas Mitchell, *The Changing Idea of a Teachers' Union* (Philadelphia: Falmer Press, 1988), p. 6.

Notes

37. Anthony Cresswell and Michael Murphy, *Teachers, Unions, and Collective Bargaining in Public Education* (Philadelphia: Falmer Press, 1988), p. 6.
38. Michael Moskow, "Teacher organizations: An analysis of issues," in Myron Lieberman and Michael Moskow, eds., *Readings on Collective Negotiations in Education* (Chicago: Rand McNally, 1967), p. 243.
39. Stephen Cole, *The Unionization of Teachers: A Case Study of the UFT* (NY: Praeger, 1969), p. 4.
40. See Tawney, *American Labour Movement*, pp. 46–47, for an account of the early organization and growth of the CIO.
41. Commons, *Trade Unionism and Labor Problems*, pp. 8–9.
42. Steve Fraser, "From the 'New Unionism' to the New Deal," *Labor History*, 25 (1984), p. 407.
43. For an account of labor's involvement in the unionization of public school teachers, see Allan West, *The National Education Association: The Power Base for Education* (NY: Free Press, 1980), pp. 52–55.
44. Quoted in West, *National Education Association*, p. 55.
45. National Education Association, *Addresses and Proceedings of the Representative Assembly* (Washington, D.C.: NEA, 1962), p. 52.
46. Cole, *Unionization of Teachers*, p. 21.
47. One of the most detailed studies of fiscal crisis in New York City, including an assessment of public education cutbacks and rollbacks, is provided by Joan Weitzman, *City Workers and Fiscal Crisis: Cutbacks, Givebacks, and Survival* (New Brunswick, NJ: Rutgers University Press, 1979).
48. Myron Lieberman, *Beyond Public Education* (NY: Praeger, 1986), p. 26.
49. Lieberman, p. 33.
50. Kerchner and Mitchell, p. 214.
51. For a discussion of Weber's notion of "negative" politics, see David Beetham, *Max Weber and the Theory of Modern Politics* (Cambridge, Mass.: Polity Press, 1985), pp. 96–98.
52. See Michael Apple, *Teachers and Texts; a Political Economy of Class and Gender Relations in Education* (NY: Routledge & Kegan Paul, 1986), p. 142.
53. Alice Kessler-Harris, *Out to Work; a History of Wage-Earning Women in the United States* (NY: Oxford University Press, 1982), p. 146.
54. Apple, *Teachers and Texts; a Political Economy of Class and Gender Relations in Education* , p. 45.
55. Susan Rosenholtz, "Effective schools: Interpreting the evidence," *American Journal of Education*, 93 (1985), pp. 371 and 368.
56. For an examination of the new political lobbying role of the NEA in the

Notes

1970s and its political agenda see David Stephens, "President Carter, the Congress, and the NEA: Creating the Department of Education," *Political Science Quarterly*, 98 (1983–84), pp. 641–663.
57. Jill Blackmore, "Educational leadership: A feminist critique and reconstruction," in John Smyth, ed., *Critical Perspectives in Educational Leadership* (New York: Falmer Press, 1989), p. 223.

3 Teachers and Basic Skills Restructuring in Midstate

1. See Dennis Carlson, "Curriculum planning and the state: The dynamics of control in education," in Landon Beyer and Michael Apple, eds., *The Curriculum; Problems, Politics, and Possibilities* (Albany, NY: State University of New York Press, 1988), pp. 98–115; and Michael Apple, "State bureaucracy and curriculum control; a review essay of *Legislated Learning: The Bureaucratization of the American Classroom*, by Arthur Wise," *Curriculum Inquiry*, 11 (No 4, 1981), pp. 382–383.
2. See Henry Giroux, "Public philosophy and the crisis in education," *Harvard Educational Review*, 54 (May, 1984), pp. 186–194.
3. Michel Foucault, *The Archaeology of Knowledge* (NY: Vintage Books, 1972).
4. I have fictionalized the names of these school districts in this account.
5. For a discussion of the national debate on the decline of the "credential value" of the high school diploma, see Michael Sedlak, *et al.*, *Selling Students Short; Classroom Bargains and Academic Reform in the American High School* (New York: Teachers College Press, 1986), pp. 21–35.
6. Of course, Stanley Kaplan and Princeton Review have specialized in preparing middle-class, college-bound students with the skills needed to pass the Scholastic Aptitude Test (SAT), Law School Admission Test (LSAT), Medical College Admission Test (MCAT), and other exams. The same basic approach was used by state officials in Midstate in their teach-to-the-test campaign in urban school districts. For a discussion of Stanley Kaplan and Princeton Review approaches to test preparation see Robert Klitgaard, *Choosing Elites: Selecting the "Best and the Brightest" at Top Universities and Elsewhere* (New York: Basic Books, 1985); David Owen, *None of the Above: Behind the Myth of Scholastic Aptitude* (Boston: Houghton Mifflin, 1985); and Deirdre Carmody, "Cram courses for S.A.T. are a booming business," *New York Times* (November 7, 1987), p. L32.
7. Erving Goffman, *The Presentation of Self in Everyday Life* (Garden City, NY: Doubleday, 1959), p. 17.

Notes

8. Stanley Aronowitz and Henry Giroux, *Education Under Siege; the Conservative, Liberal and Radical Debate Over Schooling* (Boston, MA: Bergin & Garvey, 1985), p. 64.
9. While I have focused on the state tier of government in this chapter, I do not mean to downplay the significance of the federal role in promoting bureaucratic managerial models in education and an economically functional curriculum. For an analysis of the federal role in education, see Joel Spring, *The Sorting Machine Revisited; National Educational Policy Since 1945* (New York: Longman, 1989).
10. See Roberto Suro, "Courts ordering financing changes in public schools," *New York Times* (March 11, 1990), p. 1.
11. John Goodlad, *A Place Called School; Prospects for the Future* (New York: McGraw-Hill, 1984), p. 294.
12. See Michael deCourcy Hinds, "Cutting the dropout rate: high goal but low hopes," *New York Times*, (February 17, 1990), p. 1.
13. We must be careful not to take this criticism of big government and more spending as an endorsement of the social agenda of the New Right, with its emphasis upon "starving" essential public institutions and privatizing social services.
14. See W. Norton Grubb and Marvin Lazerson, *Broken Promises: How Americans Fail Their Children* (Chicago: University of Chicago Press, 1982).
15. Thomas Peters and Robert Waterman, *In Search of Excellence: Lessons from America's Best-Run Companies* (NY: Warner Books, 1984).

4 Teachers and Basic Skills Restructuring in Urbanville

1. The name of the research and development center has been fictionalized.
2. See Harry Braverman, *Labor and Monopoly Capital* (London: Monthly Review Press, 1974) for a critical history of Taylorism and scientific management in industry.
3. David Tyack, *The One Best System* (Cambridge, Mass.: Harvard University Press, 1974).
4. James B. Conant, *Slums and Suburbs; a Commentary on Schools in Metropolitan Areas* (NY: McGraw-Hill, 1961).
5. National Education Association, *Cardinal Principles of Secondary Education: A Report of the Commission on the Reorganization of Secondary Education* (Washington, D.C.: US Government Printing Office, 1918).
6. Of a French bureaucratic agency, Michel Crozier writes: "The staff's dissatisfaction and pessimism do not prevent a satisfactory basic pattern

Notes

of adjustment. Indeed, they can be viewed as a specific way, a 'grumbling way,' of achieving it" (Crozier, *The Bureaucratic Phenomenon* [Chicago: University of Chicago Press, 1964], p. 50).
7. Henry Giroux, "Rethinking the boundaries of educational discourse: Modernism, postmodernism, and feminism," *College Literature*, 17 (Nos. 2/3, 1990), p. 45.

5 Role Formalization and "Playing the Game" in Urbanville Schools

1. The contribution of game theory to economics has been considerable. The classic work in this field is John von Neumann and Oskar Morgenstern, *Theory of Games and Economic Behavior* (Princeton, NJ: Princeton University Press, 1944). In political science game theory has also been employed to analyze military campaigns, international relations, and voting patterns. See Steven Brams, *Game Theory and Politics* (New York: Free Press, 1975). The application of game theory in sociology has been associated with "ethnomethodology" and dramaturgical or "self-presentation" analysis. See Harold Garfinkel, *Studies in Ethnomethodology* (Englewood Cliffs, NJ: Prentice-Hall, 1967); and Erving Goffman, *The Presentation of Self in Everyday Life* (Garden City, NY: Doubleday, 1959).
2. Brams, introductory note.
3. Erving Goffman, *Frame Analysis; an Essay on the Organization of Experience* (New York: Harper & Row, 1974), p. 455.
4. Goffman, *Frame Analysis*, p. 457.
5. Brams, p. 4.
6. Herve Moulin, *Game Theory for the Social Sciences* (New York: New York University Press, 1982).
7. Brams, p. 8
8. See Andrew Levine, Elliot Sober, and Erik Olin Wright, "Marxism and methodological individualism," *New Left Review* (No. 162, March–April, 1987), pp. 67–84.
9. Levine, Sober, and Wright, p. 68.

6 "Classroom Management" in the Basic Skills Era

1. Michael Apple, "Curricular form and the logic of technical control: building the possessive individual," in Apple, ed., *Cultural and Economic*

Notes

Reproduction in Education; Essays on Class, Ideology and the State (Boston: Routledge & Kegan Paul, 1982), p. 256.
2. Lee Canter (with Marlene Canter), *Assertive Discipline: A Take-Charge Approach for Today's Educator* (Los Angeles: Canter & Associates, 1979).
3. Daniel Duke and Adrienne Meckel, *Teacher's Guide to Classroom Management* (NY: Random House, 1984), pp. 10–11.
4. Duke & Meckel, pp. 11–13.
5. Duke & Meckel, p. 34.
6. U. S. Department of Education, *Research in Brief* (Washington, D.C; June, 1988).
7. Gerald Levy, *Ghetto School; Class Warfare in an Elementary School* (New York: Pegasus Press, 1970).
8. Levy, pp. 48–49.
9. Jonothan Kozol, *Death at an Early Age* (New York: Houghton Mifflin, 1967).
10. Kozol, pp. 9–10.
11. See Harry Braverman, *Labor and Monopoly Capital* (London: Monthly Review Press, 1974); and Richard Edwards, *Contested Terrain: The Transformation of the Workplace in the Twentieth Century* (New York: Basic Books, 1979).

7 Beyond the Crisis in Urban Schooling

1. See Ira Shor, *Culture Wars: School and Society in the Conservative Restoration, 1969–1984* (Boston: Routledge & Kegan Paul, 1986).
2. I am indebted to Stephen Haymes, Sociology Department, University of Wisconsin-Milwaukee, for helping me understand the spatial politics of urban school reform in the basic skills era.
3. For a discussion of "authoritarian populism" as applied generally to recent political developments, see Stuart Hall, "Popular democratic versus authoritarian populism: Two ways of taking democracy seriously," in Alan Hunt, ed., *Marxism and Democracy* (London: Lawrence and Wishart, 1980), pp. 190–191. See also, Michael Apple, "Redefining equality: Authoritarian populism and the conservative restoration," *Teachers College Record*, 90 (No. 2, Winter, 1988), pp. 167–184.
4. Thomas Timar & David Kirp, *Managing Educational Excellence* (NY: Falmer Press, 1988), p. 67.
5. See William Bickel, "Knowledge, Dissemination, Inquiry," *Educational*

Notes

Researcher, special issue on Effective Schools, 12 (No. 4, 1983), pp. 3–5.

6. Cleo Cherryholmes, *Power and Criticism; Poststructural Investigations in Education* (NY: Teachers College Press, 1988), p. 152.
7. See Raymond Callahan, *Education and the Cult of Efficiency* (Chicago: University of Chicago Press, 1962).
8. Timar & Kirp, p. 6.
9. See, for example, The Carnegie Foundation for the Advancement of Teaching, *A Nation Prepared: Teachers for the 21st Century* (NY: Carnegie Forum Task Force on Teaching as a Profession, 1986), and *An Imperiled Generation: Saving Urban Schools* (Lawrenceville, NJ: Princeton University Press, 1988); The Holmes Group, *Tomorrow's Teachers* (East Lansing, Michigan: The Homes Group, 1986); and Theodore Sizer, *Horace's Compromise; the Dilemma of the American High School* (Boston: Houghton-Miflin, 1984).
10. *A Nation Prepared*, p. 45. (All citations are from excerpts from the report published in the *Chronicle of Higher Education*, 32 [May 21, 1986], pp. 43–51).
11. *A Nation Prepared*, p. 44.
12. *A Nation Prepared*, pp. 46–47.
13. *An Imperiled Generation*, p. xii.
14. *An Imperiled Generation*, p. xv.
15. *An Imperiled Generation*, pp. 5–7.
16. *An Imperiled Generation*, p. 4.
17. *An Imperiled Generation*, p. 19.
18. *An Imperiled Generation*, p. 13.
19. *An Imperiled Generation*, p. 29.
20. *An Imperiled Generation*, p. 9.
21. *An Imperiled Generation*, pp. 10–11.
22. *An Imperiled Generation*, p. 13.
23. James Traub, "Fernandez takes charge: New York City's blunt new schools chancellor is shaking up the bureaucracy," *New York Times Magazine* (June 17, 1990), p. 25. See also, Felicia Lee, "New school chief: An innovator and taker of risks," *New York Times* (September 25, 1989), p. B1; and Joseph Berger, "Can the star of Miami save New York City schools?" *New York Times* (January 7, 1990), Section 4, p. 1.
24. John Dewey, *Democracy and Education* (New York: Macmillan, 1966) (first printing, 1916), p. 338.
25. Dewey, p. 339.
26. John Dewey, "The underlying philosophy of education," Chapter IX in William H. Kilpatrick, ed., *The Educational Frontier* (NY: The Century Co., 1933), pp. 316–317.

Notes

27. Charles Silberman, *Crisis in the Classroom: The Remaking of American Education* (NY: Random House, 1970).
28. Silberman, *Crisis in the Classroom*, p. 95.
29. Svi Shapiro, *Between Capitalism and Democracy; Educational Policy and the Crisis of the Welfare State* (New York: Bergin & Garvey, 1990), p. 66.
30. Herbert Gintis, "Communication and politics: Marxism and the 'problem' of liberal democracy," in *Socialist Review*, 10 (Nos. 2/3, 1980), p. 198.
31. See Antonio Gramsci, "Some problems in the study of the philosophy of praxis," in *Selections from the Prison Notebooks*, trans. and ed. Quintin Hoare & Geoffrey Smith, (NY: International Publishers, 1980), pp. 381–419
32. Peter McLaren, "Culture or canon? Critical pedagogy and the politics of literacy," *Harvard Educational Review*, 58 (May, 1988), p. 214.
33. Henry Giroux, "Rethinking the boundaries of educational discourse: Modernism, postmodernism, and feminism," *College Literature*, 17 (No. 2/3, 1990), p. 42
34. Critical Pedagogy, as Giroux and others have developed it within an American context, owes much to the work of the Brazilian educator, Paulo Freire. See Freire, *Pedagogy of the Oppressed* (New York: Seabury Press, 1970), and *The Politics of Education: Culture, Power, and Liberation* (South Hadley, Mass.: Bergin & Garvey, 1985). See also Peter McLaren, "Review article—postmodernity and the death of politics: A Brazilean reprieve," *Educational Theory*, 36 (Fall, 1986), pp. 389–401.
35. See Jürgen Habermas, *The Theory of Communicative Action, Volume I: Reason and the Rationalization of Society*, trans. Thomas McCarthy (Boston: Beacon Press, 1984).
36. See Thomas McCarthy, *The Critical Theory of Jürgen Habermas* (Cambridge, Mass.: MIT Press, 1978), p. 280.
37. Jürgen Habermas, "A reply to my critics," in John Thompson and David Held, *Habermas: Critical Debates* (Cambridge, Mass.: MIT Press, 1982), p. 246.
38. Robert Young, *A Critical Theory of Education; Habermas and Our Children's Future* (New York: Teachers College Press, 1990), p. 71.
39. Cameron McCarthy, *Race and Curriculum; Social Inequality and the Theories and Politics of Difference in Contemporary Research on Schooling* (New York: Falmer, 1990), p. 132.
40. McCarthy, *Race and Curriculum*, p. 133.
41. William Bigelow, "Inside the classroom: Social vision and critical pedagogy," *Teachers College Record*, 91 (Spring, 1990), pp. 437–448.
42. Bigelow, p. 438.

Notes

43. Bigelow, p. 439.
44. Bigelow, p. 443.
45. Karl Marx and Frederick Engels, *The German Ideology, Part One* (NY: International Publishers, 1974), p. 42.
46. See Tom Schuller, *Democracy at Work* (NY: Oxford University Press, 1985), p. 4.
47. See Ed Davis and Russell Lansbury, "Democracy and control in the workplace: An introduction," in Davis and Lansbury, eds., *Democracy and Control in the Workplace* (Melbourne, Australia: Longman Cheshire, 1986), pp. 1–29.
48. See Schuller, Chapter 9: "Dividing labour and ruling skills," pp. 132–149.
49. See Kenneth Zeichner, "Contradictions and tensions in the professionalization of teaching and the democratization of schools," *Teachers College Record*, 92 (Spring, 1991), pp. 363–379.
50. John Dewey, *The Sources of a Science of Education* (New York: Horace Liveright, 1929), pp. 46–48.
51. Joe Kincheloe, *Teachers as Researchers: Qualitative Inquiry as a Path to Empowerment* (New York: Falmer, 1991), p. 18.
52. Kincheloe, *Teachers as Researchers*, p. 20.
53. Quoted by John Holusha, "The man who is fighting the U.A.W. from inside," *New York Times* (October 23, 1988), p. F6.
54. Albert Shanker, "What's wrong with schools? Ask the kids," a column in the AFT *Where We Stand* series in the *New York Times* (September 22, 1989), p. E7.
55. See Nancy Burstein and Beverly Cabello, "Preparing teachers to work with culturally diverse students: A teacher education model," *Teacher Education*, 40 (September–October, 1989), pp. 9–16.
56. See "Educators advocate steps to lure minority teachers," *New York Times* (May 30, 1990), p. B9.
57. See Albert Shanker, "Disincentives for change," *New York Times* (May 27, 1990), p. E7.
58. Amitai Etzioni, *The Semi-Professions and their Organization* (Glencoe, Ill.: The Free Press, 1969).
59. See Michael Apple, *Teachers and Texts; a Political Economy of Class and Gender Relations in Education* (NY: Routledge & Kegan Paul, 1986). Apple notes: The very program of rationalizing all important social relations in our major institutions is, in fact, pre-eminently a masculine discourse.... [S]uch a hierarchical conception is not neutral. It disenfranchises alternative concerns for human relations, connectedness, and care" (p. 142).
60. See David Montgomery, *The Fall of the House of Labor: The Workplace,*

Notes

the State and American Labor Activism, 1865–1925 (Cambridge, UK: Cambridge University Press, 1987).

61. For an analysis of the 1988 presidential election and the role of the Rainbow Coalition see Andrew Kopkind, "The Jackson movement," *New Left Review*, No. 172 (November–December, 1988), pp. 83–91.

Index

Absenteeism, teacher: morale and classroom management, 208; preparation periods, 172, 174
Abuse, student, 214–15
Accountability, 231–32
Administration: NEA and power relations, 89; Professional Improvement Plans (PIPs), 139–40; review of case study data, 220; teachers and otherness, 81
Adult Proficiency Level (APL) Study, 34–35
Affirmative action, 250
AFL-CIO: company family ideology, 90; craft unionism, 86; industrial unionism, 92, 93, 94–95; organization of teachers, 95–96
Alienation, student: student/teacher racial disparities, 250; technical control, 58
Alternative school programs: barriers to liberal and humanistic experiments, 238; basic skills restructuring and vicious cycle of control, 13–14, 59–60
Althusser, Louis, 68–69
American Federation of Teachers (AFT): AFL-CIO and teacher organization, 96; teacher professionalism, 84, 248

Anger, student, 195–96
Apathy, teacher, 166–67
Apparatus, discourse, 18
Apple, Michael: construction of interests by teachers, 7; deskilling of teachers and classroom management, 186; deskilling of teachers and proletarianization thesis, 73; hidden curriculum of classroom life, 38; popularization and limitations of Willis' research, 267; role formalization and decision-making, 100–101
Apprenticeship, 83
Aronowitz, Stanley, 121
Art, 149
Assault, teacher/student, 191–95
Assertive Discipline, 188–89, 190
Authoritarianism, 206–207
Authoritarian populism, 222, 251–52
Authority: bureaucratic control, 56–57; charismatic, 55–56; rationalization of institutional, 214–15; restrictions on discipline options, 204; traditional form, 54–55

Backloading, 160, 161
Basic skills: author's objectives, 22–23;

277

Index

bureaucratic-rational forms of control, 186; classroom management and order, 24;
conservative state discourse on reform, 221–25; control crisis, 54–62; crisis tendencies and reform, 62–63; defined in context, 1; disempowerment of teachers and bureaucratic-hierarchical discourse, 4; effective schools movement, 47–48, 201; end-of-ideology thesis, 10–11; fiscal crisis and cost-effective curriculum, 52–54; hidden curriculum and work norms, 39–40; literacy and semi-skilled job market, 35; Midstate and rise of educational state, 120–25; Midstate diploma exam, 118–19; poststructural analysis of discourse, 18–19; review of case study data, 219–20; student motivation, 36–37; technical controls, 60–61; unionism and coextensive development, 2–3; Urbanville teachers and restructuring, 136–43, 151–53; vicious cycle of control, 13–14, 60–61

Behavioralism: basic skills restructuring in Urbanville, 137–39; effective schools research and student motivation, 46
Bell, Daniel, 11
Bennett, William, 44
Biddle, Bruce, 46–47
Bigelow, William, 244–45
Bilinguality, 205–206
Bipolar oppositions, 19, 258
Black Power movement, 196–97
Blacks: illiteracy, 36; males and hidden curriculum, 198. *See also* Minorities; Race
Boston, 229, 250
Bowles, Samuel, 6, 38–39
Boyer, Ernest, 226
Brams, Steven, 157
Braverman, Harry, 57
Breaks, teacher, 174
Buildings, physical conditions, 171–72
Bureaucracy: forms of authority, 56–57; liberal and leftist neo-Weberians, 58; staff dissatisfaction and adjustment, 270–71; vicious cycle of control, 13–15
Burn-out, teacher, 181

Capitalism: as discursive practice, 27–28; ideology of advanced, 29–30; worker motivation, 58–59
Carey, James, 96–97
Carnegie Foundation: conclusions on crisis tendencies, 25; liberal discourse on reform, 226–33
Cavazos, Lauro, 63
Centralization, 222. *See also* Decentralization; Decision-making
Charismatic leaders, 55–56
Cheating, 120
Cherryholmes, Cleo: definition of power, 54; poststructural perspectives on educational research, 17; vulgar pragmatism, 224
Chicago, 229
Chicago Teachers' Federation, 87
Civil rights: centralization of state power, 222; problem of order, 220; traditional form of authority, 55
Class: hidden curriculum and work norms, 39; legitimation crisis, 41–48; liberal discourse on reform, 237; Marxism and capitalist society, 28; Marxism and conceptual limitations, 5; repressive forms of control, 220; teachers' work culture, 2; Urbanville Education Association organization and leadership, 134, 136, 152–53. *See also* Middle class
Class-cutting, 61–62, 229
Classroom: additional classes and working condition contract disputes, 179–81; author's objectives, 24; class size, 53; official model, 200–203; self-contained, 85; teacher morale, 207–11. *See also* Classroom management; Control; Working conditions
Classroom management: bureaucratic rationalization, 186–87, 213–15; efficiency discourse, 186; McKinley School and problem of order, 203–207; Urbanville teachers and control, 188–98. *See also* Control; Order
Coalition of Essential Schools, 226
Cole, Stephen, 90
Coleman report, 263–64
Collective bargaining: conservative state discourse on reform, 225; end-of-ide-

Index

ology thesis, 12; industrial unionism, 93–94, 97–98; public employees, 95; terms and conditions of employment, 164–65; urban school crisis of mid 1960s, 2–3

College: basic skills and lack of preparation for, 223; graduates as percent of work force, 260; minimum competency tests and Midstate diploma exam, 119, 124; preparatory programs and legitimation crisis, 42; teacher training and state, 84

Committees, union, 133–34

Commons, John, 92

Communicative rationality, 242–43

Community, 135, 152–53

Company unionism, 88–91

Competency tests: college entry exams and standardized testing, 119; functional literary crisis, 35, 37–38. *See also* Standardized testing

Conant, James, 149

Conference Board, 39

Conflict management, 11–12

Conservatism: collective bargaining and teachers, 98; end-of-ideology thesis, 10–11; legitimation crisis and minority failure, 42–43; models of state reform, 125; social agenda of New Right, 270; state discourse on reform, 221–25; work skills and educational reform, 32. *See also* Right

Contract: end-of-ideology thesis, 181–83; game theory and employment terms and conditions, 162–81; game theory and teacher orientation, 23–24; game theory and wage package, 159–62

Contradiction, 8–9

Control: authoritarian and repressive forms, 185–86; basic skills and crisis of order, 54–62; bureaucratic rationalization, 186; review of case study data, 220; teachers and job, 82–88; Weberian concept of vicious cycle, 12–15, 58, 59–61. *See also* Classroom management; Order

Cooperation: charismatic model of teaching, 56; game theory, 158

Cost-effective curriculum, 49–54

Counter-hegemony, 8

Courts: affirmative action and teaching, 250; assault cases involving students and teachers, 192–94; Midstate and fiscal crisis, 108–109, 110–11; teachers and collective bargaining rights, 164–65

Craft unionism, 82–88

Cresswell, Anthony, 89

Crime, 198

Crisis: author's objectives, 21–22; basic skills and reform, 62–63; bureaucratic rationalization of classroom control, 186; democratic-progressive discourse, 239–53; fiscal and cost-effective curriculum, 49–54; game theory, 183; legitimation and effective schools, 41–48; Marxist analysis, 8–9; Midstate case study, 106–12; order and basic skills, 54–62; review of case study data, 218–19; teachers' work culture, 102–104; teacher unionism, 82; theoretical grounding, 26–31; work skills and curriculum reform, 31–41

Culture: contract in secular American, 179; Hispanic and classroom management, 206; multiculturalism, 243–44

Curriculum: comprehensive and teaching of basics in Urbanville, 147–53; crisis tendencies and reform, 31–41; fiscal crisis and cost-effective, 49–54; hidden and work norms, 38–39; poststructuralism and studies of, 257

Cynicism, teacher, 181

Data: classroom management, 187–88; longitudinal study of basic skills, 106; sources for Midstate case study, 256; sources for Urbanville case study, 128, 156, 256

Decentralization: decision-making and accountability, 231–32; New York City experience, 234–35; vicious cycle of control, 13, 14. *See also* Centralization; Decision-making

Decision-making: decentralization and accountability, 231–32; unions and collaborative, 248–49; workplace democratization, 245–46. *See also* Centralization; Decentralization

279

Index

Deconstruction, 19–21
Democracy: Weber and substantive, 10; workplace democratization, 245–46
Democratic party: decline of American political liberalism, 252; Midstate reform agenda, 123–25; teachers' unions and partisan politics, 101
Democratic-progressivism, 239–53
Derrida, Jacques, 19
Deskilling, teacher: behavioral objective movement, 138–39; bureaucratic-rational forms of student control, 186; proletarianization thesis, 72–74
Detention, 210
Determinism: reproductive theory of teaching, 71; structural Marxism, 259
Dewey, John: experimental schools and progressive methods, 236, 237; Midstate Educational Association and progressive ideals, 113; teacher as investigator, 246
Diagnosis, educational, 114
Difference, 19
Diploma exam. *See* Standardized testing; TEaching-to-the-test
Discipline. *See* Classroom Management; Control; Order
Discourse: conservative on reform, 221–25; construction of reality and identities and bipolar oppositions, 258; deconstruction, 19–21; democrative-progressive on reform, 239–53; liberal on reform, 226–39; poststructuralist concept, 17–19; power relations, 54; sources of discursive data, 106; systemic theory of practices, 26–27
Drop-out rates: Midstate and diploma exams, 119; Urbanville and diploma exams, 148. *See also* Class-cutting; Truancy
Drugs, 203

Economics: as cause of crisis, 2; conceptual grounding of commission reports on education, 260; game theory, 271; infrastructure as structure of dominance, 69; liberal discourse on reform, 233–34
Educational Testing Service, 115

Effective schools research: classroom management and McKinley School, 201; conservative state discourse, 224; legitimation crisis, 44–48; Midstate Educational Association and standardized testing, 117–18; role formalization, 101; time-on-task and control, 61; time-on-task and instructional efficiency, 140–41
Elections committee, 133
Elementary and Secondary Education Act (ESEA), 49–50
Elementary teachers: preparation periods, 173–74; scans and basic skill reforms, 142–43; teacher-administrator conflict, 168–169
Elites: critical analysis of crisis tendencies, 28; defining of teachers' interests, 155–56; hegemony and crisis management, 9
Ellena, William, 46–47
Emotionally disturbed, 196
Employment: as cause of crisis, 2; college graduates and job outlook, 260; Midstate and crisis, 107–108; Urbanville teachers and terms and conditions contract, 162–81. *See also* Semi-skilled employment; Work skills
Empowerment: classroom management and rationalization of authority, 215; patriarchal ideology and teachers, 4; professional and craft of teachers, 87
End-of-ideology thesis: classroom management and efficiency discourse, 186; conservative state discourse on reform, 224; elites and teachers' interests, 156; labor-management relations, 24; progressive experimentalism, 237; Urbanville teachers and game theory, 181–83; vicious cycle of control, 14–15; Weberian concept, 10–12
Environment, 27
Equality: elementary and secondary teachers and gender, 143; legitimation crisis, 41–42; state funding for education, 108–11. *See also* Gender; Racism; Sexism
Ethnicity, 2. *See also* Minorities; Race
Etzioni, Amitai, 251

Index

Evaluation, student: liberal discourse on reform, 232; working condition contract disputes, 177–79

Evaluation, teacher: "One Best Way" of teaching, 143–47; teachers and role formalization, 100; scans and basic skills reforms in Urbanville, 142

Expectations: middle class and work, 239; positive thinking and classroom behavior, 202–203

Family, company unionism, 88–91
Federal Government, 121. See also Courts; Fiscal crisis; State
Feminism, 99. See also Gender
Fernandez, Joseph, 235
Fine, Michelle, 42
Fiscal crisis: cost-effective curriculum, 49–54; liberal response, 122–23; Midstate case study, 108–11; wage roll-backs and teachers, 74
Ford, Henry, 57, 83
Foucault, Michel: discourse terminology, 17–18, 106; professionalization of discipline and normalizing of deviants, 263
Frankfurt School: elites and crisis tendencies, 28; end-of-ideology thesis, 12; mass culture, 30; one-dimensionality of modern life, 15
Free school, 238
Friends for Education Inc., 262
Functionalism, 6–7

Game theory: conceptual framework, 157–59; contract orientation, 23–24; contributions to economics, political science, and sociology, 271; review of case study data, 219; theoretical grounding for study, 16–17
Urbanville teachers: end-of-ideology thesis, 181–83; terms and conditions of employment, 162–81; wage-labor contract, 159–62
Gender: democratic-progressive alternative, 251; elementary teachers and scans, 143; liberal discourse on reform, 237; rationalizing of social relations as masculine discourse, 275; resistance to innovation, 99; teacher professionalism, 103; teachers' work culture, 3–4; Union leadership, 221; Urbanville Education Association and contract negotiations, 167; Urbanville Education Association and power relations, 134, 136, 152. See also Sexism

Getting over, 211–13
Gintis, Herbert: concrete political struggles and neo-Marxism, 240; hidden curriculum and work norms, 38–39; social justice and liberal discourse, 20–21; structural-functional reproductive theory of schooling, 6
Giroux, Henry: critical pedagogy and teaching, 242; democratic coalition for change, 153; literacy and economic functionalism, 121; teachers as transformative intellectuals, 66
Goal displacement, 182–83
Goffman, Erving, 120, 157
Gouldner, Alvin, 58
Government. See Courts; Federal government; State
Grace, Gerald, 78
Grade books, 146
Gramsci, Antonio, 240, 257
Grievances, teachers': after-school meetings and parent conferences, 175–76; as data source, 128; Urbanville Education Association and contract negotiations, 167–68
Gulf War, 251

Habermas, Jurgen: capitalism and worker motivation, 59; concept of crisis, 8; crisis tendencies, 28–30; critical literacy curriculum and critical pedagogy, 242; critical reading of Weber, 15
Haley, Margaret, 87
Hallinger, Philip, 45–46
Harris, Kevin, 66, 70
Hegemony, 7–8, 257
Hispanics, 205–206. See also Minorities; Race
History: determinism and structural Marxist reproduction theory, 240; re-

281

Index

visionist on urban schools and ethnic minorities, 262
Holmes Group, 226
Homophobia, 251
Houston, 229
Hunter, Madeleine, 100

Identity: poststructuralism and construction, 19; teacher formation and occupational movement, 80–82
Ideology: Habermas and advanced capitalism, 29–30; limitations, 76–77; resistance theory, 79; scientific management and social interests, 215; standardized testing and Midstate, 114; state apparatuses and education, 69. See also End-of-ideology thesis
Image, 120
An Imperiled Generation: Saving Urban Schools (1988), 226, 229–33
Incorporation thesis, 75–80
Individualized Educational Plan, 43
Industrial relations, 11–12
Industrial unionism, 91–102, 103–104
Information, perfect, 158
Innovation, 98–99
Institutionalization, 1
Instrumentalism, 16–17
Intercoms, 209–10
Interest construction, 7–8

Jackson, Jesse, 94, 252
Jackson, Philip, 38
Japan, 227
Jencks, Christopher, 47
Johnson administration, 34, 49

Kaplan, Stanley, 117, 269
Kennedy, John, 95
Kerchner, Charles, 89, 98
Kessler-Harris, Alice, 100
Kilpatrick, William Heard, 55
Kincheloe, Joe, 246–47
Kindergartens, 38
King, Nancy, 38
Kirp, David: conservative state discourse on reform, 223, 225; neo-Weberian study of basic skills reforms, 14
Kozol, Jonothan, 35–36, 214

Labeling, student, 119–20, 196
Language, 163, 205. See also Discourse
Lead Teachers, 228, 235
Lee Canter & Associates, 188
Left, 90. See also Liberalism
Legislation, 191–92. See also State
Legitimation: crisis and effective schools, 41–48; fiscal crisis, 51; teacher job control, 85–86
Leninism, 28
Lesson planning: role formalization and job control, 100; teacher evaluation, 146
Levy, Gerald, 213–14
Liberalism: decline of American political, 252; deconstruction of discourse, 20–21; discourse on reform, 226–39; end-of-ideology thesis, 11; funding and discourse on reform, 122–23; minority failure, 43; models of state reform, 125
Liegerman, Myron, 98
Limitations, ideological, 76–77
Lindbloom, Charles, 259–60
Literacy: competency tests, 37–38; democratic-progressive discourse, 241–45; economic functionalism, 121; increase in 1980s, 35–36; Midstate and crisis, 108; Midstate and diploma exam, 118–19; semi-skilled job market, 33–35
Lobbying, 101, 112
Lockwood, David, 75
Lortie, Dan: company family ideology in public education, 89; spatial power relations of schooling, 85; teachers and job control, 84

McCarthy, Cameron, 43, 243
McKinley Middle School: "chronic" urban school teachers, 213–14; description of, 198–99; "getting over" by teachers and students, 211–13; order problem, 200–13; review of case study data, 219–21; teacher morale and classroom management, 207–11
McLaren, Peter, 66, 241
McNeil, Linda, 61
Mainstreaming, 191
Management: principles of enlightened

Index

business, 124–25; scientific, 57, 144, 215
Manufacturing, 107
Marxism: capitalism as discursive practice, 27–28; class analysis, 3; determinism and structural, 259; lack of constructive alternatives, 239–40; theoretical grounding for study, 5–9. *See also* Marx, Karl
Marx, Karl: trade union movement, 75–76; Weberian analysis, 9–10; work and culture, 245; worker alienation, 58. *See also* Marxism
Massachusetts, 50
Mathematics, 115
Media, 56
Meetings, after-school, 174–77
Merton, Robert, 238
Middle class: liberalism and work expectations, 239; proletarianization thesis, 72–73; structural neo-Marxism, 69–70; terminology, 266
Midstate case study: basic skills and rise of educational state, 120–25; review of case study data, 218–19; sources of crisis, 106–12; standardized testing and teachers, 112–20. *See also* Midstate Education Association (MEA)
Midstate Education Association (MEA): behavioral objectives, 138–39; classroom management, 189–92; courts and collective bargaining, 165; courts and strikes, 165–66; effective schools research, 117–18; game theory and wage-labor contract, 159–62; standardized testing, 112–13, 115; state funding and fiscal crisis, 111–12
Minorities: revisionist historians on urban schools, 262; Urbanville Education Association and community, 135. *See also* Race; Racism
Mitchell, Douglas, 89, 98
Morale, teacher: classroom management, 207–11; comprehensive curriculum, 151
Motivation, student: basic skills and work norms, 40; crisis tendencies, 30; effective schools research, 46; functional literary crisis, 36–37; problem of order, 205; technical control, 58–59
Multiculturalism, 243–44
Murphy, Joseph, 45–46
Murphy, Michael, 89
Music, 149

National Board for Professional Teaching Standards, 228
National Civic Federation (NCF), 88, 90
National Education Association (NEA): company family ideology, 89–90; comprehensive high school curriculum, 150; craft and professional orientations, 86; industrial unionism, 96–97; teacher professionalism and collaborative decision-making, 248; UniServ and contract bargaining, 160
National Labor Relations Board, 93
A Nation at Risk, 226, 260
A Nation Prepared: Teachers for the 21st Century (1986): liberal discourse on reform, 226–29, 232–33, 260
Negativism: teachers and politics, 99
Neo-Marxism: class analysis, 3; crisis tendencies, 28; lack of constructive alternatives, 240; new middle class, 69–70; theoretical grounding for study, 5–9
New Right, 270. *See also* Conservatism; Right
New York City: class-cutting and truancy rates, 61–62, 229; experience with decentralization, 234–35; fiscal crisis, 49, 50; student/teacher racial disparities, 250
New York City Teachers' Union, 87–88
New York Times, 36, 110
Nixon administration, 34

Occupational movement, 80–82
O'Connor, James, 50–52
Oligarchy, 221
"One Best Way" of teaching, 143–47
Open classroom, 13–14, 59–60
Oppositions, bipolar, 19, 258
Order: crisis and basic skills, 54–62; McKinley Middle School and problem of, 200–13; perspective of author and

Index

participant observer, 199–200. *See also* Classroom management; Control
Otherness, 19, 81

Parent conferences, 175–76
Parsons, Talcott, 262
Participant observer, 199–200, 256
Patriarchy: bureaucratic-hierarchical discourse, 3–4; democratic-progressive alternative, 251; gender and innovation, 99; union leadership, 221
Pedagogy. *See* Teaching
Peters, Thomas, 125
Phenomenology, 15–16
Physical conditions, buildings, 171–72. *See also* Working conditions
Planning-Programming-budgeting system (PPBS), 77–78
Poland, 94
Political action committees (PACs), 101
Political science, 271
Politics: Democratic reform agenda in Midstate, 123–25; power of trade unionism, 94; negative, 99; reproductive theory of teaching, 68–71; resistance theory of teaching, 74–80; teacher deskilling and proletarianization thesis, 72–74; teachers and theoretical grounding, 67–68; teachers' unions and partisan, 101–102. *See also* Conservatism; Left; Liberalism; Right
Positive thinking, 202–203
Poststructuralism: basic skills and motivation, 37; crisis of order, 54; curriculum studies, 257; resistance theory, 79; teacher identity formation and occupational movement, 80–82; theoretical grounding, 17–21
Post-traumatic stress syndrome, 206
Poverty: functional literacy crisis, 36; liberal approach to reform, 124; minority failure, 43. *See also* War on poverty
Power: discourse and relations, 54; industrial unionism, 92; legitimation crisis, 41–48; local school districts and state education agencies, 121; state and decision-making, 105–106
Pragmatism, vulgar, 224

Praxis, philosophy of, 240
Preparation periods, 172–74
President, union, 132–33
Princeton Review, 117, 269
Principals: effective schools research, 45; "getting over," 212–13; official model of classroom management, 200–203; teacher morale and classroom management, 207–10
Prison, 165–66
Professional Improvement Plans (PIPs), 139–40
Professionalism, teacher: after-school meetings and events, 176; craft unionism and teacher job control, 82–88; discipline and normalizing of deviants, 263; elementary and secondary teachers compared, 169; liberal discourse and promotion, 228–29; preparation periods, 174; reform efforts and salaries, 235; teachers' work culture and crisis tendencies, 102–103
Progressivism, educational: experimentalism, 236–38; teacher evaluations and "One Best Way" of teaching, 146–47
Proletarianization, 72–74. *See also* Deskilling, teacher
Property taxes, 49
Pupil Engagement Rate, 141
Purposive-rational thinking, 57

Race: democratic-progressive alternative, 249–50; legitimation crisis, 42–48; liberal discourse on reform, 237; repressive forms of control, 220; teacher-student conflicts and power relations, 196–98; teachers' work culture, 3; urbanization and segregation, 107; Urbanville Education Association organization and leadership, 134–36; Urbanville in basic skills era, 129, 152–53, 221. *See also* Ethnicity; Minorities; Racism
Racism: critical pedagogy, 243–44; liberal approach to reform, 124; Urbanville Education Association and institutional, 136; vocational education, 135. *See also* Minorities; Race
Rationality, 15

Index

Reading: liberal discourse on reform, 229; Midstate diploma exam, 115. *See also* Literacy
Reagan administration, 44, 226
Reality, situational, 15–17
Record-keeping, 146
Referrals, educational, 114
Reform: conservative state discourse, 221–25; Democratic party definition of role of schools, 124; discourse on in Midstate, 113–14; hegemony and crisis management, 8–9; liberal discourse, 226–39. *See also* Basic skills
Report cards, 177–79
Reproductive theory: craft model of teaching, 84; historical determinism, 240; Marxist and neo-Marxist educational analysis, 6–7; teaching and politics, 68–71
Republican party, 252–53
Research, 246–47
Resistance theory of teaching, 74–80
Reuther, Walter, 95
Right: company family ideal, 90; criticism of big government and social agenda, 270. *See also* Conservatism
Role formalization, 99–101, 156–57
Role models, 250
Roosevelt administration, 93
Rules, game, 158–59

Salary. *See* Wages
Satisficing strategy, 31
Scans, teacher, 141–43
School-based management, 91
School Evaluation Teams, 232
Scientific management: deskilling of labor, 57; legitimating ideology, 215; "One Best Way," 144
Secondary teachers: preparation periods, 173, 174; teacher-administrator conflicts, 169
Security guards, 210
Segregation: socioeconomic, 149–50; white flight and urban, 107. *See also* Race
Self-contained classrooms, 85
Semi-skilled employment: crisis and curriculum reform, 33–35; Midstate and crisis, 107–108

Seniority, teacher, 171
Sexism: critical pedagogy, 243; Urbanville Educational Association and administrators, 167. *See also* Gender
Shanker, Albert, 84, 249
Shapiro, Svi, 239
Shop programs, 149
Silberman, Charles, 60, 238
Simon, Herbert, 30–31
Site-based management, 245
Socialism, 70. *See also* Marxism; Neo-Marxism
Social justice, 20–21
Socioeconomic status (SES), 45–46
Sociology, 271
South Korea, 227
Spanish language, 205
Standardized testing: Midstate and diploma exam, 112–20, 124; teaching-to-the-test and test scores, 262; Urbanville and comprehensive curriculum, 147–48. *See also* Competency tests; Teaching-to-the-test
State: basic skills and rise of educational, 120–25, 218–19; conservative discourse on reform, 221–25; decision-making, 105–106; fiscal crisis and cost-effective curriculum, 49–54; legitimation crisis and effective schools, 41–48; school restructuring and reform, 62–63
Stephens, J. M., 47
Stress, work-related, 207, 230
Strikes: industrial unionism, 92; restriction of teachers' rights, 97–98, 165
Structuralism: reproductive theory of teaching, 68–71; teacher deskilling and proletarianization thesis, 72–74
Students: assault charges against teachers, 192–95; authoritarian and repressive forms of control, 185–86; critical literacy, 241; McKinley School and challenges to teachers' authority, 203–204; McKinley School and "getting over," 211–13; unionism, 249. *See also* Classroom; Control
Student-to-teacher ratio, 53
Substitute teachers, 172
Suburbs: fiscal resources of urban

Index

schools, 2; teacher working conditions compared to urban, 230; white flight and segregation, 107
Support staff, 130–31
Suspension, in-house, 209
Systems theory: conservative state discourse on reform, 225; discursive practices, 26–27; interpretation of Weber, 262

Taxation, 49, 51–52
Taylor, Frederick: craft unionism, 83; deskilling of labor and scientific management, 57; "One Best Way," 144
Teacher Effectiveness Training (T.E.T.), 190
Teachers: alienation and disaffection of urban, 230; authoritarian and repressive forms of student control, 185–86; author's objectives, 22; benign view of state role, 123; "chronic" urban, 213–14; company unionism and professional educational family, 88–91; conservative state discourse on reform, 224–25; contract orientation and role formalization, 156–57; craft unionism, professionalism, and job control, 82–88; critical theory of education, 65–66; curriculum and instructional reform, 151–53; deskilling and proletarianization thesis, 72–74; elites and defining of interests, 155–56; fiscal crisis and basic skills, 52–53; identity formation and occupational movement, 80–82; industrial unionism, 91–102; as political actors and theoretical grounding, 67–68; promotion of professionalism, 228–29; race, class, gender and work culture, 3–4; reskilling as classroom managers, 186–87; review of case study data, 218–19; transformative intellectual, 66; unionism and urban school crisis, 2–3, 82. *See also* Teaching; Unions and unionism; Work culture
McKinley School case study: "getting over," 211–13; problem of order, 203–207; teacher morale, 207–11
Midstate case study: democratic reform Midstate Education Association, 130–31; standardized testing, 112–20
Urbanville case study: basic skills restructuring, 136–43; classroom management, 188–98; end-of-ideology thesis, 181–83; game theory, 159–81; leadership positions in Urbanville Educational Association, 130–31; professional ideals, 128
Teaching: charismatic model, 56; comprehensive curriculum in Urbanville, 147–51; critical pedagogy, 66; democratic-progressive discourse, 241–47; "One Best Way" and evaluations, 143–47; reproductive theory, 68–71; resistance theory, 74–80
Teaching-to-the-test: functional literacy crisis, 37–38; increases in test scores, 262; Midstate diploma exam, 116–17, 119; Stanley Kaplan and Princeton Review, 269
Technical controls, 57–59, 60–61
Technology, 32–33
Television, 56
Testing. *See* Competency testing; Standardized testing; Teaching-to-the-test
Theft, 197–98
Theory: crisis tendencies and management, 26–31; groundings for study, 4–21; teachers as political actors, 67–68
Thinking: higher-order skills, 231; purposive-rational, 57
Timar, Thomas: conservative state discourse on reform, 223, 225; neo-Weberian study of basic skills reforms, 14
Time on Task: basic skills reforms and Urbanville, 140–43, 145–46; problem of order and McKinley School, 200
Transfers, building and/or grade, 170–71
Truancy, 61–62, 229
Tyack, David, 144

Unions and unionism: author's objectives, 23; company and professional educational family, 88–91; craft, professionalism, and job control, 82–88; democratic-progressive agendas, 247–49; incorporation thesis, 75–76; industrial and "Great Bargain," 91–

Index

agenda, 125; leadership positions in Midstate Education Association, 130–31; standardized testing, 112–20

Urbanville case study: basic skills restructuring, 136–43; classroom management, 188–98; end-of-ideology thesis, 181–83; game theory, 159–81; leadership positions in Urbanville Educational Association, 130–31; professional ideals, 128

Teaching: charismatic model, 56; comprehensive curriculum in Urbanville, 147–51; critical pedagogy, 66; democratic-progressive discourse, 241–47; "One Best Way" and evaluations, 143–47; reproductive theory, 68–71; resistance theory, 74–80

Teaching-to-the-test: functional literacy crisis, 37–38; increases in test scores, 262; Midstate diploma exam, 116–17, 119; Stanley Kaplan and Princeton Review, 269

Technical controls, 57–59, 60–61

Technology, 32–33

Television, 56

Testing. *See* Competency testing; Standardized testing; Teaching-to-the-test

Theft, 197–98

Theory: crisis tendencies and management, 26–31; groundings for study, 4–21; teachers as political actors, 67–68

Thinking: higher-order skills, 231; purposive-rational, 57

Timar, Thomas: conservative state discourse on reform, 223, 225; neo-Weberian study of basic skills reforms, 14

Time on Task: basic skills reforms and Urbanville, 140–43, 145–46; problem of order and McKinley School, 200

Transfers, building and/or grade, 170–71

Truancy, 61–62, 229

Tyack, David, 144

Unions and unionism: author's objectives, 23; company and professional educational family, 88–91; craft, professionalism, and job control, 82–88; democratic-progressive agendas, 247–49; incorporation thesis, 75–76; industrial and "Great Bargain," 91–102, 103–104; oligarchic style of leadership, 4; resistance theory of teaching, 78; review of case study data, 221; urban school crisis, 2–3, 82. *See also* Midstate Education Association (MEA); Urbanville Educational Association (UEA)

UniServ, 160

United Auto Workers, 248

United Federation of Teachers (UFT), 95–96, 97

U.S. Department of Education, 202

University of Chicago, 236

University of Texas, 34

Urbanization, 106–107

Urbanville case study: basic skills restructuring and teachers, 136–43; classroom management and teachers, 188–98; description of schools during basic skills era, 129; end-of-ideology thesis and teachers, 181–83; game theory and teacher wage package, 159–62; restructuring of teachers' work through curriculum and instructional reform, 151–53; review of case study data, 219–21. *See also* Urbanville Educational Association (UEA)

Urbanville Educational Association (UEA): classroom management, 189; collective bargaining and power, 136; comprehensive high school curriculum, 150–51; description of during basic skills era, 129–36; game theory and employment terms and conditions, 162–81; game theory and wage package, 159–62; gender and power structure, 152; limitations to effectiveness, 127–28; verbal and/or physical confrontations between students and teachers, 192

Valium, 206

Video display terminal, 33

Violence: challenges to teachers' authority, 203–204; teachers and assault charges, 191–95

Index

Vocational education: employment opportunities and declining enrollment, 149; Urbanville and racism, 135
Vulgar pragmatism, 224

Wages, teacher: deskilling and cheapening, 73–74; professionalism, 235; salary steps, 160–61; Urbanville and game theory, 159–62
Wagner Act, 93
War on poverty, 49–50. *See also* Johnson administration
Waterman, Robert, 125
Weapons, 203–204
Weber, Max: bureaucratic control, 56–57, 58; charismatic leaders, 55, 56; forms of authority, 54–55; legitimation, 41; negative politics, 99; rationalization of institutional authority, 214–15; systems theory and interpretation, 262; theoretical grounding for study, 9–15
Wexler, Philip, 71
What Works (Dept. of Education), 44
Willis, Paul: limitations of research, 267; resistance theory of teaching, 74–77, 79–80

Winterowd, W., 35
Wolcott, Harry, 77–78
Work culture, teachers': company unionism and professional educational family, 88–91; craft unionism, professionalism, and job control, 82–88; crisis tendencies, 102–104; democratic-progressive discourse, 245–47; identity formation and occupational movement, 80–82; industrial unionism, 91–102; race, class, and gender, 3–4; review of case study data, 218–21
Working conditions: game theory and negotiation of teacher, 162–81; urban and suburban compared, 230
Workload, teacher, 179–81
Work skills: crisis of and curriculum reform, 31–41; literacy and economic functionalism, 121; Midstate and crisis, 107–108; Midstate and diploma exam, 118–19
Writing, 115–16

Young, Robert, 242

Zero-sum game, 158, 219